P9-DMY-225

$2.00 a Day

$2.00 a Day

Living on Almost Nothing in America

Kathryn J. Edin
H. Luke Shaefer

Houghton Mifflin Harcourt
BOSTON   NEW YORK
2015

Copyright © 2015 by Kathryn J. Edin and H. Luke Shaefer

All rights reserved

For information about permission to reproduce selections from this book,
write to Permissions, Houghton Mifflin Harcourt Publishing Company,
215 Park Avenue South, New York, New York 10003.

www.hmhco.com

Library of Congress Cataloging-in-Publication Data is available.
ISBN 978-0-544-30318-8

Book design by Rachel Newborn

Printed in the United States of America
DOC 10 9 8 7 6 5 4 3 2 1

To our children,
Bridget, Kaitlin, Marisa, and Michael

Contents

$2.00 a Day

Introduction

DEEP ON THE SOUTH SIDE of Chicago, far from the ever-evolving steel skyline of America's third-largest city, sits a small, story-and-a-half white clapboard house clad in peeling paint. That's where Susan Brown lives with her husband, Devin, and their eight-month-old daughter, Lauren, the three of them sharing the home with Susan's grandmother, stepgrandfather, and uncle.*

Wooden steps lead up to the age-worn threshold of an enclosed front porch, which slumps noticeably to the left. To enter the house, visitors must sidestep a warped, mold-stained plywood board that covers a large hole in the porch floor. The front door opens into a small, dark room furnished with a worn couch, a shaky wooden coffee table, and a leatherette easy chair with stuffing escaping from the left arm. Up and to the left, you can see a dark patch where the wall meets the ceiling. It seems like the spot is at best damp and at worst crumbling.

The air is dense. It is well above ninety degrees outside, but it feels even hotter inside the house. None of the windows open, although gaps between the frames and their casings let in a little bit of air. The carpeting in the front room has been discolored by footsteps and

---

* To protect the individuals who are written about in this book, the names of people, organizations, places, and some minor details that do not substantively affect the stories have been changed throughout.

spills, and its matted surface feels a bit sticky. Where the carpet has worn away, there are the crumbling remains of black-and-white linoleum. Where the linoleum has worn through, there are the vestiges of once-fine hardwood floors.

At the back of the house, a giant 1980s-era refrigerator dominates a small kitchen outfitted with open shelving and a porcelain sink that may well be a century old. Inside the refrigerator, there are just a few bottles of baby formula that Susan has gotten from the Special Supplemental Nutrition Program for Women, Infants, and Children, called WIC. She says of baby Lauren, "She gets WIC, but it don't last . . . They give her, like, seven cans, but it's like the *little* cans." Otherwise, she says with a shrug, "we don't have no food in the freezer right now." The fridge groans as it works to keep its mostly empty shelves cold.

In the heart of all the chaos that is inevitable when six people share a cramped, worn three-bedroom home, there is a small dining area sandwiched between the front room and the empty fridge in the back. In it sits a round dining table covered with a pristine white linen tablecloth, intricately embroidered around the edges. Four place settings are outfitted with gold-rimmed china and silver flatware. Four bright white napkins embellished with the same embroidery as the tablecloth have been carefully folded and placed in large crystal goblets. It is hard to imagine a more elegant table at which to share a meal. Yet here it sits — never used, never disturbed — accompanied by a single chair.

This table harks back to a different era, a better time in the life of Susan's family, when owning this house in this part of Chicago signaled the achievement of middle-class African American respectability. Before the economic anchors of this far South Side neighborhood closed down — the steel yards in the 1960s, the historic Pullman railway car company by the early 1980s, and the mammoth Sherwin-Williams paint factory in 1995 — Roseland was a community with decent-paying, stable jobs. It was a good place to raise your kids.

As the jobs left, the drugs arrived. "It got worse, it's changed,"

Susan says. There's "too much violence . . . unnecessary violence at that." Given what her family has been through, this is more than a bit of an understatement. Susan's brother was shot in broad daylight just one block away. Her great-grandmother, in whose house they are living, has fled for a meager retirement out west. Susan's family would like nothing more than to find another place to live, safer streets and a home that isn't crumbling around them. Yet despite all of its ills, this house is the only thing keeping Susan, Devin, and Lauren off the streets. They have spent the past few months surviving on cash income so low that it adds up to less than $2 per person, per day. With hardly a cent to their names, they have nowhere else to go.

Two dollars is less than the cost of a gallon of gas, roughly equivalent to that of a half gallon of milk. Many Americans have spent more than that before they get to work or school in the morning. Yet in 2011, more than 4 percent of all households with children in the world's wealthiest nation were living in a poverty so deep that most Americans don't believe it even exists in this country.

Devin has a high school diploma. A clean record. Some work history. He spent most of the past year working construction gigs off the books for an uncle, until he got a temp job up in the northern suburbs. But that job lasted only a few months, and now he's gone half a year without finding another. After two months at home following the birth of baby Lauren, Susan began a frantic search for work, but it hasn't been going well. "I've been looking for jobs for forever," she says, clearly demoralized. "It's gonna drive me crazy!" Before she became pregnant with Lauren, Susan earned her GED and spent more than a year in community college, completing the remedial courses that would allow her to finally begin earning credits toward a certification in early childhood education. Yet she can't afford to return to college right now. Somebody has to find work.

Devin speaks with more confidence than Susan. He believes that any day now, things are bound to turn around. On his way to apply for a position at the Save-A-Lot grocery store nearby, his blue jeans are clean and crisp, his short-sleeved button-down shirt pressed. He has heard that there is an opening for part-time work in the produce department, paying $8.50 an hour. Despite six months of rejections, he is confident that he's got this one. At only twenty hours a week, it won't get his family above the poverty line, but it's a start. Now if only Susan can find something. At least child care isn't a worry. Susan's grandmother has had to leave her job to care for her husband, just home after a long hospitalization. She says that while she's nursing him at home, she can babysit Lauren if Susan finds a job.

Susan is sick of going hungry, sick of eating instant noodles morning, noon, and night. She's tired of falling further and further behind on her bills, tired of being a freeloader in her own home. With no cash coming in, the whole family is in hock to Susan's absentee landlord, her great-grandmother, who charges each of her tenants a modest rent to cover the property taxes and supplement her Social Security check. Susan's uncle has been scraping together just enough to pay the utilities with his slim earnings from the occasional side job fixing cars in the backyard. The whole household depends on Susan and Devin's food stamp benefits in order to eat. So as Susan goes about the work of caring for her baby and searching for a job, she is also learning another skill — the art of surviving on virtually nothing.

The Rise of $2-a-Day Poverty

By 2010, Kathryn Edin had spent more than twenty years canvassing poor communities all over the country, sitting with low-income parents at their kitchen tables or as they went about their work, talking about their economic lives. Beginning in the early 1990s, she and her colleague Laura Lein detailed the budgets of hundreds of the nation's welfare recipients. They showed how, despite receiving a few hundred dollars in welfare benefits each month, these families still struggled to survive. Typically, they were able to cover only about three-fifths of their expenses with the cash and in-kind assistance they received from the welfare office. Each month, they had to scramble to bridge the large gap in their budgets. Yet on the whole, Edin and Lein found that by deploying grit and ingenuity, these families were usually able to stave off the most severe forms of material deprivation.

In the summer of 2010, Edin returned to the field to update her work on the very poor. She was struck by how markedly different things appeared from just fifteen years before. In the course of her interviews, she began to encounter many families living in conditions similar to those she would find when she met Susan and Devin Brown in 2012—with no visible means of cash income from any source. These families weren't just poor by American standards. They were the poorest of the poor. Some claimed food stamps, now called SNAP, for the Supplemental Nutrition Assistance Program. A few had a housing subsidy. Most had at least one household member covered by some form of government-funded health insurance. Some received an occasional bag of groceries from a food pantry. But what was so strikingly different from a decade and a half earlier was that there was virtually no cash coming into these homes. Not only were there no earnings, there was no welfare check either. These families didn't just have too little cash to survive on, as was true for the welfare recipients Edin and Lein had met in the early 1990s. They often had no cash at all. And the absence of cash permeated every aspect of their lives. It seemed as though not only cash was missing, but hope as well.

The question that began to keep Edin up at night was whether something had changed at the very bottom of the bottom of American society. Her observations could have been a fluke. To know for sure, she had to find a survey representative of the U.S. population that asked just the right questions. And it had to have asked them over many years so she could see whether extreme destitution had been growing, especially since the mid-1990s, when the country's main welfare program, Aid to Families with Dependent Children (AFDC), was replaced by a system of temporary, time-limited aid.

It was entirely a coincidence that in the fall of 2011, Luke Shaefer came to Harvard, where Edin was teaching, for a semester. Shaefer is a leading expert on the Survey of Income and Program Participation (SIPP), the only survey that could answer Edin's question. The SIPP, administered by the U.S. Census Bureau, is based on survey interviews with tens of thousands of American households each year. Census Bureau employees ask detailed questions about every possible source of income, including gifts from family and friends and cash from odd jobs. A key goal of the survey is to get the most accurate accounting possible of the incomes of the poor and the degree to which they participate in government programs. No one claims these data are perfect: people may not want to tell a stranger "from the government" about the intimate details of their finances, especially if they think it could get them in trouble with the law. But the SIPP can tell us more about the economic lives of the poorest Americans than any other source. And because it has asked the same questions over many years, it is the only tool that can reveal if, and how much, the number of the virtually cashless poor has grown in the years since welfare reform.

That fall, during an early morning meeting in her office in Cambridge, Edin shared with Shaefer what she had been seeing on the ground. Shaefer immediately went to work to see if he could detect a trend in the SIPP data that matched Edin's observations. First, though, he needed to determine what income threshold would capture people who were experiencing a level of destitution so deep as to be unthought-of in America. Accordingly, he borrowed inspiration from one of the World Bank's metrics of global poverty in the developing world — $2 per person, per day. At the time, the official poverty line for a family of three in the United States worked out to about $16.50 per person, per day over the course of a year. The government's designation of "deep poverty"— set at half the poverty line — equated to about $8.30 per person, per day. As far as Shaefer and Edin could tell, no one had ever looked to see whether any slice of the American poor fell below the even lower threshold of $2 a day for even part of a year. With the SIPP, it was fairly easy to estimate how many American families with children were reporting cash incomes below this very low threshold in any given month.

Like any good social scientist, Shaefer tried hard to prove Edin's observations wrong. He wouldn't just focus on family income (as our official poverty measure does). Instead, any cash coming to anyone in the household — related or not — would be included. He would include any government benefits that came in the form of cash. He'd add private pensions. Gifts from family and friends would be counted as well. Even cash from occasional odd jobs would be added in. In short, any dollar that made it into the house — no matter what the source — would be counted toward a family's income. And after he made his initial calculations, he'd do another set of calculations, adding in the value of tax credits plus some of the nation's biggest in-kind assistance programs for the poor, particularly SNAP. SNAP is more like cash than any of the government's noncash programs aimed at helping the poor.

The results of Shaefer's analysis were staggering. In early 2011, 1.5 million households with roughly 3 million children were surviving on cash incomes of no more than $2 per person, per day in any given month. That's about one out of every twenty-five families with children in America. What's more, not only were these figures astoundingly high, but the phenomenon of $2-a-day poverty among households with children had been on the rise since the nation's landmark welfare reform legislation was passed in 1996 — and at a distressingly fast pace. As of 2011, the number of families in $2-a-day poverty had more than doubled in just a decade and a half.

It further appeared that the experience of living below the $2-a-day threshold didn't discriminate by family type or race. While single-mother families were most at risk of falling into a spell of extreme destitution, more than a third of the households in $2-a-day poverty were headed by a married couple. And although the rate of growth was highest among African Americans and Hispanics, nearly half of the $2-a-day poor were white.

One piece of good news in these findings was that the government safety net was helping at least some households. When Shaefer added in SNAP as if it were cash — a problematic assumption because SNAP cannot legally be converted to cash, so it can't be used to pay the light bill, the rent, or buy a bus pass — the number of families living in $2-a-day poverty fell by about half. This vital in-kind government program was clearly reaching many, though not all, of the poorest of the poor. Even counting SNAP as cash, though, Shaefer found that the increase in the number of families with children living in $2-a-day poverty remained large — up 70 percent in fifteen years. And even after throwing in any tax credits the household could have claimed in the prior year, plus the cash value of housing subsidies, the data still showed a 50 percent increase. Clearly, the nation was headed in the wrong direction.

Reflecting on these numbers, we, Shaefer and Edin, sought out even more confirmation that what we had found represented a real shift in the circumstances of families at the very bottom. With this in mind, we began to look for other evidence, beyond the SIPP, of the rise of $2-a-day poverty. Reports from the nation's food banks showed a sizable rise in the number of households seeking emergency food assistance since the late 1990s. A look at government data on those receiving SNAP revealed a large increase in the number of families with no other source of income. And reports from the nation's public schools showed that more and more children were facing homelessness. Taken together, these findings seemed to confirm the rise of a new form of poverty that defies every assumption about economic, political, and social progress made over the past three decades.

Trends Meet Real Lives

Statistics can help identify troubling trends like these, but they can't tell us much about what's going on beneath the numbers. In fact, these statistics led to more questions than answers. What had caused the rise in $2-a-day poverty among households with children? Was the landmark welfare reform of 1996 partly to blame? Were these families completely detached from the world of work? Or were they enmeshed in a low-wage labor market that was itself somehow prompting spells of extreme destitution? How was it even possible to live without cash in modern America? What were families in $2-a-day poverty doing to survive? And were these strategies different from those poor families had been using prior to welfare reform, when AFDC still offered such families a cash cushion against extreme destitution? What was so indispensable about cash — as opposed to in-kind resources such as SNAP — for families trying to survive in twenty-first-century America?

To better understand the lives being lived beneath the numbers, we needed to return to where this exploration started — to the homes of people like those Edin had met in 2010. Only families who were themselves living in $2-a-day poverty could tell the story of how they had ended up in such straits. Only their stories could reveal what it actually takes to survive with virtually no cash in the world's most advanced capitalist economy.

In the summer of 2012, we launched in-depth ethnographic studies in locations across the country. If the $2-a-day poor truly constituted more than 4 percent of all households with children — about a fifth of all families living below the poverty line — then it wouldn't exactly be easy to find families in such circumstances. But it shouldn't be impossible either. The first question was where to start the search.

We wanted one of our sites to represent the "typical" American city. Another site would be chosen because it represented "old poverty"—a rural locale that had been deeply poor for half a century or more. We also wanted to explore the lives of the $2-a-day poor in a place where widespread poverty was a somewhat more recent phenomenon. With that in mind, we looked for a city that had, up until the 1970s, been characterized by widespread affluence but had experienced severe economic decline in the decades since. Finally, we wanted to include a place that had been very poor in prior decades but had recovered in recent years.

With these criteria in mind, we set up field sites in Chicago; in a collection of small, rural hamlets in the Mississippi Delta; in Cleveland; and in a midsize city in the Appalachian region — Johnson City, Tennessee. As we spent time in each locale, we began by reaching out to local nonprofits, especially those with deep roots in the communities they served. We hung flyers in their lobbies, volunteered in their programs, and approached the most destitute of families who walked through their doors. Because many among the $2-a-day poor are isolated from such sources of aid, we also enlisted the help of trusted community members embedded in neighborhoods where we knew many families were struggling.

Our work began in Chicago, the "City of the Big Shoulders," according to the poet Carl Sandburg. We were attracted to Chicago for our first site because of the research of the eminent sociologist William Julius Wilson, who used Chicago as his case study for *The Truly Disadvantaged,* the most important book written about poverty in the past three decades. It was Wilson who first observed, famously, that a poor child fared worse when she grew up among only poor neighbors than she would have if she'd been raised in a neighborhood that included members of the middle class, too. Wilson argued that the reason poverty had persisted in America even in the face of the War on Poverty declared by President Lyndon Johnson in 1964 was that in the 1970s and 1980s, poor African Americans had become increasingly isolated, relegated to sections of the city where their neighbors were more and more likely to be poor, and less and less likely to find gainful employment. For Wilson, it was the rise of joblessness among a black "ghetto underclass" that had left poverty rates so stubbornly high despite billions spent on antipoverty efforts.

As we started looking for families who were living below the $2-a-day threshold — walking the streets of some of the very same neighborhoods that Wilson had studied — we worried that our efforts might be something akin to looking for a needle in a haystack. But, in fact, it turned out that the extreme poor were surprisingly easy to find. Within just a few weeks in Chicago, we had identified multiple families who qualified. The same would prove true in each of our other sites.

Cleveland's precipitous fall from grace over the past half century is an emblem of the decline of America's once-great manufacturing economy. With industry booming in the 1950s, the city was dubbed by its businesses "the best location in the nation." But the jobs in the steel factories that had driven that wealth disappeared over the decades that followed. The city's Cuyahoga River caught on fire (a couple of times). The glory days of Cleveland Indians baseball and Browns football gave way to decades of losing sports teams, adding to the impression that Cleveland was a place in decline, a "mistake on the lake." The city still boasts world-class cultural institutions such as the Cleveland Museum of Art and a national leader in health care, the Cleveland Clinic. Even so, in 2010 Cleveland was ranked number one in *Forbes*'s list of "America's Most Miserable Cities."

Several hundred miles south, in the foothills of the Appalachian Mountains, lies Johnson City, Tennessee. Due to the collapse of coal mining and the prevalence of subsistence farming, the Appalachian region as a whole numbered among America's very poorest places by 1965, with fully a third of its populace below the poverty line. Now, due to economic diversification, current figures put the poverty rate at half that level — a rate that is now in line with the rest of the nation's. Yet the central portion of the Appalachian region, where Johnson City lies, still has pockets of deep need. Just to the north and west of Johnson City, on the Kentucky side of this tristate region, are six of the nation's ten "hardest places to live," according to the *New York Times*. Johnson City thrives due to its "eds and meds" — education and health care — plus the ongoing strength of manufacturing in nearby Kingsport. Elderly migrants from the North are attracted by its very low cost of living. Yet economic need is readily apparent in the city's trailer parks, cheap apartments, and government housing developments.

Even farther south, the Mississippi Delta has long been among America's poorest places, dubbed "the most southern place on earth" by the historian James C. Cobb, due to the fact that its cultural and economic history is so characteristic of the region. Once dependent on generations of black laborers to plant and harvest its highly prof-itable cash crop, cotton, the Delta's economy has been largely given over to production agriculture—more often corn and soybeans now—which does very little to support local employment. In many of the region's small cities and towns, some with populations of only a few thousand, or even a few hundred, child poverty can top 60 per-cent or even higher, more than three times the national average. In some of these towns—including the hamlets of Jefferson and Percy, in the central Delta's Sunshine County—you can pretty much throw a stone in any direction and strike the home of someone who is living among the $2-a-day poor.

In each of these places, we looked for families with children who had spent at least three months living on a cash income of less than $2 per person, per day. In most cases, these spells of such dire pov-erty proved to be much longer. We visited with these families over the course of many months—and, in some cases, years—talking with them frequently, sharing meals, and observing their daily lives. As common themes emerged from their stories—such as their surpris-ingly high level of attachment to the formal labor market and the fre-quency with which doubling up with family or friends precipitated a spell of $2-a-day poverty—we looked back to the SIPP and to other sources of data to see if we could see them there as well.

In the end, we followed eighteen families, eight of them featured here. As had been true of those Edin first encountered in the summer of 2010, some of these households received SNAP or lived in subsi-dized housing. But others weren't getting even those benefits. During the course of our fieldwork, some of these families escaped $2-a-day poverty; others did not. Most escaped only to fall back into destitution again.

Recent public discussions of rising inequality in the United States have largely focused on the biggest winners of the past decade, the top one percent. But there is a different inequality at work at the other end of the income scale.

In 1995, Senator Daniel Patrick Moynihan famously predicted that the proposed welfare reform would result in children "sleeping on grates." Most observers think history proved him wrong. But does the rise in the number of the $2-a-day poor represent the (until now unexamined) great failure of welfare reform? Perhaps Moynihan was not so far off after all. Perhaps his only mistake was in assuming that this failure at the very bottom of the economic distribution would be visible and obvious, when in fact, throughout history, American poverty has generally been hidden far from most Americans' view.

America's cash welfare program — the main government program that caught people when they fell — was not merely replaced with the 1996 welfare reform; it was very nearly destroyed. In its place arose a different kind of safety net, one that provides a powerful hand up to some — the working poor — but offers much less to others, those who can't manage to find or keep a job. This book is about what happens when a government safety net that is built on the assumption of full-time, stable employment at a living wage combines with a low-wage labor market that fails to deliver on any of the above. It is this toxic alchemy, we argue, that is spurring the increasing numbers of $2-a-day poor in America. A hidden but growing landscape of survival strategies among those who experience this level of destitution has been the result. At the community level, these strategies can pull families into a web of exploitation and illegality that turns conventional morality upside down.

None of the people whose stories appear in this book see a handout from the government — the kind that the old system provided prior to welfare reform — as a solution to their plight. Instead, what they want more than anything else is the chance to work. They would like nothing better than to have a full-time job paying $12 or $13 an hour, a modest dwelling in a safe neighborhood, and some stability above all else. In the 1990s, we, as a country, began a transformation of the social safety net that serves poor families with children. More aid has been rendered to a group that was previously without much in the way of government assistance—the working poor. Extending the nation's safety net in this way has improved the lives of millions of Americans. But there are simply not enough jobs, much less good jobs, to go around. And for those without work, there is no longer a guarantee of cash assistance.

$2.00 a Day shows that the transformation of the social safety net is incomplete, with dire consequences. We believe the time has come to finish the job. Doing something more to help these families won't be easy; it will require a commitment by all of us. The government's emphasis on personal responsibility must be matched by bold action to expand access to, and improve the quality of, jobs. But there will always be circumstances in which work as a primary approach to alleviating poverty won't work. In those cases, we need a system that truly acts as a safety net for families in crisis, catching them when they fall.

Chapter 1

Welfare Is Dead

IT IS ONLY 8:00 A.M., half an hour ahead of opening time, but already a long line has formed outside the Illinois Department of Human Services (DHS) office, which sits on a barren block west of Chicago's Loop. It is a wet summer morning, one of those odd times when the rain is falling but the sun still shines. People are hunkered down, some shielding themselves from the rain with umbrellas or hoods, others holding sodden newspapers and thin plastic grocery bags over their heads. This two-story, yellow-brick office building — windowless on the first floor — is where those seeking help come to apply for programs such as SNAP and Medicaid. But traditionally it has been linked most closely to the nation's now nearly moribund cash assistance program, what many refer to as welfare.

Modonna Harris shuffles to the end of the line. A friend, noticing that Modonna had no food in her tiny apartment, convinced her to make the trip. She and her fifteen-year-old daughter, Brianna, have been living in a North Side homeless shelter for several months. The shelter provides dinner during the week, and Brianna gets breakfast and lunch through a local nonprofit recreation program, but Modonna and Brianna often go hungry on weekends. The shelter's residents can usually count on a "guy who drops off some surplus food" from an unknown source, but recently all he's brought is nasty-smelling milk well beyond its expiration date.

When asked why she hasn't applied for welfare, Modonna shrugs. Actually, it hasn't even occurred to her. She explains, "I've been through this before, and I've been turned down . . . They did send me a letter. But they just say, 'You're not eligible,' they don't explain why." How could she not be eligible, she wondered, without even one cent in cash income and a child to provide for? Her aunt's explanation is simple: Hasn't she heard? They just aren't giving it out anymore. To Modonna, that seemed as good an answer as any. "I don't actually know anybody who is getting it. And, you know, when my auntie was saying that, I'm thinking, 'Okay, well maybe that's making sense of why I didn't get it' . . . I'm like, 'Okay, maybe that's it.'" Despite her now desperate circumstances, Modonna was deeply reluctant even to go to the DHS office and apply for the cash welfare program. Finally, after much persuasion, she relented.

Much of the time, when you ask for help from the government, you can expect the process to take a long time. First, you wait in line to "get a number." (In places like Chicago, you have to get to the DHS office early, because the line can stretch down the block even before the doors open.) Once you get a number, you wait for your name to be called so you can see the caseworker and provide the required documentation. Then you go home to wait while they process your paperwork. Finally, if your application is approved, you wait for the mail carrier to deliver your electronic benefit transfer (EBT) card, which works like a bank debit card.

One way the poor pay for government aid is with their time.

Modonna has a proud, even regal, air about her. Her voice is smooth and her diction precise. Her posture is perfect, her dark skin smooth, her smile warm. But most of the other folks waiting in line look to be in rough shape, with worn, dingy clothing, decaying teeth, painful infirmities, and an air of desperation. The kind-looking woman in front of Modonna seems prematurely old. She turns to Modonna and relates how she struggled to get Medicaid for her oldest adult son, desperately ill and then hospitalized with AIDS. Roadblock after roadblock held up the process; months passed and he died — the day before his medical card arrived in the mail. Now she is here again, this time to apply for Medicaid on behalf of her younger adult son, who is also chronically ill and in need of treatment.

Modonna is visibly uncomfortable in this line. She would probably say that she's one of the people who doesn't belong here (although you'd perhaps hear that from many of the people in line). Both of her parents worked steadily while she was growing up. She had close to a middle-class upbringing, although it was far from idyllic. Her parents divorced when she was young, and she lived mostly with her unsupportive mother, who suffered from depression. This was better than being with her dad — who was controlling and demeaning. Despite all this, Modonna managed to graduate from one of the better high schools in Chicago and to start college at a decent private university specializing in the arts. But she attended for only two years. With her family unwilling to provide financial assistance, she maxed out on student loans and had to drop out, with a boatload of student debt and no degree to show for it. She left hoping that one day she might go back to complete her degree. But love intervened.

Brianna arrived about a year into Modonna's marriage to Brian, who had swept Modonna off her feet with his drive to make it in the music production business. He had a dream, and he seemed to be doing the work to make it happen. Yet after a few years, it became painfully clear that he was a pathological liar with an addiction to hard-core porn. He would hide his dirty magazines under the rug and deny they were his. "They must have been here when we moved in," he'd claim. One time, the family was evicted because Brian just stopped paying the rent and didn't tell Modonna until it was too late. Brian cheated first, and then Modonna got wrapped up in a turbulent, all-consuming love affair. The marriage broke up about the time Brianna entered the first grade.

Modonna had worked off and on over the years before the marriage ended. Now on her own, she needed a full-time job. With no college degree and a sporadic work record, the best position she could find was a daytime shift as a cashier at Stars Music downtown, which paid $9 an hour. She would hold that job for the next eight years. Modonna loved the work. "I learned so much at Stars," she recalls. The mother-daughter pair found a tiny studio apartment in the South Shore neighborhood, near Lake Michigan, and for a while things were good. The two scraped by on a combination of Modonna's paycheck, a small amount of SNAP, and whatever child support Brian managed to provide. Brianna was doing well in school—she even made honor roll one semester. Modonna felt proud to be the provider for her little family.

Then their apartment building started going downhill, fast. Deferred maintenance became no maintenance at all. Modonna couldn't handle the "roaches, the size of . . . big water bugs," and the other obvious hazards. She tried to get out of her lease and asked that her security deposit be returned. The tension between her and her landlord escalated, and she ended up calling a lawyer, who requested a list of the building's code violations from the city. When it came, Modonna says, it was "eight pages long!"

Right when it seemed as if she might win some concessions from her landlord, Modonna's cash drawer at Stars came up $10 short, and she couldn't account for it. She was summarily dismissed, given no benefit of the doubt, despite her years of service and the small amount of money involved. "Ten dollars short, and they found it after they fired me," she says. But no call of apology came, no invitation to return to work.

That's when things really started to fall apart. Modonna was approved for unemployment insurance, which is fairly rare among low-wage workers in the service sector, where low earnings and unstable work hours can make it hard to meet the program's eligibility criteria. She knows she was lucky in this regard. But her benefits—which didn't begin to approach what she was making at Stars—weren't enough to cover the cost of her rent.

She fell behind, and her landlord, usually willing to work with a tenant in a tough situation, used the opportunity to get rid of a troublemaker. Six days after her rent was due, he slipped an eviction notice under her door.

Out on the streets, Modonna and Brianna bounced around, forced to double up with family member after family member, a hard pill to swallow. Her father's new wife didn't want her and Brianna around, so they couldn't stay with them. Her sister, a cop who lived in the western suburbs, had little patience: after just a few days, they were told they had to go. After moving in with her mother, her mother's boyfriend began coming on to Modonna. Meanwhile, the foster child Modonna's mother had taken in — and now doted on — began taunting Brianna, ridiculing her over her late-to-develop figure, her "nappy hair," and the fact that she didn't have a home. Finally, Brianna broke. After a particularly vicious verbal attack by the girl, Brianna grabbed a knife from the kitchen counter and threatened to cut her own throat. The incident was deemed a suicide attempt, and Brianna was admitted to a psychiatric hospital and remained there for nearly a month. Desperate to find a new living situation, Modonna made plans to move down to Mississippi to stay with a friendly aunt once Brianna was released, but Modonna's father blocked them from leaving. Still controlling, he told her that she would be breaking the law by taking Brianna so far away from Brian.

Needless to say, all of these factors made it hard for Modonna to search for a job. Even so, she managed to submit dozens upon dozens of job applications, pounding the pavement week after week. Yet a new job didn't materialize. At one point, Modonna found a temporary gig as a teacher's assistant at a day camp based in her church. This job ended badly for her, though. When she went to pick up her first paycheck, she was told they didn't have the money to pay her because the government grant they had been expecting hadn't come through. "I never got that check. Never."

Finally, with nowhere else to go and just a little money left from unemployment, Modonna and Brianna spent a few special nights at the Marriott downtown. While hardly practical, those few days were some of the happiest the two ever spent together. The mini-vacation repaired some of the damage done by the past few months. Those were days they wouldn't trade for anything. "Oh my God, we loved it there . . . That was cool. That was awesome." Joy radiates from Modonna's and Brianna's faces and animates their words when they talk about their stay at the Marriott. The next stop was the homeless shelter — a succession of them, actually, all across Chicago.

Today, the day she finally visits the DHS office at the urging of her friend, Modonna finds herself in a line she doesn't want to be in, asking the government for help she doesn't think it will give her. After about a half hour, the doors open. After another half hour, the queue has advanced enough to allow Modonna to escape the rain and move inside. Those at the front of the line have checked in at the desk and now claim chairs in the waiting area, which is painted a dispiriting green, the color of pea soup.

After another few minutes, an official-looking woman with a clipboard emerges from a closed door at the side of the waiting room. She approaches those remaining in line, person by person, quietly informing each of the day's "latecomers" that caseworkers will be able to see only those who arrived by 7:30 a.m. and got a number from the staff person who was on duty at the time. Finally, she reaches Modonna. "Do you have a number?" Modonna shakes her head no. "Well, you'll have to come back tomorrow," she says. She urges Modonna to arrive earlier next time, her tone implying, *What were you thinking, showing up at 8:00 a.m.? Everyone knows you have to get here by at least 7:30, a full hour before the office opens.*

As the woman moves on, delivering the same grim message over and over, most people shuffle off. A few hold on to their places until they reach the front desk. Modonna sticks it out, just to see what will happen. Once she makes it to the front of the line, a carefully coiffed woman with eyes glued to a computer screen tells her that there are no appointments left today. "Why don't you consider applying online?" she suggests, making only brief eye contact. When queried, the woman admits that an online application won't get Modonna very far. She will still have to come in for an appointment.

Modonna was right, and her friend was wrong. This was a waste of time.

Modonna is convinced now more than ever that they just aren't giving out cash at the DHS office anymore, and to a certain degree she's right. Out of every one hundred Americans, fewer than two get aid from today's cash welfare program. Just 27 percent of poor families with children participate. There are more avid postage stamp collectors in the United States than welfare recipients.

In 1996, welfare reform did away with a sixty-year-old program that entitled families with children to receive cash assistance as long as they had economic need. It was replaced with a new welfare program, called Temporary Assistance for Needy Families (TANF)—the one Modonna waited in line for—which imposes lifetime limits on aid and also subjects able-bodied adult recipients to work requirements. If they fail to meet those requirements, they risk being "sanctioned"—losing some or even all of their benefits.

At the old welfare program's height in 1994, it served more than 14.2 million people—4.6 million adults and 9.6 million children. In 2012, the year Modonna took her trip to the DHS office, there were only 4.4 million people left on the rolls—1.1 million adults (about a quarter of whom were working) and 3.3 million kids. That's a 69 percent decline. By fall 2014, the TANF caseload had fallen to 3.8 million.

Before 1996, welfare was putting a sizable dent in the number of families living below the $2-a-day threshold. As of early 1996, the program was lifting more than a million households with children out of $2-a-day poverty every month. Whatever else could be said for or against welfare, it provided a safety net for the poorest of the poor. In the late 1990s, as welfare reform was gradually implemented across the states, its impact in reducing $2-a-day poverty began to decline precipitously. By mid-2011, TANF was lifting only about 300,000 households with children above the $2-a-day mark.

One reason families in $2-a-day poverty — whose incomes are far beneath the threshold TANF requires — often fail to claim benefits is because it just doesn't occur to them to do so. Many, like Modonna, believe that getting cash from the government is no longer a viable option, no matter how desperate the need.

Take Susan Brown in Chicago's Roseland community, about twenty miles south of the shelter where Modonna and Brianna are living. Asked if she plans to apply for welfare, Susan recoils a bit, shaking her head emphatically, as if to say, *Of course not.* When pressed to explain her reluctance, she explains, "I just don't want to get rejected again." Every time she gets turned down by a prospective employer, she cries uncontrollably. Why open herself up to certain failure by applying for welfare?

Welfare's virtual extinction has gone all but unnoticed by the American public and the press. But also unnoticed by many has been the expansion of other types of help for the poor. Thanks in part to changes made by the George W. Bush administration, more poor individuals claim SNAP than ever before. The State Children's Health Insurance Program (now called CHIP, minus the "State") was created in 1997 to expand the availability of public health insurance to millions of lower-income children. More recently, the Affordable Care Act has made health care coverage even more accessible to lower-income adults with and without children.

Perhaps most important, a system of tax credits aimed at the working poor, especially those with dependent children, has grown considerably. The most important of these is the Earned Income Tax Credit (EITC). The EITC is refundable, which means that if the amount for which low-income workers are eligible is more than they owe in taxes, they will get a refund for the difference. Low-income working parents often get tax refunds that are far greater than the income taxes withheld from their paychecks during the year. These tax credits provide a significant income boost to low-income parents working a formal job (parents are not eligible if they're working off the books). Because tax credits like the EITC are viewed by many as being pro-work, they have long enjoyed support from Democrats and Republicans alike. But here's the catch: only those who are working can claim them.

These expansions of aid for the working poor mean that even after a watershed welfare reform, we, as a country, aren't spending less on poor families than we once did. In fact, we now spend much more. Yet for all this spending, these programs, except for SNAP, have offered little to help Modonna and Brianna during their roughest spells, when Modonna has had no work.

To see clearly who the winners and losers are in the new regime, compare Modonna's situation before and after she lost her job. In 2009, the last year she was employed, her cashier's salary was probably about $17,500. After taxes, her monthly paycheck would have totaled around $1,325. While she would not have qualified for a penny of welfare, at tax time she could have claimed a refund of about $3,800, all due to refundable tax credits (of course, her employer still would have withheld FICA taxes for Social Security and Medicare, so her income wasn't totally tax-free). She also would have been entitled to around $160 each month in SNAP benefits. Taken together, the cash and food aid she could have claimed, even when working full-time, would have been in the range of $5,700 per year. The federal government was providing Modonna with a 36 percent pay raise to supplement her low earnings.

Now, having lost her job and exhausted her unemployment insurance, Modonna gets nothing from the government at tax time. Despite her dire situation, she can't get any help with housing costs. So many people are on the waiting list for housing assistance in Chicago that no new applications are being accepted. The only safety net program available to her at present is SNAP, which went from about $160 to $367 a month when her earnings fell to zero. But that difference doesn't make up for Modonna's lost wages. Not to mention the fact that SNAP is meant to be used only to purchase food, not to pay the rent, keep the utility company happy, or purchase school supplies. Thus, as Modonna's earnings fell from $17,500 to nothing, the annual cash and food stamps she could claim from the government also fell, from $5,700 to $4,400.

Welfare pre-1996 style might have provided a lifeline for Modonna as she frantically searched for another job. A welfare check might have kept her and her daughter in their little studio apartment, where they could keep their things, sleep in their own beds, take showers, and prepare meals. It might have made looking for a job easier — paying for a bus pass or a new outfit or hairdo that could help her compete with the many others applying for the same job.

But welfare is dead. They just aren't giving it out anymore.

Who killed welfare? You might say that it all started with a charismatic presidential candidate hailing from a state far from Washington, D.C., running during a time of immense change for the country. There was no doubt he had a way with people. It was in the smoothness of his voice and the way he could lock on to someone, even over the TV. Still, he needed an issue that would capture people's attention. He needed something with curb appeal.

In 1976, Ronald Reagan was trying to oust a sitting president in his own party, a none-too-easy task. As he refined his stump speech, he tested out a theme that had worked well when he ran for governor of California and found that it resonated with audiences all across the country: *It was time to reform welfare.* Over the years, America had expanded its hodgepodge system of programs for the poor again and again. In Reagan's time, the system was built around Aid to Families with Dependent Children (AFDC), the cash assistance program that was first authorized in 1935, during the depths of the Great Depression. This program offered cash to those who could prove their economic need and demanded little in return. It had no time limits and no mandate that recipients get a job or prove that they were unable to work. As its caseload grew over the years, AFDC came to be viewed by many as a program that rewarded indolence. And by supporting single mothers, it seemed to condone nonmarital childbearing. Perhaps the real question is not why welfare died, but why a program at such odds with American values had lasted as long as it did.

In fact, welfare's birth was a bit of a historical accident. After the Civil War, which had produced a generation of young widowed mothers, many states stepped in with "mother's aid" programs, which helped widows care for their children in their own homes rather than placing them in orphanages. But during the Great Depression, state coffers ran dry. Aid to Dependent Children (ADC), as the program was first called, was the federal government's solution to the crisis. Like the earlier state programs, it was based on the assumption that it was best for a widowed mother to raise her children at home. In the grand scheme of things, ADC was a minor footnote in America's big bang of social welfare legislation in 1935 that created Social Security for the elderly, unemployment insurance for those who lost their jobs through no fault of their own, and other programs to support the needy aged and blind. Its architects saw ADC as a stopgap measure, believing that once male breadwinners began paying in to Social Security, their widows would later be able to claim their deceased husbands' benefits.

Yet ADC didn't shrink over the years; it grew. The federal government slowly began to loosen eligibility restrictions, and a caseload of a few hundred thousand recipients in the late 1930s had expanded to 3.6 million by 1962. Widowed mothers did move on to Social Security. But other single mothers — divorcées and women who had never been married — began to use the program at greater rates. There was wide variation in the amount of support offered across the states. In those with large black populations, such as Mississippi and Alabama, single mothers got nickels and dimes on the dollar of what was provided in largely white states, such as Massachusetts and Minnesota. And since the American public deemed divorced or never-married mothers less deserving than widows, many states initiated practices intended to keep them off the rolls.

Poverty rose to the top of the public agenda in the 1960s, in part spurred by the publication of Michael Harrington's *The Other America: Poverty in the United States.* Harrington's 1962 book made a claim that shocked the nation at a time when it was experiencing a period of unprecedented affluence: based on the best available evidence, between 40 million and 50 million Americans — 20 to 25 percent of the nation's population — still lived in poverty, suffering from "inadequate housing, medicine, food, and opportunity." Shedding light on the lives of the poor from New York to Appalachia to the Deep South, Harrington's book asked how it was possible that so much poverty existed in a land of such prosperity. It challenged the country to ask what it was prepared to do about it.

Prompted in part by the strong public reaction to *The Other America,* and just weeks after President John F. Kennedy's assassination, President Lyndon Johnson declared an "unconditional war on poverty in America." In his 1964 State of the Union address, Johnson lamented that "many Americans live on the outskirts of hope — some because of their poverty, and some because of their color, and all too many because of both." He charged the country with a new task: to uplift the poor, "to help replace their despair with opportunity." This at a time when the federal government didn't yet have an official way to measure whether someone was poor.

In his efforts to raise awareness about poverty in America, Johnson launched a series of "poverty tours" via Air Force One, heading to places such as Martin County, Kentucky, where he visited with struggling families and highlighted the plight of the Appalachian poor, whose jobs in the coal mines were rapidly disappearing. A few years later, as Robert F. Kennedy contemplated a run for the presidency, he toured California's San Joaquin Valley, the Mississippi Delta, and Appalachia to see whether the initial rollout of the War on Poverty programs had made any difference in the human suffering felt there.

RFK's tours were organized in part by his Harvard-educated aide Peter Edelman. (Edelman met his future wife, Marian Wright — later founder of the Children's Defense Fund — on the Mississippi Delta tour. "She was really smart, and really good-looking," he later wrote of the event.) Dressed in a dark suit and wearing thick, black-framed glasses, Edelman worked with others on Kennedy's staff and local officials to schedule visits with families and organize community hearings. In eastern Kentucky, RFK held meetings in such small towns as Whitesburg and Fleming-Neon. Neither Edelman nor anyone else involved anticipated the keen interest in the eastern Kentucky trip among members of the press, who were waiting to hear whether Kennedy would run for president. Since the organizers had not secured a bus for the press pool, reporters covering the trip were forced to rent their own vehicles and formed a caravan that spanned thirty or forty cars. Edelman remembers that "by the end of the first day we were three hours behind schedule."

Kennedy's poverty activism was cut short by his assassination in June 1968. But Johnson's call to action had fueled an explosion in policy making. More programs targeting poor families were passed as part of Johnson's Great Society and its War on Poverty than at any other time in American history. Congress made the fledgling Food Stamp Program permanent (although the program grew dramatically during the 1970s under President Richard Nixon) and increased federal funds for school breakfasts and lunches, making them free to children from poor families. Social Security was expanded to better serve the poorest of its claimants, Head Start was born, and new health insurance programs for the poor (Medicaid) and elderly (Medicare) were created.

What the War on Poverty did not do was target the cash welfare system (by then renamed Aid to Families with Dependent Children, or AFDC) for expansion. Yet the late 1960s and early 1970s marked the greatest period of caseload growth in the program's history. Between 1964 and 1976, the number of Americans getting cash assistance through AFDC nearly tripled, from 4.2 million to 11.3 million. This dramatic rise was driven in part by the efforts of the National Welfare Rights Organization (NWRO). A group led by welfare recipients and radical social workers, the NWRO brought poor families to

welfare offices to demand aid and put pressure on program adminis-
trators to treat applicants fairly.

The NWRO was also the impetus behind a series of court decisions in the late 1960s and the 1970s that struck down discriminatory
practices that had kept some families over the prior decades off the
welfare rolls, particularly those headed by blacks, as well as divorced
and never-married mothers. Through "man in the house" rules, state
caseworkers had engaged in midnight raids to ensure that recipients
had no adult males living in the home. In addition, "suitable home"
requirements had enabled caseworkers to exclude applicants if a
home visit revealed "disorder." Some instituted "white glove tests"
to ensure "good housekeeping." An applicant could be denied if the
caseworker's white glove revealed dust on a windowsill or the fire-
place mantel. When these practices were struck down, the caseloads
grew bigger, and with rising caseloads came rising expenditures. No
longer was cash welfare an inconsequential footnote among government programs. It was now a significant commitment of the federal
and state governments in its own right. As costs increased, AFDC's
unpopularity only grew.

The largest, most representative survey of American attitudes, the
General Social Survey, has consistently shown that between 60 and
70 percent of the American public believes that the government is
"spending too little on assistance for the poor." However, if Americans are asked about programs labeled "welfare" in particular, their
support for assistance drops considerably. Even President Franklin
D. Roosevelt claimed that "welfare is a narcotic, a subtle destroyer of
the human spirit." Although there is little evidence to support such a
claim, welfare is widely believed to engender dependency. Providing
more aid to poor single mothers during the 1960s and 1970s likely
reduced their work effort somewhat. But it didn't lead to the mass
exodus from the workforce that the rhetoric of the time often sug-
gested. Sometimes evidence, however, doesn't stand a chance against
a compelling narrative.

Americans were suspicious of welfare because they feared that it sapped the able-bodied of their desire to raise themselves up by their own bootstraps. By the mid-1970s, with the country grappling with what seemed like a fundamental societal shift, another reason for wariness toward welfare arose. In 1960, only about 5 percent of births were to unmarried women, consistent with the two previous decades. But then the percentage began to rise at an astonishing pace, doubling by the early 1970s and nearly doubling again over the next decade. A cascade of criticism blamed welfare for this trend. According to this narrative, supporting unwed mothers with public dollars made them more likely to trade in a husband for the dole.

Once again, no credible social scientist has ever found evidence that the sharp rise in nonmarital childbearing was driven by welfare. While welfare may have led to a small decrease in the rate of marriage among the poor during those years, it could not begin to explain the skyrocketing numbers of births to unwed women. Yet Americans were primed to buy the story that AFDC, a system that went so against the grain of the self-sufficiency they believed in, was the main culprit in causing the spread of single motherhood.

And so it was that Ronald Reagan, preparing his run for the presidency during a period when discontent with this stepchild of the welfare state was particularly high, found an issue with broad appeal and seized on it as a way to differentiate himself from his more moderate opponent. His stump speech soon began to feature the "welfare queen"—a villain who was duping the government in a grand style. Unlike the average American, she wasn't expected to work or marry. The father or fathers of her offspring were given a pass on the responsibility of caring for the children they sired.

The campaign even found a woman who became the symbol of all that was wrong with welfare. In a speech in January 1976, Reagan announced that she "[has] used 80 names, 30 addresses, 15 telephone numbers to collect food stamps, Social Security, veterans benefits for four nonexistent, deceased veteran husbands, as well as welfare. Her tax-free cash income alone has been running $150,000 a year." As he punctuated the dollar value with just the right intonation, audible gasps could be heard from the crowd.

Reagan's claims were loosely based on a real person. Hailing from Chicago, Linda Taylor was a character as worthy of the big screen as Reagan himself. In a profile in *Slate,* Josh Levin wrote that in the 1970s alone, "Taylor was investigated for homicide, kidnapping, and baby trafficking." She was implicated in multiple counts of insurance fraud and had numerous husbands, whom she used and discarded. Without a doubt, she was a real villain. But she was very far from a typical welfare recipient.

Although negative racial stereotypes had plagued welfare throughout its existence, the emphasis on race was more widespread and virulent after Reagan turned his focus to the system. His welfare queen soon became deeply ingrained in American culture. She was black, decked out in furs, and driving her Cadillac to the welfare office to pick up her check. None of these stereotypes even came close to reflecting reality, particularly in regard to race. It was true that as of the late 1960s and beyond, a disproportionate percentage of blacks participated in AFDC. But there was never a point at which blacks accounted for a *majority* of recipients. The typical AFDC recipient, even in Reagan's day, was white.

Reagan lost the Republican primary to Ford in 1976 but defeated President Jimmy Carter in 1980. As president, Reagan took a somewhat softer tone, rhetorically portraying the welfare recipient as more of a victim of bad public policy than a villain. Like FDR, President Reagan viewed the poor as caught up in a system that acted like a narcotic. He was buoyed by the work of the libertarian social scientist Charles Murray, whose influential 1984 book *Losing Ground* argued that social welfare policies had increased long-term poverty. Murray's logic was simple: Pay women to stay single and have babies, and more of them will do so. Pay them not to work, and you have a double disaster on your hands. Murray laid the blame for continuing high rates of poverty squarely at the feet of the welfare system.

By discouraging both work and marriage, the system was ensuring that millions of American women and children remained poor. In his second inaugural address, Reagan argued for Murray's thesis; his call was to help the poor "escape the spider's web of dependency."

Despite this grand narrative and call to action, the changes Reagan was able to make to the welfare system were not extensive. The most notable legislative accomplishment of the 1980s was the Family Support Act, a bipartisan effort by conservatives and New Democrats who sought to distance themselves from the tax-and-spend image that was losing them seats in Congress. Arkansas governor Bill Clinton was a leader among the latter group. The act was the most significant attempt to date to put teeth into a work requirement for the welfare poor and to enhance child support enforcement. Those with new requirements imposed upon them were supposed to work at least part-time or to participate in a training program, but there were numerous exemptions. In the end, the program amounted to little more than an unfunded mandate. There was a jobs program with a catchy acronym (JOBS, standing for "job opportunities and basic skills"), but few states took their part seriously, and life changed for only a small fraction of welfare recipients.

President Reagan famously quipped that "we waged a war on poverty, and poverty won." Judged by the size of the welfare rolls, Reagan's campaign against welfare was at least as futile. By 1988, there were 10.9 million recipients on AFDC, about the same number as when he took office. Four years later, when Reagan's successor, George H. W. Bush, left office, the welfare caseloads reached 13.8 million — 4.5 million adults and their 9.3 million dependent children. How was it that welfare, an immensely unpopular program, could withstand such an offensive? If welfare's chief nemesis, Ronald Reagan, had failed, who possibly stood a chance?

David Ellwood was comfortable in his role as Harvard professor. He had sharp blue eyes, a scruffy beard, and a slight wave to his hair when it needed a trim. He was the smart kid who came to Harvard for college and never left, landing his first job as a professor there right after graduate school. The son of an influential Minnesota physician (who is credited with inventing the concept of the health maintenance organization, or HMO), Ellwood was raised to be a shaper of policy. Early on in his career, he established himself as one of the nation's leading experts on welfare policy, one who was unafraid to step into the public sphere.

Before Ellwood, no one had produced reliable estimates of how long the typical welfare recipient stayed on welfare. Armed with data from America's longest-running longitudinal survey—a survey that had followed the same families for well over a decade—Ellwood and his colleague Mary Jo Bane released a study in 1983 showing that the typical welfare spell lasted less than two years. It was also true, they found, that at any given time there were people on AFDC who did fit the picture of the long-term user, either staying on chronically for years and years or cycling on and off, over and over again. Because such families stayed on for longer periods, it created the inaccurate impression that the program served mostly long-term dependents. The real story supported by Ellwood and Bane's findings was that most families used welfare as a temporary hand up during a crisis or transition. The majority did not seem to be trapped in Reagan's "spider's web of dependency."

Releasing these results just as Charles Murray's indictment of welfare in *Losing Ground* gained traction, Ellwood found himself thrust into the limelight, cast into the role of welfare's defender, arguably the most thankless task in America. Angry letters and phone calls poured in. His appearance on *The Oprah Winfrey Show* even sparked a screaming match between audience members, caught on tape. Producers, politicians, and others apparently found it easy to find welfare recipients who were willing to claim that the program made people lazy. Ellwood was shocked by the vitriol that his defense of welfare inspired. He wondered how a system that engendered such hate—even among many of those whom it was supposed to help—could ever survive. There had to be a better way.

During this time, Ellwood came to a critical realization: Americans didn't hate the poor as much as they hated welfare. In fact, during the very years that Reagan was fighting his war on welfare, the number of Americans who thought we were spending *too little* on help for the poor actually rose, up from 63 percent in 1986 to 70 percent in 1988. The public's concern with welfare was not about how much it cost, but rather about the terms under which aid was given. Many scholars argued that Murray's claims weren't credible, but even so, no one could really assert that the current welfare program was either pro-work or pro-marriage. Ellwood concluded that if government aid to the poor could be restructured in such a way as to promote work and promote family, perhaps the American public would come to be more generous.

In his book *Poor Support*, Ellwood explained how he saw the problem. Welfare, he wrote, "is a flawed method of helping people who are poor and disadvantaged. Welfare brings some of our most precious values — involving autonomy, responsibility, work, family, community, and compassion — into conflict." If a new model was to have a chance at success, it had to involve a social compact of some sort that was in line with American values. Help should be rendered, but work should be required as well.

Ellwood called for a major revamping of America's approach to alleviating poverty, one that would turn the welfare system upside down. First, he wanted to boost the payoff for low-wage work by raising the minimum wage and greatly expanding a small and then little-known program called the Earned Income Tax Credit, a program that, through a refundable tax credit, offered a wage subsidy to the working poor. He also proposed converting AFDC "into a transitional system designed to provide serious but short-term financial, educational, and social support for people who are trying to cope with a temporary setback." In Ellwood's vision, this program might provide assistance for a few years while recipients pursued education and training. After that, they would be required to work. For those who were unable to find work before the time limit expired, a public, minimum-wage job would be provided. Ellwood acknowledged that providing high-quality education and training opportunities, and even public jobs, would be costly. But he believed that if such a program fit into core American values, the public would pay for it.

Ellwood's plan was comprehensive and multidimensional. Yet of all the recommendations, there were but two that received widespread attention: one of welfare's primary defenders was proposing that the U.S. cash welfare program should (1) impose time limits and (2) require work, reforms that went further even than Reagan's.

In 1992, a new presidential hopeful sought to break away from the pack of contenders by taking up issues that resonated with voters. Hailing from Arkansas, a state as far removed from Washington as any, at least in a cultural sense, Bill Clinton had long been a proponent of changing the welfare system. His position had, in fact, been shaped by the thinking of David Ellwood. When Ellwood presented a paper titled "Reducing Poverty by Replacing Welfare" to the National Governors Association in the late 1980s, Clinton was eager to tell Ellwood how much he admired the professor's work. Clinton's view going into the presidential campaign was that the poor should receive ample help, but that help should be geared toward those who were working. The cash welfare "entitlement," offering indefinite support without anything expected in return, should end.

Once again, a charismatic presidential candidate decided to make welfare reform one of his major issues. Clinton had the broad brushstrokes of a policy position, but not the specifics. Nor did he yet have the language that would capture people's attention. Those elements came from his aide Bruce Reed, who coined the phrase that would serve as a defining idea for the Clinton campaign and presidency. A skinny thirty-one-year-old with no expertise in welfare policy, but with a burning desire to win back the White House for a party that he thought had swung too far to the left, Reed saw welfare reform as a clear political winner. He went searching for the phrase that could put the issue front and center.

Clinton first announced that it was time to "end welfare as we know it" in a speech at Georgetown University in October 1991. In the days before the Georgetown speech, as Reed fervently worked to flesh out what exactly this meant, he happened upon one of the papers in which Ellwood laid out his proposal. Reed seized on the only conservative tenet of Ellwood's plan and proposed that in the Clinton program, families would get up to two years of cash aid coupled with job training and other services. After that, they had to work, either in a private sector job or by fulfilling a significant community service requirement. "Two years and you're out" became Clinton's other catchphrase, making it quite clear which part of the Ellwood plan was to be featured most prominently in the campaign.

The popularity of his pledge to end welfare was perhaps the only bright spot in an otherwise brutal few months of campaigning for the southern governor. New allegations seemed to arise almost weekly — that Clinton had engaged in sexual infidelities, dodged the draft, and smoked marijuana (but famously never inhaled). It was arguably his pledge to end welfare that kept him in the race. Nothing polled better for Clinton than welfare reform. The *New York Times'* Jason DeParle reported that a campaign staffer called the issue "pure heroin."

Clinton's plans for welfare reform were featured prominently when he accepted the Democratic Party's nomination for president. And in his first major address to a joint session of Congress, in 1993, the new president made it clear that he planned to act on his pledge, declaring, "I want to offer the people on welfare the education, the training, the child care, the health care they need to get back on their feet, but say after 2 years they must get back to work, too, in private business if possible, in public service if necessary. We have to end welfare as a way of life and make it a path to independence and dignity."

Drawing on Ellwood, the new president's plan would add time limits to AFDC, but it would also increase the benefits of work to poor parents through a dramatic expansion of the EITC. By doing this, he argued, the country would "make history. We will reward the work of millions of working poor Americans by realizing the principle that if you work forty hours a week and you've got a child in the house, you will no longer be in poverty." As Clinton was announcing plans to bolster the efforts of the working poor — whom many saw as deserving, but for whom there was little to no aid — he once again borrowed from Ellwood, making the case that the working poor "play by the rules" but "get the shaft." It was time to "make work pay."

According to Jason DeParle, however, Ellwood worried that Clinton's rhetoric on welfare time limits was too harsh. Were Ellwood's own words going to be used to push families with children off the rolls and into deep poverty? Ellwood had more than once tried to clarify that he promoted time limits only in the context of an overall expansion of aid to the working poor. Bruce Reed's feverish desire that the new president live up to his pledge to "end welfare as we know it" caused Ellwood to wonder what exactly the Clinton reform was going to look like.

Still, when the call came asking him to serve in the new administration as an assistant secretary in the U.S. Department of Health and Human Services, Ellwood immediately packed his bags for Washington. Within days of arriving in the capital, he and a colleague were asked to develop a plan to expand the EITC in a big way. This expansion was included in Clinton's 1993 budget plan and became law in August of that year. In just a few years, the federal government would be spending many billions of dollars more on the EITC — to aid workers — than it ever had on AFDC.

Making good on the promise to reform the welfare system itself was far more daunting. It quickly became apparent that the administration — and, most important, the president — didn't have a specific plan for how to approach the issue. There was a clear charge to "end welfare as we know it," but no one knew exactly how this campaign rhetoric was to be transformed into a concrete proposal. David Ellwood's plan would cost a great deal more than the current system, because of its investments in education, training, and the provision of public jobs. Bruce Reed's goal, which was more closely aligned with the language that had gotten the president elected, was to spend a great deal *less* on welfare, not more. Which approach would the president endorse?

An interagency task force was formed, cochaired by Ellwood, Reed, and Mary Jo Bane, Ellwood's colleague from Harvard who had also taken a leave to join the administration. It included more than thirty members, from every federal department with a possible stake in the effort. But forming this task force was little more than a PR move to show that the Clinton administration was committed to the issue. A smaller work group, drawn heavily from the Department of Health and Human Services but including Reed and some others, was charged with developing the actual proposal. This smaller group would do the heavy lifting, meeting several times a week over the course of many months. Ellwood's deputy, Wendell Primus, a well-respected, long-term Democratic staffer in the House of Representatives with an encyclopedic knowledge of welfare policies and a commanding physical presence, was tapped to organize the group. Struggling under the weight of the competing agendas of its members, however, the work group found it all but impossible to achieve its goal.

It wasn't until June 1994, after the new administration had taken a beating on its proposed health care reform effort, that the Clinton team released its welfare reform package. Adults receiving cash assistance could stay on the program for two years without any work requirement. After that, they had to work, preferably in the private sector, but if not there, then in a subsidized job. There were numerous exemptions to the work requirement. So many, in fact, that the administration's projections showed that by the end of the 1990s, only a tiny fraction of those on cash assistance would be working. There was a time limit but it also had many exemptions. In short, it wasn't a bill that would end welfare as we knew it.

The bill was essentially dead on arrival to Congress. In the summer of 1994, both sides of the aisle were preparing for Republican gains in the midterm elections that fall. Democrats didn't want to engage in a debate on welfare that might divide and further weaken them, and Republicans assumed they'd be in a much better position to negotiate after the election. Neither side wanted to touch the issue.

Most observers expected Republicans to do well in the 1994 midterm elections, but virtually no one predicted the extent of the landslide. The GOP made historic gains in both houses and took full control of Congress for the first time since 1954. As Newt Gingrich prepared to take over as Speaker of the House, no Republican then in office had ever served under a Republican Speaker.

For the first time in AFDC's sixty-year history, there was a Republican-controlled Congress paired with a Democratic president on record as favoring welfare reform. If ever a window for major reform had opened, it was in 1995. And no one was more enthusiastic about that than House Ways and Means Committee staffer Ron Haskins, a former marine with a doctorate in child psychology who had come to Washington in the 1980s on a congressional fellowship and never left. Brash and imbued with boundless energy, Haskins was up at 5:00 a.m. on the day after what he referred to as the "glorious" 1994 election, absolutely elated by the Republican victory and ready to get to work to make welfare reform a reality.

With Haskins's help, Republicans seized the opportunity to craft their own version of welfare reform, building on what they had proposed in the Contract with America, the Republican policy document used as a blueprint for the 1994 campaign. The program they envisioned would be brought closer to the people, so to speak, by passing all federal welfare funds to the states in the form of block grants (spending on which could be capped at the federal level). This would allow states greater latitude in how they spent the money, which would not all have to go to providing cash aid to the poor.

Yet for congressional Republicans, it wasn't acceptable simply to send money down to the states with no strings attached. To keep all of its block grant, a state would be required to meet stringent benchmarks for workforce participation among recipients. At first, governors balked at this demand. Everyone knew that work programs cost money, and a lot of it. But then a critical compromise was struck, based on an idea hatched by Robert Rector of the conservative Heritage Foundation. The work participation requirements could be met by reducing the welfare rolls, *by any means.* It didn't matter if recipients left cash assistance for work or not, they would still be counted as meeting the work requirement.

Perhaps even more important than the new work requirements was the fact that the new block grant structure essentially capped funding for the program, so a state couldn't be expected to provide assistance if the cost exceeded its allotment. Now it could say, "Sorry, we've run out of money." The plan also mandated that states impose a five-year lifetime benefit cap for cash assistance using federal funds, but they could choose to impose shorter time limits if they wished. Recipients who exceeded the time limit would have no access to any cash assistance at all. Furthermore, there were no provisions to ensure former recipients subsidized or public jobs. Most important, under the new plan, no one with children would have the *legal right* to receive a dime of cash welfare from the government, even if the family had no other means of support. The old welfare program, AFDC, had ensured that right.

David Ellwood watched from his perch at Health and Human Services, believing that these welfare "reform" efforts had veered completely off the rails. The new plan wasn't a hand up, it was a hand off — off the rolls, off assistance — with no attempt to make sure families landed in a better place. It was, in effect, his worst nightmare, his ideas used in a way that he had never intended. Perhaps making the calculation that there was no longer any opportunity to create a change for the better in Washington, he resigned from the administration in July 1995 to return to his post at Harvard, where he would observe the new developments from afar.

Ellwood's replacement was Peter Edelman, RFK's former aide. Edelman had been serving in the administration as counselor to Secretary of Health and Human Services Donna Shalala but hadn't been involved in the welfare reform efforts at all until he took over Ellwood's job. He and his wife, Marian Wright Edelman, a well-respected child advocate, had known the Clintons for more than two decades. First Lady Hillary Clinton herself had previously served as chairwoman of the board of Marian Wright Edelman's Children's Defense Fund.

By the time Peter Edelman entered the picture, congressional Republicans had seized the ball. Already, Congress was well on its way to passing a bill, but no one knew exactly where the president stood or what he was willing to accept. Edelman, Mary Jo Bane, and the other top brass at Health and Human Services urged the president simply to reintroduce the administration's bill from the previous year in an effort to offer an alternative to the Republican-led efforts. But Clinton was unwilling.

The bills that came out of the House and Senate not only turned AFDC into a block grant, but they also converted Medicaid into a block grant and levied cuts to the Food Stamp Program. These latter provisions turned out to be steps that, in the end, the president wasn't willing to take, and he would veto them. But in the fall of 1995, even insiders in the Clinton administration had no idea what kind of bill coming out of Congress the president would sign. How far would he be willing to go?

While her husband was working inside the administration, Marian Wright Edelman published an op-ed in the *Washington Post* in November 1995, telling the president that "irreparable damage will be inflicted on children if you permit to be destroyed the fundamental moral principle that an American child, regardless of the state or parents the child chanced to draw, is entitled to protection of last resort by his or her national government." Then an internal administration report authored by Wendell Primus and Sheila Zedlewski of the Urban Institute was leaked to the *Los Angeles Times*. It projected that the Senate version of the welfare reform bill — the more moderate of the two — would nonetheless "push 1.1 million more children into poverty, an increase of almost 11 percent."

Thus, by the fall of 1995 it was public knowledge that Marian Wright Edelman was vehemently opposed to the bill. Further, a respected analyst within the president's own administration predicted that the bill would send more than a million children into poverty. The White House braced for public outrage. Yet calls did not flood the White House switchboard, nor did angry letters overflow the mailroom. In fact, in the weeks following the release of Primus's report, Clinton's job approval rating spiked to its highest level in more than a year and a half.

It seemed more and more likely that a welfare reform bill would get through Congress. Peter Edelman recalls Wendell Primus telling him, "If [Clinton] signs the bill, I'm going to quit the next day." Edelman thought there remained some chance that the legislation would fail, or that Clinton might veto it if it passed. In the end, the bill that Congress passed in the summer of 1996 wasn't that different from the version Clinton had vetoed earlier in the year. It didn't turn Medicaid into a block grant, although it did include new restrictions on access to food stamps, mainly for legal immigrants, who, unlike undocumented immigrants, had access to the program. Most important, the bill ended AFDC in favor of a new program that required work and imposed lifetime limits. Designed as a block grant, the new program gave states much more latitude in how they spent the money from the federal government than AFDC allowed. While the federal government imposed a five-year lifetime limit on benefits using federal funds, states were free to impose even shorter time limits, and some of them did so. The legislation slashed cash and noncash benefits for immigrants (although these benefits were largely restored in later years). At the same time, though, it increased funding for child care subsidies for recipients who found jobs and for otherwise eligible families. But there was no backstop, no Ellwood-like public jobs program for those who couldn't find work in the private sector. Nor was there much in the way of additional dollars for education and training.

After an intense morning meeting with his cabinet and closest advisers, President Clinton announced that he would sign the bill, and he did so on August 22, 1996, the day after he signed into law the first increase in the federal minimum wage in five years. The president was making good on his promise to end welfare as we knew it. But at the same time, he was giving poor working families a raise through a modest minimum-wage hike and a substantial wage supplement now provided through a refundable tax credit, the EITC. This was the Clinton compromise.

It was a watershed in America's commitment to the poor. True to his word, Wendell Primus immediately resigned from his post. In short order, so did Mary Jo Bane and Peter Edelman. Edelman and Bane made the decision together. After they spotted each other across the table at a Health and Human Services meeting, Edelman remembers saying, "Are you thinking what I'm thinking?" It would have been their responsibility, as members of the administration, to implement the new legislation, which they had opposed. They left without public statement, sending e-mails only to their respective staffs explaining their decisions. Yet the act garnered front-page coverage across the country. The *Washington Post* noted that the twin resignations amounted to "an unusually public move that underscores the deep divisions within the administration over the legislation." The *New York Times* highlighted "the resignation of Mr. Edelman" as a "particular rebuke."

Yet other than the resignation of a few top officials, Clinton suffered no significant fallout from signing the bill. After doing so, his job approval rating shot up to 60 percent and remained high through the 1996 presidential election. The Democratic National Convention did not dissolve in protest as some had predicted, and the president was reelected by a wide margin in November. If Clinton owed his first presidential election to welfare reform, making good on his campaign pledge probably helped solidify his election to a second term.

Perhaps the most surprising fact, though, is how quickly the issue faded from view. A federal program in existence for sixty years, a system that had survived would-be reformers for decades — including a full frontal attack by Ronald Reagan — was terminated by Congress and the stroke of the president's pen in the summer of 1996 without much fuss at all. Welfare, as the country knew it, was dead, and very few people seemed to care.

Daniel Patrick Moynihan, then a long-serving Democratic senator from New York who had played a leading role in every national welfare discussion since the early 1960s, famously admonished his colleagues during the 1995 congressional debate over reform, in words befitting a biblical prophet: "If, in ten years' time, we find children sleeping on grates, picked up in the morning frozen, and ask, 'Why are they here, scavenging, awful to themselves, awful to one another,' will anyone remember how it began? It will have begun on the House floor this spring and the Senate chamber this autumn." In an *Atlantic Monthly* article published in early 1997, Peter Edelman warned that when the new cash assistance program's time limits took effect, there would be "more homelessness, for example, with more demand on already strapped shelters and soup kitchens."

The reform's supporters were similarly dramatic but told a very different story, one of liberating the poor from a deeply flawed program. And in the years following welfare reform's passage, it looked to almost everyone as if the pro-reform advocates were right. Writing in the *New York Times* in 2006, former president Clinton boasted about what he saw as a landmark achievement: "Welfare reform has proved a great success" and "shows us how much we can achieve when both parties bring their best ideas to the negotiating table and focus on doing what is best for the country."

There were important signs pointing to success. Poor single mothers left welfare and went to work in numbers that virtually no one expected. In 1993, 58 percent of low-income single mothers were employed. By 2000, nearly 75 percent were working, an unprecedented increase. Rates of employment declined during the 2000s as the economy slowed but have remained above pre-reform levels, although not by much during the years of high unemployment around the 2007–2009 Great Recession. As the welfare system changed, cash assistance caseloads plummeted and have remained low ever since, even during the Great Recession.

Child poverty rates fell for four consecutive years after 1996 and have never again reached the pre-reform peak, belying the prediction that the changes would throw more than a million more kids into poverty. The EITC's expansion, coupled with the 1996 increase in the minimum wage and the increased availability of child care dollars, made government provision for working-poor parents far more generous than ever before. The booming economy of the late 1990s meant that jobs were plentiful right at the time that Temporary Assistance for Needy Families was implemented. The national unemployment rate dropped to a low of 4 percent in 2000. In a sense, welfare reform couldn't have been better timed for success.

Yet even as President Clinton and House Republicans were taking their victory laps, signs of the dark underbelly of welfare reform were already beginning to emerge. Most of those who left welfare did so for a job, but 40 percent of them did not have a job at exit, some because of the new requirements, but most for reasons that no researcher could discern. Among those who found work, the wages, benefits, and overall quality of their jobs were typically low. As a result, poverty among these "welfare leavers" remained high.

Of even greater concern was the fact that a series of studies in the 2000s showed that the number of single mothers who were neither working nor on welfare — a group that researchers referred to as "disconnected"—had risen substantially. One in five single mothers was in such circumstances during the mid-2000s. Disconnected welfare leavers experienced substantially higher rates of material hardship than those who left welfare for jobs.

Other problems for families at the very bottom also began to surface. Starting in 2001, more and more families with children who were receiving SNAP began to report that they had no other source of cash income to live on — not from work, not from public assistance. By 2006, the number of such families had grown 143 percent from a decade before. By 2012, 1.2 million families on SNAP told eligibility workers they had no other income. Private charities began to feel the pinch, too. According to Feeding America, an antihunger organization and national network of food banks that conducts the nation's largest study of charitable food distribution in the United States every few years, pantries and other emergency food programs nationwide served roughly 21.4 million Americans in 1997. By 2005, that number was higher by 3.9 million, and it ballooned even further during the Great Recession, to 37 million Americans in 2009.

Daniel Patrick Moynihan's hometown of New York City experienced a sharp and sustained rise in the need for family homelessness services when the economy soured in 2001, and there was evidence of higher rates of family homelessness nationally by mid-decade. Beginning in 2004, public schools were mandated to count the number of homeless children in their classrooms. (This is the number of children whose parents or guardians could not afford permanent housing but were still attending school.) In 2004–2005, there were 656,000 such children. This number spiked temporarily in 2005–2006 because of Hurricanes Katrina and Wilma, but then gradually increased over time, reaching 795,000 in 2007–2008 and 1.3 million in 2012–2013. Thus, though it was not immediately apparent, the claims of Moynihan, Edelman, and the other top officials who resigned in protest when the 1996 bill was signed have proved remarkably prescient.

Linked to all these disturbing indicators was the rise of American households with children living on $2 a day, a trend that cannot be separated from the fact that welfare — the cash assistance system — was no longer catching families when they fell.

No one really knows for sure why the TANF rolls have remained so low, even during the Great Recession. The most obvious explanation is that families who have fallen off the rolls have hit their time limits. But as it turns out, such cases account for a rather small number and don't explain the trend. Researchers can't fully explain why so many families who are eligible for TANF, like Modonna, never get on the program in the first place, which is a far more important factor in explaining the low caseload levels. Those who have not yet come up against the time limits and are still eligible may be dissuaded from applying because the process is so time-consuming. And as Modonna learned, there is no guarantee that proving your need will earn you a place on the rolls. Even if you are approved for TANF, the payoff is questionable, given that benefit levels have fallen so much in value over the years. In addition, you are now expected to engage in work activities in exchange for your benefits, in some cases with unpaid community service, unless you are exempt for some reason. Prospective applicants might reasonably determine that their time would be better spent hitting the streets in search of a real employer — and such a choice isn't all bad from a policy perspective, of course.

Perhaps more important, though, is evidence that welfare reform coincided with a fundamental shift in the way low-income single mothers thought about parenting. In the years prior to welfare reform, in-depth conversations with hundreds of single mothers on welfare illuminated their belief that taking a full-time job would greatly detract from their ability to be a good parent, especially if they had young children. Then came the roaring 1990s, when an unprecedented number of these single mothers found themselves going to work, "pushed" by the changes in the welfare rules and "pulled" by the EITC expansions, minimum-wage increase, and unprecedented strength of the economy.

Years after welfare reform, when researchers engaged in a further series of in-depth conversations with former welfare recipients, the typical single mom talked about work in a very different way from those interviewed just a few years before. Now she was telling researchers that to be a good parent, she had to model the value of education by getting a job. For these single mothers, the idea of returning to welfare violated their views of what being a good parent required, adding a self-imposed stigma to the potent societal stigma that came with claiming benefits from the program.

The simplest explanation of all, however, for why families are not turning to the assistance that can be gleaned from TANF comes from Modonna Harris back in Chicago. That is, as the cash assistance rolls plummeted in just a few years' time, TANF receipt became rare enough among the poor that it has simply faded from view. No one in Modonna's network of family and friends knew anyone who was getting welfare — even those in obvious need.

Had the Ellwood plan gone into effect in the mid-1990s, Modonna and Brianna might have been able to get some cash assistance during their long spell of living on nothing. Or perhaps they would have had access to something that Modonna would have preferred far more: a subsidized job. Modonna sees herself as a worker, a provider, and she's proud of that. Had the Ellwood plan passed, perhaps her downward spiral into $2-a-day poverty, and her repeated spells of homelessness, could have been avoided. No one will ever know for sure.

What is known, though, is that the way things turned out, the 1996 reformers didn't merely "replace" welfare. They killed it. By 2012, welfare was far from the minds of the $2-a-day poor. So far, in fact, that Modonna Harris, living in a shelter on the Near West Side of Chicago, and Susan Brown, living in the dilapidated family home on the South Side — both eligible for the program — thought they just weren't giving it out anymore.

Chapter 2

Perilous Work

A THIRTY-FIVE-MINUTE RIDE on a city bus headed east across Chicago's South Side and a few blocks' walk brought Jennifer Hernandez — who had recently escaped her second spell of $2-a-day poverty in two years — to the main office of Chicago City Custodial Services. She arrived each weekday at 7:00 a.m., shortly after sunrise. After announcing herself by intercom to Debra, her boss, the mother of two was buzzed in and climbed the steep flight of wooden steps to Chicago City's second-floor office. In the beginning, Jennifer thought of it as "a pretty good job, you know, I liked it, I enjoyed it." That is, at least until it landed her and the kids in the emergency room a couple of times.

Chicago City specialized in the deep cleaning of condos and office suites between tenants and, more recently, of foreclosed homes being readied for resale. The daily workload varied dramatically. "One day we might do one home, and one day we might do, like, seven or [even] twelve!" Jennifer says. Her "team" never knew where the day's assignments would take them. "Sometimes we'd be doing condos on the Gold Coast, other times we'd be cleaning a[n abandoned] house out in West Pullman," a dilapidated neighborhood on Chicago's South Side. "We were all over the city."

Jennifer and the other "custodians" would clock in and then begin to pack up the day's allotment of sponges, white rags turning brownish from use, and cleaning solvents carefully parceled out by Debra. The supplies went into dingy pink plastic tubs so they could be hauled around from place to place. The team would then cart these tubs down the narrow stairwell, along with a worn vacuum cleaner, brooms, mops, and buckets. Everything was loaded into the back of a car supplied by one of the team's members, who would get a little extra in her paycheck for its use. All the while, Jennifer and her crew would be hounded by Debra to speed up. "She was very pushy. She wanted everything, you know, 'Let's go! Let's go! Let's go!'"

Upon arrival at the first job, the crew would lug the supplies through the front door. They would sweep, then vacuum, then mop the floors, often scrubbing on their hands and knees to remove scuff marks and grime. They would scour the sinks, showers, and toilets until they glistened. Every surface, including the walls, doors, and window frames, had to be free of dust, fingerprints, and streaks. The crew was supposed to make do with the same daily allotment of cleaning supplies no matter how many addresses were on the list and no matter how big the jobs. Running out would earn a reprimand from Debra, who watched the company's bottom line with an eagle eye. Most important, though, was that the team keep to a tight schedule: there was no going home until each and every job on the day's list was done.

At the end of the day, Jennifer would sometimes rub her aching hands as she collected her children, Kaitlin and Cole, from their after-school program, often just before it closed at 6:00 p.m. Kaitlin, a slender ten-year-old with thick glasses and chin-length dark hair who is always in motion, would be bursting with news of her school day. Cole, a quiet seven-year-old with a buzz cut and a warm smile, is less chatty, but he would eagerly grasp his mother's hand as they walked.

For Jennifer's labor, she was paid $8.75 an hour. If she was lucky enough to get full-time hours (which didn't always happen), her bi-weekly check, after taxes, totaled roughly $645. With rents on two-bedroom apartments in the Chicago area averaging around $960 per month, Jennifer and the two kids could not have come close to surviving without the one-year housing subsidy offered by the homeless shelter where they had stayed for three months. She had qualified for the subsidy, what the shelter called "stage two" for shelter residents who found jobs (stage one was the intensive job search the shelter required of all adults), when she'd landed the position at Chicago City. Combining her paycheck, SNAP, and the rent subsidy, she could finally breathe a little. First paycheck in hand, she and the kids relocated to one of the nonprofit's apartments, a modest one-bedroom in the down-market Marquette Park neighborhood. With the subsidy, she paid only 30 percent of her net income in rent. Her plan was to work hard and get ahead. With extraordinary luck, maybe she really *could* be self-sufficient in a year's time, when her rent subsidy lapsed.

The phone call with a job offer from Chicago City had come just days before La Casa — Jennifer's third shelter in ten months — was about to evict her and the kids. They were approaching the facility's three-month maximum stay, and she had no job. During her ten-month job search, the family had found themselves among America's $2-a-day poor: they had no earnings, no help from family or friends, not a single dollar from welfare, no cash income at all. Jennifer was entirely reliant on her SNAP, the roof over her head that La Casa and her previous shelters provided, and an unusual talent for finding all the "free stuff" that the city of Chicago and its charities have to offer. Jennifer loved to see Kaitlin and Cole smile when they were outfitted with new backpacks filled with school supplies and new outfits for school — red polo shirts and blue chinos. Her favorite score was the free outdoor performance of *Hamlet* that she had taken the kids to, courtesy of Chicago's Shakespeare in the Parks series.

Diligently, over the summer months of 2012, she had searched for work while living at La Casa, just as she had during her stay at the shelter on North Avenue and the one on the Southwest Side. Each day she would spend hours in the stuffy basement computer lab filling out applications online, and each day she would hit the streets to hand-deliver dozens of résumés to store after store, trying to make eye contact, attempting to leave a favorable impression. Yet her appearance undoubtedly put her at a disadvantage. Her smile revealed badly decayed teeth and stained gums, while her glasses, missing a temple, sat askew on her nose. Jennifer suffered from asthma and was overweight, so she found it hard to catch her breath as she moved from store to store along the Clybourn Corridor, the Magnificent Mile, and other retail strips on the Near North Side and Near West Side of the city.

By the time she landed the interview with Debra at Chicago City, it was mid-August and she was getting desperate. During her two-and-a-half-month stay at La Casa, she had applied for more than one hundred positions and hadn't gotten a single offer. Either she got a job and advanced to stage two, or she and the kids would be out on the streets. She had exhausted all of the family shelters she knew of in the city. Where would they go this time?

Luckily, unlike other service sector employers with whom she had interviewed, Debra didn't seem to mind Jennifer's lopsided gaze or even her discolored gums. Nor did she seem to mind that Jennifer's address, "c/o La Casa," marked her as homeless. Chicago City's workers were largely invisible to the customers they served. Only those job seekers who were at the very end of the hiring queue ended up here — people with criminal records, drug problems, or a shelter address like Jennifer's. A willingness to work hard for little pay was all this occupation required, and Jennifer was more than willing.

During the fall, most of the assignments were not so bad. Typically, they involved cleaning vacant units in large apartment complexes and office buildings. Sure, the work could be punishing, the hours uncertain, and the management demanding. But in those early months, Jennifer's only real complaint was the high turnover rate. "Every week I'd come in and I'd see new faces," she says. Given Debra's fast-paced timetable, it was hard for the team to stay on schedule when the new folks didn't know the drill. Each new hire slowed them down. Still, Jennifer felt a sense of accomplishment when they were done with a job and had polished everything to a shine, a visible sign that she had made a difference that day.

Jennifer's real problems didn't start until winter, when the workload shifted from a mix of jobs to a steady stream of foreclosed homes. The Chicago area registered tens of thousands of foreclosures in 2012 alone, making it one of the hardest-hit cities that year. A large fraction of these houses were in the poorer black and Hispanic neighborhoods south of the Loop, where Jennifer's crew was routinely assigned. Chicago's minority homeowners, often victims of predatory lending practices by some of the biggest names in banking, had been badly affected by the foreclosure crisis. Thousands of vacant houses were scattered along the streets of Chicago's poorer neighborhoods, imbuing these communities with an aura of abandonment. As the days grew cold and dark, Jennifer found herself spending more and more of her work hours in these derelict homes, many of which had "been shuttered for a long time. No power, no working lights, no heat, the dead of winter." And yet, she says, "we were expected to come in and make it . . . look beautiful!"

Jennifer never knew what they would encounter when they entered through the padlocked metal doors the banks installed in a futile attempt to keep out squatters, addicts, thieves, and scrappers. "People would break in and, basically, they'd turn them into crack houses." Weathered plywood boards covered up windows on the outside, but often shattered glass littered the floors inside — glass that was hard to see with no working lights. Would they find a junkie or a destitute family huddled upstairs? Wildlife? A drug den?

The houses that Jennifer and her team found themselves cleaning were in various states of disrepair, but all were covered in dirt and grime. "A lot of work, a lot of dirt, a lot of cleaning that had to be done." Fresh graffiti was often the first signal to the Chicago City crew that someone had broken in. Sometimes scrappers had already stripped the home of anything of value. "They took everything. They took the toilets, they took the sinks." Appliances were gone, cabinets ripped out of the kitchen and bathroom, tile torn off the floors, and copper wiring and other valuable metals extracted through gaping holes in the walls.

Water is key to any cleaning job, but for Chicago City's crews, access to water presented a major challenge. These properties had long since had the water shut off, so Jennifer's team had no choice but to bring their own, hauling it in from the car via heavy covered buckets. If the water hadn't already cooled down on the way over, it would quickly do so in an unheated house on a winter's day in Chicago. The crew couldn't possibly bring enough water to complete even one of these big jobs, let alone a dozen. As they worked, the water in their buckets turned pitch-black, leaving streaks on the counters, windows, and floors. Off they would go with the buckets — to a neighbor's house or up to the nearest gas station or restaurant. Avoiding eye contact at commercial establishments, they would sneak into the restroom to fill the buckets and then carry them, once more heavy with gallons of water, back to the work site.

Then there were the cleaning supplies, which could be stretched only so far. Once they ran out, Jennifer, who after only a few months was one of the more senior employees, would pack up the empty bottles and head back to the office to get more. As she restocked at headquarters and prepared to return to the site, Debra would pepper her with questions — How did you run out? What were you using it on? — as if cleaning a boarded-up house took the same amount of bleach as cleaning a swanky apartment at the end of a corporate lease.

As Jennifer and her team worked away in these homes, they saw their breath in the cold. "We'd have sweaters, we'd have coats. You had to have gloves." Routinely, Jennifer had to make a run to the Salvation Army to fetch an extra coat to pile on top of the one she already had on. After weeks of working in the freezing cold, scrubbing with the cooling and then frigid wash water mixed with harsh solvents, Jennifer watched as the skin on her hands first blistered and then began to peel. "They really didn't supply us with things for our health. It really wasn't a safe environment."

Then Jennifer, an asthmatic, started getting sick, repeatedly. Just breathing in the dank air inside foreclosure after foreclosure left her light-headed and prompted that familiar tightening in her chest, leaving her with a noticeable shortness of breath all night long. She started coming down with colds, then developed a hacking cough that wouldn't go away. After that, she contracted a series of nasty viruses. She would try to go in to work when she was sick, but Debra would send her home, fearing for the health of the rest of the crew. Even when Jennifer started to feel better, her kids were sure to catch whatever bug she had. Both of them suffered from asthma as well, and on a couple of winter nights the family rushed to the emergency room for a shot of adrenaline after one or another of them began to turn blue.

Debra soon grew impatient. "Why are you missing so much? Why are you missing so many days?" she demanded. Jennifer explained that working in the cold, moldy foreclosed homes, with their "broken windows, broken glass," was making her ill. She asked if there were other tasks she could do until the weather got warmer. But cleaning foreclosed homes was the only work Chicago City had.

As January turned into February, Jennifer watched as her hours on the weekly schedule started to get whittled away — thirty-five, thirty, twenty-five, twenty, and below. Once at the top of the scheduling list because of the quality of her work, Jennifer's absences had moved her to the bottom. By the beginning of March, she was making barely $200 every two weeks, a bit over $400 for the month. Subtract the percentage of her earnings she had to put toward rent, plus the $84 for the monthly bus pass she needed to get to Chicago City's headquarters, and this job just "wasn't a good situation." With only seven months left of the subsidy she was getting from La Casa — by which time she was supposed to have become self-sufficient through work and no longer in need of that help — Jennifer realized she would have to devote all of her efforts to looking for a better job. But past experience had taught her that even the worst jobs in Chicago weren't easy to find for someone like her.

At the beginning of March, Jennifer called Debra to give her notice, ending what had been a relatively long tenure for an employee at Chicago City. For six months, the job had provided an escape from $2-a-day poverty. The memory of the previous, harrowing nine months she had spent living on less than $2 a day was the only thing that had kept her there that long. As her earnings fell to zero, so did her share of the rent. Even though she'd quit her job, La Casa's policy stipulated that she could keep the subsidy until it expired. With no rent to pay and a tax refund coming, she hoped she could manage to survive while she looked for a new job. The kids wouldn't need school clothes and supplies until August, winter coats until October. The rent subsidy wouldn't run out until the beginning of November. Meanwhile, she needed to rest, get well, and ensure that the kids were healthy enough to complete the school year. Mostly, she needed to find another job, with luck one that wouldn't make her sick. It had taken her ten months to find the job at Chicago City. How long would it take her to find the next one?

Few families in $2-a-day poverty are chronically disconnected from the workforce. Rather, most of them are workers who fall into extreme poverty only when they can't manage to find or keep a job. Like Jennifer and her children, Kaitlin and Cole, the typical family in $2-a-day poverty is headed by an adult who works much of the time but has fallen on hard times. In fact, roughly 70 percent of children who experienced a spell of $2-a-day poverty in 2012 lived with an adult who held a job at some point during the year.

Yet even when working full-time, these jobs often fail to lift a family above the poverty line. Even if Jennifer had worked a forty-hour week at Chicago City for an entire year — not taking a single day off (not even Christmas or Thanksgiving) — her annual earnings of $18,200 would still have left her family below the poverty threshold, set at $18,769 for a family of three in 2013. She would have gotten a substantial boost at tax time, thanks to the Earned Income Tax Credit and other refundable tax credits. But even after adding this in, her family would have escaped poverty by only a few thousand dollars. And, of course, it is unrealistic to think that she could have gone an entire year without taking a day off. Beyond holidays, when

Chicago City was closed, the chances that neither of her children would need to stay home from school even one day during the year were slim to none. Jennifer didn't have paid sick leave or personal days.

Thus, even when she was working full-time at $8.75 an hour — a full $1.50 above the federal minimum wage — and had a generous temporary housing subsidy to boot, Jennifer struggled to pay her share of the rent and utilities, buy food, pay for the bus pass she needed to get to work, put minutes on her phone, and still somehow manage to keep her kids in respectable school clothes and winter coats, hats, gloves, and boots. Without the housing subsidy, an extraordinarily rare commodity available to only a tiny fraction of Chicago's homeless families, she never could have afforded their apartment — and there was little chance that she would secure such a subsidy again. Even if she were to find another job before the subsidy lapsed, how could she possibly make enough to cover the full cost of the rent with her wages alone?

Jennifer's circumstances are not rare. About one in four jobs pays too little to lift a family of four out of poverty. Low-wage workers are concentrated in the service sector; the typical American experiences direct benefit from their labor. Like Jennifer at Chicago City, some are all but invisible to the nine-to-five professional worker or daytime shopper. Others are constantly interacting with people, taking lunch orders, selling groceries or clothing, or caring for the elderly in nursing homes. Few of these jobs offer workers much autonomy, and many extract a physical or psychological toll, as Jennifer's job at Chicago City did. Not only do they pay low wages, but those who work them are often subject to variable hours and are seldom offered benefits such as affordable health insurance, paid vacations, or retirement plans.

The sectors of the economy populated by low-wage workers now dwarf those that the country once relied on to provide jobs in the working-class trades that paid a respectable wage. Manufacturing, which once accounted for more than 30 percent of all jobs in the

United States, now provides less than 10 percent of jobs. The country had roughly 12 million manufacturing jobs as of 2012, 7 million fewer than at the sector's peak in the late 1970s. In contrast, there were about 15 million jobs in the retail sector and almost 14 million in leisure and hospitality. And in the economy that Jennifer's children will inherit, low-wage employment is projected to grow, not shrink. Thus, Kaitlin and Cole may find themselves grappling with many of the same challenges their mother struggles with today—wondering how to survive on a low-wage job that pays too little and offers too few hours.

Despite the low quality of the jobs available, Jennifer and others among the $2-a-day poor envision themselves first and foremost as workers. Like most poor children in America today, Kaitlin and Cole have grown up watching their mother spend much of her time either holding down a job or hunting for one. Kaitlin, who knows what it means to work for a living, and Cole, who has seen his mother's blistered hands after a hard day of scrubbing in a foreclosed home, have been raised to believe that work is the best way to provide for a family. For the $2-a-day poor, whose home lives are often incredibly stressed, work can even offer an escape of sorts. Before things went completely south—while she was still cleaning corporate apartments on Chicago's Gold Coast—Jennifer appreciated the routine of going to Chicago City. She valued the challenge of rendering an apartment spotless, ready to welcome its next occupant.

Yet Jennifer's devotion to work has not been enough to shield her family from multiple spells of life on less than $2 a day. Cashier, sandwich maker, waitress, laundress, general laborer, custodian—these are all occupations Jennifer has held. And she's been judged a good worker in many of these jobs, offered small promotions, given the occasional extra shift as a reward. None of that, however, has protected her family from intermittent stays in one or another of the city's homeless shelters. In this way, the Hernandez family is typical of those we find in $2-a-day poverty—caught in an endless cycle of jobs that don't pay nearly enough and periods of living on virtually no income.

How is it that a solid work ethic is not an adequate defense against extreme poverty? Some might point to the personal failings of the people who hold these jobs. Perhaps Jennifer should have stuck it out at Chicago City. Maybe she should have used more lotion to soothe her peeling skin and accepted the cycle of illness that engulfed the family as a result of her working conditions. Maybe if she had stayed, she could have leveraged that job into something better, eventually. She did quit, after all.

Yet laying the blame on a lack of personal responsibility obscures the fact that there are powerful and ever-changing structural forces at play here. Service sector employers often engage in practices that middle-class professionals would never accept. They adopt policies that, purposely or not, ensure regular turnover among their low-wage workers, thus cutting the costs that come with a more stable workforce, including guaranteed hours, benefits, raises, promotions, and the like. Whatever can be said about the characteristics of the people who work low-wage jobs, it is also true that the jobs themselves too often set workers up for failure.

The costs of paying their workers are often the only expenses over which service sector employers have any real control. They can't control consumer demand, but by using "just-in-time" scheduling practices, they can peg their labor costs as closely as possible to fluctuations in demand. In doing so, they seek to maintain flexibility in their commitments to the people they employ. If customer traffic gets heavy on weekday evenings, they can move more workers to those shifts. If fewer customers are coming in on Sundays, they can cut the number of cashiers who clock in on that day or send them home early.

The basic strategy behind these practices explains why wide scheduling availability across days and times has become the key qualification for getting and keeping a low-wage service sector job.

Work schedules are often variable, meaning that the days and times you are required to work can shift from day to day or week to week. To get enough hours at any given job, an employee has to be flexible. But such flexibility often means relying on a patchwork of child care arrangements. In one case, as we'll discuss later, Jennifer's reliance on a relative to care for Kaitlin and Cole backfired in the most serious of ways.

Even more challenging for workers than an unpredictable schedule are abrupt ups and downs in the number of hours a worker gets. Many employers with a large low-wage workforce engage in a practice termed "work loading," which responds to downturns in demand with informal layoffs: employers keep employees on the payroll but reduce their scheduled hours, sometimes even to zero. A worker who usually gets thirty-two hours might find that the next week's schedule has her listed only for five. Or she might be sent home in the middle of a shift if the foot traffic is slow.

The extreme of this phenomenon is the growing prevalence of "on-call" shifts. In recent years, many service sector employers have begun requiring workers to be available on certain days and at certain times even when they aren't working. They might be expected to call in (or even show up) each day and, if a supervisor demands it, report to work in short order. If they are not needed, they get no compensation for the time spent on call.

The allocation of hours can also be a way for managers to reward "good" workers and punish "bad" ones. If, for example, a worker were to block off weekend or evening hours during which she would be unavailable for work — so that she could be home with her children, perhaps, or work a second job — she might see her hours reduced as a result. As was true for Jennifer, even if it's the job that is making a worker ill, calling in sick can result in the shrinking of work hours to only a fraction of those previously awarded.

As Jennifer's hours were cut in half in response to the sick days she was accruing, the size of her paycheck fell by half as well. The following February, when tax time rolled around, she might be penalized for this drop in earnings with a lower tax refund, because the EITC operates according to the principle that the more you work, the more you get from the government, up to the plateau point. Roughly speaking, for a single mother with two children, benefits increase as a household's earnings climb to about $13,500 — around what a full-time worker making minimum wage would earn in a year. The benefit level stays the same for earnings between $13,500 and $17,500, then slowly declines, zeroing out when earnings reach about $45,000. At zero earnings, you get zero benefits.

By contrast, SNAP goes up as wages go down. But even this program can be hard to manage with an unstable job. When someone like Jennifer starts working, her SNAP benefits are reduced by about 30 cents for every dollar she earns, not a welcome development with rent to pay and an apartment to furnish. Each fluctuation in her paycheck must be reported to the Department of Human Services (DHS) office, which administers SNAP. If she were to fail to report an uptick in hours — even if she thought it was just temporary — she would risk being accused of fraud. She might even have to pay back the "excess" benefits. Worse yet, she could be barred from the program for life. But if her hours dwindled to zero, it might take DHS a month or more to adjust her benefits upward, and her family might go hungry in the interim.

In the days after she left Chicago City, Jennifer began to search for work with the same tenacity she had brought to her job hunt during the ten months it had taken her to find the position with Debra. Jennifer rejects the idea of taking "handouts," even now in her third spell of $2-a-day poverty in as many years, and so she won't even apply for welfare. Her vision of the good life remains astonishingly humble: she dreams of a full-time job paying $13 an hour, a set schedule, and decent working conditions. She believes that at this wage, she could find a modest apartment in a safe neighborhood, perhaps even afford a reliable used car. Barely making it on $13 an hour is Jennifer's version of the American dream. Yet even this modest aspiration can seem all but out of reach.

Susan Brown's search for work was a constant source of worry during the summer of 2012. When especially stressed, she would nervously pass her refurbished iPhone from one hand to the other, over and over again. The phone was a gift (purchased used for $30) from her husband, Devin, during a time when he had steady work and was in the doghouse after disappearing for several days without explanation. This phone was Susan's most important asset as she hunted for a job. Without a computer and with no other way to access the Internet, she had managed to submit fifty job applications online via her iPhone's tiny touch screen in the past few months. While these applications had generated some interviews, they had not resulted in a single job offer.

"A lot of things don't go my way," says Susan with a hesitant smile. "My luck sucks."

A black woman in her early twenties, Susan got pregnant during her senior year of high school, and perhaps some of her pessimism can be traced back to that time. She left school before graduation when the pregnancy became high risk, and she found herself trekking across the South Side every week for doctor's appointments, fearing the loss of her baby. When she and Devin went in for her first ultrasound, she remembers, "I could tell by the way the doctor was acting that something was wrong, but she wouldn't tell me." After seeking answers at three different clinics, a doctor finally told her that the baby had a major developmental defect. At eight months, Susan delivered a stillborn child.

Susan swore off further pregnancies. "I kept saying I was never gonna get pregnant again. I was scared." Determined to get ahead, she enrolled in community college and completed her GED, with the goal of eventually earning an associate's degree in early childhood education. After a year of remedial course work to make up for the poor quality of her high school education, she was almost ready to advance to the for-credit classes that would begin to count toward her degree. But soon after she and Devin were married, Susan got pregnant again. Antibiotics she had been prescribed had apparently neutralized her birth control. "They told me, 'You have to read the packets.' But who reads the packets?"

Because of the prior stillbirth, Susan's pregnancy was considered high risk. Constant trips to the doctor made it difficult for her to keep up with a full class schedule, and so, once again, she dropped out of school. Happily, the pregnancy was uneventful, and Lauren turned out just fine—more than fine, in fact. It's hard to imagine a more alert, curious, and beautiful little girl. Lots of hair, clustered in tiny braids capped off with plastic barrettes, adding a cascade of color around her tiny face. Bright eyes darting this way and that, contrasting with her smooth dark skin. When Susan, Devin, and their daughter go shopping at Target or board the bus, Lauren turns heads. She plays it up, too, giggling, clapping her hands together, making sly eye contact, and bursting into a one-toothed smile after holding an admirer's attention just long enough. Being with Lauren is like walking around with a celebrity.

Susan would tell you that these days the first step in applying for most low-wage jobs is an online application that might take as long as two hours to complete (probably longer on an iPhone). Take the online application for Walmart, which Susan filled out in the summer of 2012. By the end of the first few screens, you have provided your name, date of birth, Social Security number, and home address; have agreed to submit to a drug test during the hiring process; and have indicated that you are willing to undergo unscheduled drug tests at any point during your employment. You have also indicated your race and ethnicity and have answered questions about whether you've ever been on TANF, SNAP, or Supplemental Security Income (SSI), although the screen assures you that the answers to these questions will not affect your chances of being hired.

While there's not much focus on the skills you would bring to your job, in multiple places you must indicate your availability for work.

A screen early on informs you that "at Wal-Mart, customer service is our priority. We must ensure that we have trained Associates available when our customer traffic is the heaviest, which includes evening and weekend hours." This is combined with a warning that if "your hours of availability do not align with the customer traffic demands for positions in which you are expressing interest, this may impact whether or not you will be considered for those positions." The application continues by asking you to list your available hours for each day of the week. You might, reasonably, find yourself thinking that every hour you block off as unavailable will reduce your chances of getting hired. To drive the point home, another screen asks whether you are able to work evening, weekend, and night shifts.

What Susan hates most about applying for jobs is the "test" such applications almost always require. Even talking about these tests seems to raise her already high anxiety level. Her streak of strikeouts has led her to question her instincts. Take, for example, Walmart's "assessment." If presented with the statement "I frequently change the way I approach job activities," should you answer "strongly disagree" to show consistency, or "strongly agree" to show that you are open to feedback? And what about the statement "When your opinion about how to solve a problem has differed from your supervisor's," are you supposed to say that you have typically "talked through the problem with your supervisor to reach a compromise"? Or should you say that you have "combined your ideas with your supervisor's to come up with a solution jointly"? Maybe the right answer is that you have "modified your opinion to satisfy the preferences of your supervisor."

Other questions are easier. It seems pretty clear that a good candidate would "feel required to make changes based on feedback" and should strongly disagree with the statement "Nothing is wrong with taking home supplies from work now and then." But some of the work-related scenarios are downright vexing. When asked about your "most common strategy for handling major disagreements with other people," do you say that you work to "find compromise options that both you and the other person will accept"? Or do you instead say that you work with your coworker to "come up with new options"? Couldn't you do both? Or how about the question "When you have been in disorganized work situations where the number of people wanting supplies is larger than the amount of supplies available" have you "proposed ways to structure the process of distributing the supplies" or, alternatively, "tried to find ways for everyone to make sacrifices to the make the supplies last"?

Human resources representatives might say that candidates shouldn't try to answer these questions strategically, but rather to be as truthful as possible. But when living on less than $2 a day, you can't afford *not* to be strategic. Even if you were to take the test simply at face value, you might begin to question your instincts after forty or fifty failed attempts to find a job online. Desperate for help, Susan has sought counsel from family members but often gets conflicting advice. Where her aunt says she should answer "very true" to show character, her grandmother advises that the right answer is "not at all true"—that shows realism, she says. There is a lot of folk wisdom exchanged across the South Side of Chicago about how to take these tests, much of it contradictory. Susan, who doesn't know whom to believe, is a nervous wreck every time she logs on to take another one. Devin has offered to take the test for her next time.

As much as these tests are an understandable focus of Susan's anxiety, she does get called for interviews. Clearly, the tests aren't the only thing keeping her from getting a job. In late July 2012, in fact, she scored an interview for a part-time position at a secondhand shop about twenty blocks north. Given her lack of cash, she had no option but to walk. So on the day of her interview, she started off well ahead of schedule, trudging along in her heavy black polyester pants and stretchy white T-shirt—her dressiest outfit—in the sweltering July sun, headed toward the store's address, which she had typed into her iPhone maps program. When she arrived, it was apparent she was in the wrong place, and she called for directions. Another twenty blocks later, she arrived at the interview, flustered and drenched in sweat. The people she talked with were nice enough, commending her perseverance in getting to the interview, even if late. But as of a week later, she hadn't heard anything back. Then she saw that the job had been re-advertised. She applied online once again. Not surprisingly, she isn't holding out much hope.

Why is it so hard for Jennifer Hernandez and Susan Brown to find work? They are both deeply devoted to their job search. Maybe their pessimism and desperation come across in job interviews, or maybe they simply don't know the proper way to act. Perhaps they don't dress appropriately, given that neither has a reliable place to wash clothes and certainly no money to buy new, interview-worthy attire. Maybe they say inappropriate things, reveal too much about their personal lives, or show up late for their appointments. Should Susan have left *two* hours before her interview at the secondhand shop rather than one, with the expectation that she might get terribly lost and have to walk twenty additional blocks in the stifling heat?

Susan's and Jennifer's job searches are likely made harder by the color of their skin. In the early 2000s, researchers in Chicago and Boston mailed out fake résumés to hundreds of employers, varying only the names of the applicants, but choosing names that would be seen as identifiably black or white. Strikingly, "Emily" and "Brendan" were 50 percent more likely to get called for an interview than "Lakisha" and "Jamal." A few years later, a researcher at the University of Wisconsin conducted a similar study in Milwaukee, but with a unique twist. She recruited two black and two white actors (college students, posing as high school graduates) who were as similar as possible in every way. She sent these "job applicants" out in pairs, with virtually identical fake résumés, to apply for entry-level jobs. Her twist was to instruct one of the white and one of the black applicants to tell employers that they had a felony conviction and had just been released from prison the month before. Even the researcher was surprised by what she found: the white applicant with a felony conviction was more likely to get a positive response from a prospective employer than the black applicant with no criminal record. When the study was replicated in New York City a few years later, she and her colleagues saw similar results for Latino applicants relative to whites.

The results from the Milwaukee study indicated that the average white applicant with no criminal record had to apply for only three jobs to get a callback, while a white job seeker with a criminal record had to apply for six. Contrast this to the findings for African Americans: the average black applicant with no criminal record had to apply for seven jobs to get a callback, while a black job seeker with a felony conviction had to put in twenty applications. The researcher noted how depressed and anxious the black actors in her study became after experiencing this degree of rejection month after month, even though they were only playing a part.

Whatever one's race or ethnicity, during the summer of 2012 in Chicago, entry-level work for someone without a college degree was pretty hard to find. Even at the height of the Great Recession, the national unemployment rate for college graduates over the age of twenty-five never surpassed 5 percent. In contrast, workers at the very bottom continued to experience double-digit unemployment through 2012, well after the recession was officially over. For low-level positions, there are often many more applicants than there are jobs. Companies such as Walmart might have hundreds of applicants to choose from, and it is not uncommon for many of these applicants to have some post–high school education, making it that much harder for a young woman of color with a GED and little previous work experience to make the cut.

How do these companies wade through so many applications? How would you do it? If given the choice, why would you take a chance on someone like Susan or Jennifer? The singular goal of companies such as Walmart, Target, and McDonald's is to make a profit. So how might we expect them to act when the potential pool of employees may well include more than one applicant who might fail to show up for work on time, might have to miss work repeatedly due to sickness or an asthmatic child, or might come to work high?

Low-wage employers look for indicators that an applicant is a good bet. With this in mind, conducting a criminal background check might seem reasonable: it's a quick check of whether the candidate can or cannot be trusted. In fact, a whole industry exists solely to conduct criminal and other types of background checks for such employers. As the Milwaukee study shows, the fact of a criminal record appears to be highly consequential. Unfortunately, it turns out that the average criminal background check can be wildly inaccurate. An employer might use only an individual's name, maybe along with her birth year. When Susan asked someone at one place where she interviewed why she didn't get the job, she was told — off the record — that when they ran her criminal background check, a Susan Brown from Texas popped up with a list of serious offenses: drugs, grand theft auto, the list went on and on. Never mind the fact that Susan has never been to Texas. With so many applicants to choose from, why would an employer go any further than that? Now that she knows about her Texas counterpart, Susan begs at every interview that they use her Social Security number to conduct the background check, warning them that otherwise, her notorious Texan doppelganger will appear. But that's one more strike against her: it seems likely that Susan has given more than one prospective employer reason for pause by making such a big deal about the criminal background check during her interview. Unfortunately, it turns out that most jurisdictions don't even include Social Security numbers on court records, so an employer couldn't use one in a criminal background check even if they wanted to.

Jennifer's job search, the one that landed her a position at Chicago City, offers another example of the multiple obstacles faced by the $2-a-day poor. Jennifer's search was conducted while she was living at three different shelters, La Casa being the third. One question she had to grapple with right off the bat was how prospective employers would get in touch with her. Jennifer did carry a pay-as-you-go cell phone, bought the last time she had a regular paycheck, but she rarely had money to load any minutes onto it. Thus, its primary purpose during the last few months of life on less than $2 a day had been as a toy for the kids, who played the free games loaded on it when they were riding the bus or waiting in line at the free dental clinic or school backpack giveaway event.

Since she couldn't put her own phone number on her résumé, Jennifer's only choice was to list La Casa's main switchboard number. That's where an employer would call if they wanted to contact Jennifer for an interview. But the minute the secretary answered the phone, "La Casa, how can I help you?" it would out Jennifer as a resident of a homeless shelter, someone without a stable address, someone whose life was most certainly in chaos. Not exactly the type of person a prospective employer is itching to take a chance on, even if she might deserve one.

You might imagine that a caller looking to offer Jennifer an interview — with dozens of applicants to choose from and a busy day ahead of him — might hang up right then and there. But let's say he saw something special in Jennifer's résumé and was willing to hold on a bit longer to speak with her. For this he would be rewarded with a long wait on hold while one of the shelter staff raced around the facility, knocking first on the door of Jennifer's second-floor unit, then checking the computer lab in the building's basement. More likely than not, Jennifer would be nowhere to be found, because she was out pounding the pavement, delivering résumés anywhere and everywhere. So the shelter staff would have to apologize to this uncommonly diligent employer, take a written message, and tape that message to the door of Jennifer's quarters.

It might be hours later before Jennifer returned home from her job hunt to get the note. Then she would have to wait for her turn on the sole phone available to residents. By this time, even the most committed prospective employer may have moved on to the next applicant, someone who answered the phone herself, someone who didn't have a reason to be living in a homeless shelter.

By July 2012, Susan and Devin Brown were getting desperate. They had entered their sixth month of $2-a-day poverty. The family had lost their apartment months ago and had moved into the old family home, owned by Susan's absentee great-grandmother but occupied by her grandmother, her grandmother's infirm husband, and an alcoholic uncle who worked in the back alley repairing cars. The circa 1920 wood-frame, one-and-a-half-story home was falling down around them. Fortunately, near the end of July, Devin finally landed a job at a nearby grocer, promising $8.50 per hour and thirty hours a week. He would be paid weekly, and he guessed that he'd be bringing home a paycheck of about $250, minus taxes, in about a week's time. When asked how they planned to spend it, they replied, in unison, "Pay bills!" That first paycheck wasn't going to put much of a dent in the debts that had piled up, but something was clearly better than nothing. Much like Jennifer, when asked about their image of the good life, Susan and Devin waxed hopefully about a good job paying $12 an hour with at least thirty hours a week guaranteed. By pooling their earnings, they believed, they would "be on the right path." To them, the American dream would be in sight.

In the meantime, even given the new job, Devin still couldn't come close to raising his family of three above the poverty line. With each dollar earned, the family lost roughly 30 cents in SNAP. Health insurance didn't come with the job. They still couldn't afford a place of their own. Devin couldn't even afford to maintain his cell phone, though he continued to pay the bill on Susan's phone. Despite the job, struggle remained their daily fare as Susan continued to search doggedly for employment.

In spite of unreliable shifts, low pay, and often poor working conditions, when the $2-a-day poor find jobs, the routine of going to work each day can be the single biggest stabilizing force in their otherwise chaotic lives. And the stability work brings is not just a matter of income. Take Rae McCormick, from the Stockyards neighborhood of Cleveland, for example. Fair-skinned, brown-haired, and slight, Rae insists that her nine-hour shifts at Walmart were the best parts of her week, aside from the fleeting moments she and her then two-year-old daughter, Azara, enjoyed together when it was just them in the house. In her life outside work, Rae lurches from crisis to crisis. At work, at least, she was in control of her own cash register, and she could find some shelter from the storm outside.

By age twenty-four, Rae had lived in more places than she was years old. For the moment, she is staying with an "uncle," George, and "aunt," Camilla, actually of no blood relation. George is an old friend of her dad's. He has proved himself to be untrustworthy time and time again, but Rae has always cut him slack because he can do what she can't: tell Azara stories about Rae's father, the father she reveres, the father she has modeled her life on, the father who died of a brain aneurysm when she was just eleven years old. Rae writes to her father most nights in a small notebook with a mottled black-and-white cover, usually starting her letters, "Dear Dad, I miss you so much! Things are bad here."

Each day, when she arrived at the Walmart store in the suburb of Parma, Ohio, she went straight to her locker to put away her purse, which contained an asthma inhaler and the meds for her thyroid disorder, depression, and anxiety. After pinning on her name tag and straightening her shirt and blue vest sporting the Walmart logo, she headed to the front of the store to get to work. She was working day shifts and usually managed to arrive early enough to claim her favorite register. After only a few months, she had become the fastest checkout clerk in the store, mainly because she quickly memorized the four-digit bar codes for several dozen of the most commonly purchased produce items — items a cashier has to pause and look up if she doesn't know them. She could key them all in from memory. She was so fast, in fact, that in her first six months, she was named "cashier of the month" twice.

Rae would never quite give her customers the open, inviting smile that her employer encouraged, instead curling the edges of her mouth up while keeping it closed. This technique masked one other important thing this then twenty-four-year-old lacked — teeth. After her father died, her mother abandoned her in the decaying

Stockyards neighborhood to pursue a new love in the mountains of Tennessee. Rae got no dental care after her mother left. By the time Azara was born, all of Rae's teeth had rotted and had to be pulled. She took the sutures out herself. She did eventually get an ill-fitting set of dentures from Medicaid, but they chafe her gums so badly that she mostly goes without them. When she laughs, she holds her hand over her mouth. Otherwise, she manages to convey most of what she feels through her eyes.

Rae is proud of her acumen with numbers. Her strategy for memorizing bar codes was to make a list of the most popular produce items and their codes. When she returned home from work at night, she would read them into a recording device on her cell phone and set it to play throughout the night as she slept. "My subconscious did the job!" she says proudly. Her supervisor encouraged her to take the exam for the position of customer service representative, which requires applicants to memorize the department codes for each item in the store. She toyed with the idea but worried about the added challenges. Plus, the raise would be only 75 cents per hour.

Even though there was a Walmart Supercenter much closer to where she lived, Rae sought out the suburban Parma store because she yearned to surround herself with the kind of people she found there—respectful and polite. Her "anger issues" made it very nearly necessary that she do so. Surviving repeated abandonment by the adults in her life and a nearly constant exposure to danger had left Rae with underlying feelings of rage. Even at the relatively calm Parma store, Rae's temper could flare up unexpectedly with slight provocation. She has many stories of times when customers pushed her to the edge.

Rae recently had "one of those days." She was working the self-checkout lanes—the least popular position in the store because "those machines don't work. They should just take them all out and hire more cashiers." Per usual, the machines were crashing right and left, due to mechanical errors, human errors, or a bit of both. Then an elderly man in a wheelchair rolled up with a dozen handpicked doughnuts fresh from the bakery. He had no idea how to scan the items. In fact, he could hardly reach the keypad on the self-checkout terminal. When Rae stepped up to help, she had to key in each doughnut separately, a slow process for even the fastest cashier. The man berated her from his wheelchair, demanding to know what was taking so long. "Excuse me, sir!" she shouted back. "If you had bought the boxed dozen, we wouldn't be in this situation. This is not my fault!" Shaking with anger, she looked up and noticed her manager walking by. Technically, she could have been fired on the spot, but the manager let the incident go. Now Rae marvels over her luck and is more than a little horrified by her behavior. "I can't believe I almost cussed out an old man . . . in a wheelchair . . . over doughnuts! Now that's crazy. It just goes to show how it gets to you — the way the customers behave."

Rae is proud of her commitment to her work. She was offered a spot on the night shift and would have made a dollar more an hour, but she turned it down, in favor of a friend, because there was too little work to do from 11:00 p.m. to 7:00 a.m. "I would rather be busy. I like to keep moving all the time." All the cashiers in the store knew that if they needed a shift covered, Rae was good for it. One thing she could rely on George and Camilla to do was watch Azara, even if that meant just putting her in front of the TV. Rae would add an early morning shift, an "evening" shift (3:00 p.m. to 11:00 p.m.), or a weekend shift whenever she could. "Yep, I'll do it" was very nearly her mantra, and maybe that, too, was a way to cope with the chaos at home.

But then came the day when she climbed into George's pickup and the gas light flashed on as she turned the key in the ignition. She had just used her entire paycheck to pay the rent, buy groceries and diapers, and give George the agreed-upon $50 for gas so she could take the truck to and from work. Yet over the weekend, George and Camilla had used all the gas running errands. When she marched back into the house to confront them, they claimed they were completely broke, unable to put anything in the tank. Frantic, Rae called her manager, explained the situation, and told him she wouldn't have any cash until the next payday, two weeks away. Could someone give her a lift? Could they float the two-time "cashier of the month" a short-term loan? In response, the store manager informed her that if she couldn't find a way to get to work on time, she shouldn't bother coming in again.

Even after all Rae had been through, this felt like one of the worst moments in her life. "I flipped . . . I don't like confrontation. I don't want to fight. But when you make me lose my job, you don't give me any of my gas money back—I completely went crazy. And my uncle sat there and told me that I'm selfish, that I don't give a shit about anybody else, that it was my fault I lost my job. All of it got put on me. And that's when I was like, 'You know what? I've had enough. I can't do it anymore.' I was like, 'I love you guys, but fuck you.'"

In the months that followed, Rae and Azara found themselves living on nothing but SNAP, plus the diaper and cigarette money slipped her now and again by her "grandma," another friend whom she and Azara lived with for a time after she left George and Camilla's place in a rage. "I've been putting out applications, trying to find another job, 'cuz I don't like sitting at home. I'm used to working and coming home and taking care of my daughter and going to bed with her and waking up with her and doing it all over. [All I want out of life] is to be financially set, honestly. To have a nice job and my own place and not have to really worry. That's my main thing. I stress myself out enough worrying about how am I going to do this and do that. I always worry about what could go wrong so I can prepare myself in case something does happen and I'll know how to approach it and deal with it."

The $2-a-day poor in this book have several characteristics in common: they've had their share of hard luck; they've made their share of bad moves; they have other personal liabilities (asthma, or the same name as a notorious ex-con, for example); and their kin pull them down as often as they lift them up. These aspects of their personal lives are bound to seep into their work lives, at least from time to time. There is just no way around it.

Yet jobs in the low-wage labor market can be exceedingly unforgiving. Rae went from two-time "cashier of the month" to fired in just a few minutes. Jennifer scrubbed away at unheated foreclosed homes in the dead of a Chicago winter until it made her and her kids sick. Her reward was seeing her hours reduced by more than half when she missed work because of it. When one job is lost, finding the next can be remarkably hard, as Jennifer, Susan, and Rae know all too well. Between them, these three women have applied for hundreds of jobs, on iPhone touch screens and in basement computer labs of homeless shelters, over months and over years.

Although the 1996 welfare reform pushed millions of low-income single moms into the workforce, it did nothing to improve the conditions of low-wage jobs. In fact, if anything, economic theory (and plain old common sense) might support the opposite conclusion: although we can't know for sure, it stands to reason that by moving millions of unskilled single mothers into the labor force starting in the mid-1990s, welfare reform and the expansion of the EITC and other refundable tax credits may have actually played a role in diminishing the quality of the average low-wage job in America. As unskilled single mothers flooded into the workforce at unprecedented rates, they greatly increased the pool of workers available to low-wage employers. When more people compete for the same jobs, wages usually fall relative to what they would have been otherwise. Employers can also demand more of their employees.

What low-wage employers now seem to demand are workers whose lives have infinite give and 24-7 dedication, for little in return. Only an employer who is guaranteed a steady stream of desperate job applicants could require a worker to be on call, ready to come in if needed, with no promise of hours. Labor practices such as work loading and on-call shifts are important tools for service sector employers, especially retail chains trying to offer the lowest prices. Simply put, in the face of this race to the bottom, it's hard for those employers who want to do right by their workers to stay in the game. Recent research has found that when a new Walmart opens in a community, it causes an overall loss in jobs in that community because other stores — including some that might pay better or offer stable hours — can't compete. That's what happened to Rae's previous job at the neighborhood Kmart. That store was shut down when a brand-new Walmart Supercenter opened close by. This left Rae, who loved that Kmart job (she had earned a little seniority even though she still lacked full-time hours and benefits), no other choice but to start over at the Parma Walmart.

Chicago City is hardly a major chain; in fact, it is a small family-owned business. Yet it is caught up in much the same phenomenon. Banks that must maintain foreclosed homes sometimes contract with outside companies to care for these properties. These contracts typically go to large maintenance companies, such as Safeguard Properties, that determine whether each home has been vacated and, if so, care for it until it is resold.

Companies like Safeguard may then subcontract maintenance to smaller entities such as Chicago City for pennies on the dollar. The large contractors often fail to live up to their commitments. For instance, in the fall of 2013, Safeguard was being sued by the State of Illinois and others for illegal practices, including evicting homeowners who still legally occupied their properties. Jennifer was at the very bottom of this system, but her employer was not much higher up on the food chain.

Many communities within our country are caught in a downward spiral of bad jobs that don't allow families to meet their basic needs or even ensure against extreme destitution. To eradicate $2-a-day poverty, or at least reverse its upward trend, the low-wage labor market has to change. As a starting point, it is worth asking what those trying to support a family on a low-wage job feel they need, at a minimum, from such a job.

Parents like Jennifer, Susan, and Rae express desires that are quite modest. Full-time hours come first. That is a prize that can be astonishingly hard to wrest from a low-wage employer who wants to avoid added costs associated with full-time employment, such as health insurance and paid time off. A predictable schedule, so parents can arrange for safe, reliable child care, comes next. A few say they would be happy if they could get just those two things. Yet finding a job with even those basic attributes is something Susan Brown feels she can only dream of, not expect.

Most parents, like Jennifer and Rae, hope for a little more. If they could just make $12 or $13 per hour, they say, they could make it; $15 per hour is really shooting the moon. Safe working conditions, and some sick or personal days, would be a real plus. The other "extras" that once came routinely with a full-time job — health insurance, vacation days, and retirement benefits — don't often come up in conversations with the $2-a-day poor. These perks are so uncommon among the jobs available to low-wage workers that they seem all but outside the bounds of reality.

Chapter 3

A Room of One's Own

LONG BEFORE HER STINT at Chicago City Custodial Services, Jennifer Hernandez and her children, Kaitlin and Cole, stayed for a time with family on Chicago's Southwest Side, in a neighborhood of well-kept, story-and-a-half Prairie-style bungalows and yellow-brick ranches. Many of the community's modest, rectangular homes hail from the 1950s era of modern design and often sport original mid-century touches, such as a porch awning artfully set at an angle. Enjoying low crime rates, reasonable prices (for Chicago), and quiet living, this community of teachers, police officers, and other civil servants is happy to be mostly hidden from view.

And in that way, the neighborhood was just the right fit for Jennifer. Always understated, she speaks quietly, with little intonation. Her own appearance may be somewhat ragged, but without fail she makes sure her kids are always neatly dressed, fussing over their clothes much as the homeowners in this neighborhood obsess over their deep-green lawns.

Jennifer and her kids were given a one-bedroom unit carved out of the back half of the first story of a two-flat home owned by Jennifer's aunt Isabelle. She lived on the second floor, and her daughter Andrea and Andrea's live-in boyfriend, Carlos, lived in an apartment that spanned the basement and front half of the first floor. Jennifer's family had a modicum of privacy (though Andrea felt she could barge in at all hours without warning), and as far as Jennifer was concerned, the one-bedroom unit was just fine. She remembers that it "had big rooms and there was enough space for us." The kids slept in the bedroom, Jennifer on the couch in the living room. She never could have afforded a place like this on her own. In fact, from 2008 to 2013 there was never a time when she and the kids lived on their own without help. They were always either doubled up with family or in a homeless shelter.

Housing costs have reached a crisis point for low-income families, eating up far more of their incomes than they can possibly afford. The U.S. Department of Housing and Urban Development (HUD) deems a family that is spending more than 30 percent of its income on housing to be "cost burdened," at risk of having too little money for food, clothing, and other essential expenses.

Today there is no state in the Union in which a family that is supported by a full-time, minimum-wage worker can afford a two-bedroom apartment at fair market rent without being cost burdened, according to HUD. When Jennifer moved in with Isabelle, even the fair market rent on a studio apartment in the Chicago area would have consumed more than half of her paycheck. But since Isabelle couldn't legally rent out the unit Jennifer's family was staying in because it lacked a private entrance — not to mention the fact that Isabelle didn't want to live with a stranger in such close quarters — she was willing to cut Jennifer a good deal on the place.

Given the options available to Jennifer, she was grateful to be living with her kids under the roof of a relative in a safe, pleasant neighborhood. And she was certainly thankful for the chance to send her kids to a decent neighborhood school and for the job Andrea had helped her land at a swanky downtown spa.

At night, though, things could veer off the tracks. Andrea's boyfriend, Carlos, was a "working drunk." Jennifer recalls that "he would go to work, come home, and basically drink all night, [then] . . . sober up enough to go to work and come back home and start the cycle over again." Andrea had a drinking problem herself, and the couple often started screaming insults at each other just as Jennifer was putting the kids to bed. Sometimes these fights lasted deep into the night. Sometimes "they would chase each other through the house, out into the street, you know."

When these fights spilled out onto the front lawn, the police would get involved. "They've both been arrested. They've had the cops called [by the neighbors]. They've called the cops on each other." Red lights would flash outside the kids' bedroom window while the officers tried to sort out the situation. Kaitlin, who was already suffering from bouts of anxiety, couldn't get to sleep until long after things had quieted down, and Cole began to have nightmares.

At first, work offered Jennifer a daytime respite. Catalina Spa & Salon was one of the city's posh places to get a facial, a massage, the latest hairstyle, a mani-pedi, or an extensive spa treatment. Jennifer was originally hired for thirty to thirty-five hours per week at $9.25 an hour. In the beginning, Jennifer and Andrea both worked behind the scenes, washing and drying the white towels and bathrobes, folding them just so, refilling the spa products, and mopping the floors. On the whole, Jennifer enjoyed the work at Catalina. "It was a pretty fun working environment, you know, wasn't dull or drab. I enjoyed going to work. I liked the people I worked with. It was a good experience."

Then Andrea was involved in a massive car crash in which both vehicles were totaled. She suffered multiple broken ribs, putting her completely out of commission. As far as Jennifer was concerned, that wasn't all bad news—at least she wouldn't be throwing things at Carlos with quite so much ferocity at night. But it did mean big changes for Jennifer at work. By law, the spa had to hold Andrea's job open while she recovered. Wanting to be a team player, Jennifer agreed to work both shifts for a week or two until the manager could find someone else to fill in. She figured she could use the extra cash anyway. Catalina wasn't paying her overtime as they should have been, but that was okay. It was only temporary.

Two weeks turned into three, three into four, and four into six. All that time, Jennifer was doing the work of two. Tack on the three hours for her daily commute, and she was spending just shy of ninety hours away from home each week, leaving her elementary school–age children in the care of Andrea before and after school. Not only was she exhausted beyond belief, but her absence was also taking a toll on Kaitlin and Cole. "Kaitlin started giving me, like, attitude, you know, she started getting angry. Cole started getting in trouble at school. He was, like, acting up in class. I finally had to sit them down and talk to them, you know, 'What's going on?'" The kids replied, "'You're never here, you're not at home anymore,' you know, 'You're always gone.'"

That got Jennifer's attention: her kids were getting the short end of the stick during the night and now during the day, too. And, increasingly, it seemed as if Catalina was perfectly happy with the situation. They saw no reason to hire another person to take on Andrea's shift, when Jennifer was doing such a good job covering both. Finally, Jennifer's manager admitted as much, claiming they couldn't afford to bring on someone else. Jennifer, usually quiet and self-contained, couldn't hide the indignation in her voice. "Really? The prices you guys charge and you can't afford to hire someone else to come help me at least a few hours a day?" Jennifer knew that even when Andrea returned, it would be a while until she was back up to speed physically. Jennifer would be carrying a lot of the burden for a long time. But there was no room to negotiate. Jennifer was issued an ultimatum: she could continue to do the work of two, putting in seventy hours a week — ninety including commuting time — until Andrea came back, or she could look for another job.

"I'm proud. I like to do my job. I do my work, but all I wanted was a little help, you know? I was overwhelmed . . . It's hard work, heavy lifting, heavy, heavy duties. There's a lot to do." Jennifer knew that if she quit, it would take her a while to find another job. In the meantime, she'd be unable to make even her modest rent. And even if she could continue living with her aunt, the arrangement was threatening to cost her and the kids their sanity.

What Jennifer and the kids needed was a place of their own, but there was no way she could afford that. Nor could she afford to pay someone to wake up her children in the morning, get them dressed and ready for school, and stay with them until she returned home at night. She needed the child care her cousin and aunt provided just as much as she needed the roof over their heads.

Families facing dilemmas like Jennifer's often learn that they have only one option: find another couch to sleep on, another spare bedroom, another relative or family member willing to take them in without exacting too high a price. Jennifer was an only child. She had never known her father, so there was no one on that side of the family she could stay with. Her mother had died some years before, but in addition to Isabelle, she had some aunts and uncles living in central Texas, in Abilene, where she'd grown up. A phone call revealed that one of these aunts, whose children were grown and living on their own, had a couple of spare bedrooms to offer. Thanks to all her double shifts, Jennifer had enough money squirreled away to pay for three bus tickets from Chicago to Abilene. With her aunt's offer in hand, she gave notice at Catalina, explaining to her boss, "I can't continue to work like this anymore."

Jennifer, Kaitlin, and Cole took off for Abilene in March. Few who have taken a two-day, round-the-clock, cross-country bus trip would relish the opportunity to relive the experience. You can't shut out the constant drone of the bus, can't get comfortable in the cramped seats, and can't avoid the smells emanating from the restroom that runs out of paper towels on day one. Nobody on the bus wants to be there.

Throughout the trip, Kaitlin, age nine at the time, never stopped moving. She flipped the seat-back tray table up and down, up and down, up and down. Luckily, she has always had a way of charming adults, so she could get away with that sort of behavior without completely infuriating her fellow passengers. Coke-bottle glasses and bobbing hair, perpetual energy and infectious smile, all come together to produce something irresistible in Kaitlin. As Jennifer puts it, "Kaitlin is a very sweet, very lovable little girl . . . People just gravitate toward her." Kaitlin's magic has gotten them out of more than one jam over the years. The owner of an after-school program was so taken with her that when Jennifer ran out of money, she let both kids stay in the program for free. Then she gave Kaitlin a brand-new scooter.

Cole, who was six at the time, is a striking child, too, with smooth brown skin and penetrating eyes. He's far more reserved than his sister. The two kids usually get along, but every now and again he lashes out, resenting all the attention that Kaitlin attracts. One day, jealousy got the best of him as Kaitlin rode her new scooter down the street, and he shoved her so hard that she fell and suffered a hairline fracture in her wrist. On the bus headed for Texas, however, he was easier to amuse than his sister. He could get lost for hours in the games Jennifer had loaded on her cell phone (no minutes, but lots of games).

When they finally got to Abilene and to her aunt's home, Jennifer remembers that "things were going pretty well there for a while . . . It's a beautiful town, you know, it's nice. I mean, there's not a lot of violence." The house had ample room to accommodate them. Another uncle and his wife lived just down the street, a partial re-creation of the close-knit community she remembered from childhood.

Jennifer was happy to leave her Chicago aunt's home with all its drama behind, but she quickly discovered that living with her Texas relatives presented its own set of challenges. Some of her cousins were in jail or on probation, while others had succumbed to drug addiction. (Jennifer sometimes jokes that she feels "like [the] black sheep [of the family] because I've never been arrested!") Few were in stable relationships or held steady jobs. Even so, they were a tight-knit family. "We grew up together, and I love my family . . . My aunts and uncles, they were always there for me, anything I needed, any problems, I could always go talk to them, and I was always staying at someone's house, you know, my cousin's house, her house, his house, you know . . . I don't have any brothers or sisters, I'm an only child. So my cousins were my brothers and sisters."

Try as she might, however, Jennifer "just couldn't seem to make a go of it out there. I couldn't get any stable work. I mean, I would work, but it was here and there, maybe a month here, maybe a month there . . . It was hard, especially down where we're from . . . If you don't have a vehicle, you're pretty much SOL." She was troubled by recurring bouts of depression, something she has suffered from for years. "I wasn't seeing anyone for my mental health issues . . . I wasn't stabilized myself." Jennifer has always found that the best medicine for her depression is a job. "When I have been working, like I said, it, it seems to help me. Gives me a sense of purpose, you know." Without work, she often finds herself in a dark place.

As the months dragged on and Jennifer struggled to find work and help her kids adjust to their new environment, tensions began to mount in the household. Her aunt blamed her for not trying hard enough to find a steady job and for not contributing her fair share to the household expenses. When Jennifer's uncle, José, offered to shelter them in his home down the street, she was tempted. She knew he drank too much, but she respected him nonetheless. He was the head groundskeeper at a local country club. He knew how to hold down a steady job, a good-paying job, one with responsibilities. Maybe he was even someone Cole could look up to as a role model, minus the drinking.

Once again, Jennifer and the kids packed up their stuff and headed to their third home in less than a year. Luckily, this time it was just down the street. Kaitlin and Cole wouldn't have to change schools, and they'd still be safe, surrounded by family members who, for all their faults, Jennifer believed had her kids' best interests at heart. Although, even as they made the move, Jennifer was starting to panic, wondering when a real job was going to appear. She was running out of moves. Her family had stood by her so far, but how long could she expect them to keep propping her up?

What happened next made her long for the twelve-hour days at Catalina, with Andrea and Carlos screaming at each other through the night. "I never expected that, you know. I mean, [José] was a grown man, he's in his fifties. He's an adult and takes care of himself, he's had a steady job, he's worked at the country club for over twenty years." When she talks about it, her voice gets even softer than usual, and the pace of her words slows, as though she can barely bring herself to say it.

"He molested Kaitlin." Walking in on the pair in a back bedroom one day, Jennifer "caught him in the act. Caught him standing over her with his pants down. He was standing over her . . . He was obviously drunk." Jennifer had been out running errands, but José should have known that she might walk in on them at any moment.

"I think I just . . . grabbed her." She remembers yanking Kaitlin away as José reeled backward. Jennifer raced around the house to find Cole and grabbed him by the back of his collar, then she "ran with them and [we] locked ourselves in [our] room."

Huddled in the bedroom for hours — panicked, dazed, and clinging to her kids for dear life — Jennifer wrestled with what to do next. Finally, she shoved what clothing she could into a single bag, and the three of them ran through the front door and out onto the street, leaving most of their things behind. They landed, shell-shocked, on the doorstep of the local Salvation Army.

Jennifer remembers the staff told her that "normally [they] only deal with recovering addicts. Basically they're taking single individuals, you know, women and men. [But] they said they would make the exception because Kaitlin was so small, because she was a child." The facility offered only open dorms, however, which given the circumstances just wasn't going to work. At a minimum, the three of them needed a private place to sleep, a door that locked at night. So the staff "converted one of their offices into a bedroom for us . . . I'm really thankful for them. They really helped us out a lot at that time, 'cuz I was, I was pretty much lost."

Jennifer half expected that one of her aunts would come to the rescue, especially when she decided to go public with what had happened and press charges. Instead, only Isabelle back in Chicago was supportive, though she had by then rented the first-floor unit to someone else. Jennifer's Texas kin accused her of destroying the family. Even now, she says, "half of the family hates me, the other half supports me." Still, she feels she did the right thing. "I did what I needed to do for my daughter, you know . . . At some point in the future, she would have blamed me, and I couldn't bear it to live with that. I needed her to know that I did what was within my power to do, to make sure she was okay."

Housing instability is a hallmark of life among the $2-a-day poor. Children experiencing $2-a-day poverty are far more likely to move over the course of a year than other kids — even than children living in less extreme poverty. Much of this instability is fueled by perilous double-ups, which mark — and often speed — the descent of those who are already suffering from the fallout from nonsustaining work into the ranks of the desperately poor. Every family whose story is told in this book has doubled up with kin or friends at some point, because their earnings haven't been sufficient to maintain a place of their own. While living with relatives sometimes offers strength and uplift, it can also prove toxic for the most vulnerable in our society, ending in sexual, physical, or verbal abuse. The trauma from this abuse is sometimes a precipitating factor in a family's fall into $2-a-day poverty, or the calamity that keeps them in such a state for far too long.

The Great Recession will long be remembered for the foreclosure crisis that accompanied it. This crisis has left millions of homes sitting empty across the country, often for years, falling into greater and greater disrepair. As housing prices plummeted and mortgages became harder to come by, fewer and fewer people were ready or able to buy a new home, while others who had lost their homes to foreclosure needed new lodging. Consequently, people who in another era might have owned their own homes flooded the rental market. As the number of people competing for rental units grew, the poor were increasingly squeezed by rising rents or pushed out of the rental market altogether, forced to double up or couch surf.

Yet it would be wrong to pin the inability of so many of today's poor to find a stable home wholly on the housing collapse of the

Great Recession. Doing so might lead to the conclusion that this is a temporary problem that will be alleviated in time. In fact, serious problems with the availability of affordable housing have been apparent for well over a decade. Already in 2001, 63 percent of very low income households were putting more than half their income toward housing, leaving too little for other necessities. As of 2011, that figure stood at nearly 70 percent.

What has caused this ongoing rise in housing costs? Taking the long view, one of the factors driving this trend is the across-the-board improvement in the quality of housing in America. Sixty years ago, lower-end housing was likely to lack such basic amenities as indoor plumbing. Since that time, these features have become standard, even in the cheapest units. This has been a great advancement for our society, but it also means that low-cost housing has become less affordable as a result.

Further, families like Jennifer's are subject to different rules today than they once were. In Chicago, as well as in virtually every other jurisdiction in the country, child welfare officials deem it inappropriate for a brother and sister to sleep in the same bedroom once they reach a certain age. At some point, if the authorities were to find out that Kaitlin and Cole were sharing a room, Jennifer would be at risk of losing custody due to "neglect." By today's standards of child well-being, Jennifer can't move into a studio apartment to help balance her family's budget.

The most obvious manifestation of the affordable housing crisis is in rising rents. Between 1990 and 2013, rents rose faster than inflation in virtually every region of the country and in cities, suburbs, and rural areas alike. But there is another important factor at work here that is an even bigger part of the story than the hikes in rent: a fall in the earnings of renters. Between 2000 and 2012 alone, rents rose by 6 percent. During that same period, the real income of the middling renter in the United States *fell* 13 percent. What was once a fissure has become a wide chasm that often can't be bridged.

Very recently, a shift in supply and demand has made the crisis even more acute. Since the advent of the Great Recession, the number of extremely low income renters has grown dramatically — up by 2.5 million — while the supply of affordable rentals has remained flat. Because one-third of these low-cost rentals were occupied by higher-income renters, in 2011 only thirty-six affordable units were available for every one hundred renters with extremely low incomes. And most affordable units are older — usually fifty years old or more — and at heightened risk for disinvestment due to the costly nature of upgrades and repairs. It follows that they are the most likely to be deemed "substandard."

Are exploitative landlords to blame? It is easy to find examples of sleazy operators. Two years before Rae McCormick lost her job at Walmart because George used all her gas money and left her with no gas, Phillip Morris of the *Cleveland Plain Dealer* detailed the tactics of a pair of notorious landlords. This dynamic duo had perfected the art of what some call "soft evictions"—a poor euphemism for outrageously abusive methods of punishing tenants who are late on the rent. They were accused of removing exterior doors, cutting off power to units by removing the electric meter, and even allegedly smearing a rental's breaker panel with feces. According to the *Plain Dealer,* one of their tenants returned home to find that the pair had changed the door locks. When she finally managed to get into her unit, the tenant claimed that someone had stolen random shoes (both hers and her kids'), family photos, and precious poems and drawings the children had brought home from school.

Though in truth, it is very hard for even a principled landlord to supply an affordable unit to a family living on the income that a low-wage job provides. In interviews with 123 landlords renting units to low-income tenants in 2013 and 2014, many claimed that in order to make any profit at all, they had to buy units only when the purchase price was very low (e.g., a unit in disrepair or one located in a low-income neighborhood), purchase it using cash or a mortgage with very favorable terms, and keep their maintenance costs very low.

One such landlord said that he capitalizes on this formula by purchasing single-family homes in Cleveland's poorer east side neighborhoods with cash and at very low cost (generally $8,000 to $10,000). He then invests minimally in repairs (one way he saves is to paint the hardwood floors brown and the walls, trim, and ceiling a uniform white). When the maintenance or repair costs on the property become too high, he abandons it and purchases another home with cash. By employing these tactics, he's able to keep his rents affordable. To date, this property owner has purchased more than fifty units on Cleveland's struggling east side and has abandoned more than a dozen. If these practices are widespread, they may be eating the supply of affordable Cleveland housing stock alive.

A husband-and-wife team with about a dozen lower-rent units on the city's west side claim they can barely break even with their rentals. Because their tenants so frequently lose hours at work, lose their jobs altogether, or break up, leaving the household with only one earner when making the rent takes two, these landlords manage to collect the full rent on their units only about half the time. When asked what she would do to change things, the wife responded, "Raise the minimum wage!"

HUD seeks to alleviate some of the burden of the high housing costs faced by low-income families through maintaining public housing developments and through the housing choice voucher program, colloquially known as Section 8. While these programs are far from perfect, there's solid evidence from the gold standard of social science research — a randomized control trial — that they reduce housing instability considerably. Access to a Section 8 voucher, in particular, reduces the chances that a family will be homeless — either doubled up or out on the streets. It lessens by half the share of families living in overcrowded units, and it greatly diminishes the average number of moves a family makes over a five-year period.

But while the cost of housing has grown and wages have stagnated, the size of government housing programs has not kept pace, a trend of reduced investment that began in the 1980s during the Reagan administration. What's more, the new government housing initiatives of the past few decades have focused on demolishing distressed high-rise public housing and replacing it with smaller, higher-quality mixed-income developments. While this may well improve the living conditions of residents, such a strategy has reduced, rather than increased, the number of affordable units available. Today there are far more people in need of help with their housing expenses than receive it. Only about a quarter of income-eligible families get any kind of rental subsidy. In 2011, a smaller fraction of Americans received any sort of rental assistance from the government than was the case two decades earlier. And twenty years ago, the need was not nearly as great.

In many places, the waiting list for a housing subsidy — or even for an address in the projects — is astonishingly long. During the summer of 2012, when Modonna and Brianna Harris were bouncing around from shelter to shelter in Chicago, the city's waiting list for a Section 8 voucher or public housing included *85,000* families. To make matters worse, the list was closed. Modonna couldn't have taken number 85,001 even if she had wanted to. That's why Jennifer Hernandez never managed to get a housing subsidy before qualifying for La Casa's program, despite three spells of $2-a-day poverty. And Chicago's backlog is short compared to New York City's, where about *268,000* families were in the queue for a voucher or public housing as of March 2013. In the United States, housing assistance is not an entitlement — families are not legally guaranteed help just because their incomes are low. In most places and for most people, rental assistance isn't something you can easily find in the event of an emergency. Rather, it's something you should expect to wait years to get. For those who receive help, the benefit is huge. Not surprisingly, those lucky enough to secure a subsidy are often loath to relinquish it.

There are, to be sure, differences in housing markets across the country. Rents in Chicago are relatively high, while those in Cleveland are a bargain in comparison. Rents in the more rural parts of eastern Tennessee and the Mississippi Delta are lower still, but much of the affordable stock consists of decrepit trailer homes. What seems to be universal, though, is that the dwellings in which America's $2-a-day poor reside are in such terrible condition that few other Americans would be willing to step foot in them, let alone call them home. Susan, Devin, and Lauren Brown's living room floor was covered with dirty, decades-old, moldy carpeting — the type of carpeting research has confirmed is linked to asthma, nausea, vomiting, and headaches. Over in Cleveland, a two-bedroom house was home to *twenty-two* extended family members for nearly six months in 2013 — and during two of those months, the water was shut off. Children were doubled up in bunk beds in virtually every room, including the basement and tiny, sweltering attic. And in Johnson City, Tennessee, a family of four was evicted in 2013 from a public housing unit when they failed to pay the minimum $25 in monthly rent demanded by the housing authority, even from those with no income. After a few weeks of couch surfing, they landed in a fleabag motel room that was overrun by bedbugs and had no kitchen, waiting for space to open up at the only family shelter in town.

When homeless families with children temporarily double up with relatives and friends, their support might turn out to be an important asset, as it was for Susan and Devin Brown on Chicago's South Side. Yet many times the kin that poor families have to rely on are not much better off financially than they are, because poverty is too often passed from one generation to the next. If the stories of the families chronicled here are any guide, this appears to be especially true among America's $2-a-day poor. For Jennifer Hernandez, falling into the arms of her family in Texas proved to be the biggest mistake she ever made, for herself and for her vulnerable children.

In the late 1990s, a team of medical researchers set out to document the prevalence of adverse childhood experiences, or ACEs, among a group of mostly middle-aged people. ACEs include emotional, physical, and sexual abuse; emotional and physical neglect; and certain adverse household characteristics. When these researchers surveyed more than 17,000 people from San Diego — most of whom were middle-class and had gone to college — they found alarmingly high rates of ACE exposure. Sixty-four percent reported at least one adverse childhood experience; more than a third had experienced two or more such events. Fully 28 percent had experienced physical abuse, while one in five had a history of sexual abuse.

The ACE study and more recent follow-up studies offer evidence that the experience of abuse, neglect, and other adverse circumstances in childhood is disturbingly common in the American population as a whole. Yet as shocking as these ACE study findings are, poor children are at far greater risk of such experiences. And among the families in $2-a-day poverty, this heightened risk too often stems from their dependence on family and friends.

This isn't surprising when you consider the circumstances under which abuse is most likely to occur. Take child sexual abuse, the kind that Kaitlin suffered. Such abuse is most often inflicted on a child by someone she or he knows. According to some estimates, roughly 60 percent of abusers are familiar to the child but are not family members, while 30 percent of abusers, like José, are related to the child. Strangers make up only 10 percent of perpetrators. Abusers are also likely to misuse alcohol or drugs. Children who have multiple caretakers are most at risk, as are children who are emotionally vulnerable (as Kaitlin and Cole were when they moved from Chicago to Texas).

Families in $2-a-day poverty who must double up with friends or relatives sometimes find themselves in a perfect storm of risk for sexual, emotional, or physical abuse. They are often powerless, having little means to protect themselves. In addition, they are often already dealing with a crisis — the crisis that drove them to double up in the first place. Parents might be anxious or depressed, not surprising given the high levels of stress related to their housing instability. And they are more likely to be situated in networks that include children and adults who have themselves experienced abuse at some point in their lives, may struggle with alcohol and drug addiction, or may have mental health challenges. Sometimes finding refuge in the mother-in-law suite or spare bedroom of a relative's home is the best thing to ever happen to the $2-a-day poor. But it can also be the worst.

Ever since her father died, Rae McCormick's life has been a search for family — family she can care for, family she can rely on. Despite her deep and abiding love for her father, Rae has only a few memories of him. Only by looking at the single photograph of him in her possession — showing a handsome, wiry man standing beside a bright red motorcycle — does Rae remember bits and pieces about him. "My dad raised me that you work for everything you have. That way, in the end of the day, you can feel good that you did that. That came from you. I believe that you should work for everything you have and people shouldn't just give you things. I don't like pity."

When Rae's father first got really sick, her brother, Jordan, ran away and her sister, Mary Lou, went south to live with extended family in Tennessee. Then Rae's dad died and her mother abandoned her, leaving the eleven-year-old to fend for herself. From then on, "it was crazy . . . I had to put myself through fifth grade, which means that I had to get myself up for school and take myself to school . . . The landlord . . . was a really good friend with my dad, so he didn't turn me in. He kind of helped me and let me live there rent-free."

Meanwhile, Rae's mother moved from boyfriend to boyfriend, bouncing back and forth between Appalachia and Cleveland. Each month, however, her mother would send her the $300 or so in Social Security survivor's benefits to which she was entitled because of her father's death. Money in hand, she would navigate the dangerous blocks between her Cleveland apartment and the local liquor store, the closest place to pay the gas and light bills. Given her tiny frame — even now, she's only five foot two — she could barely see over the counter. It was the liquor bottles on the high shelves behind the bulletproof glass and not the cashier that caught her eye as she stood on tiptoes to complete her transactions. Wherever she went, she was careful, because there were "gangs, Crips and Bloods, everywhere." She remembers a time when she called the police on an intruder who was crouching on the porch roof outside her bedroom window. They never came. Terrified to be so alone, she acquired a pit bull named Sweetie. (Because of safety concerns, pit bulls are common among the residents of Cleveland's Stockyards neighborhood. Rottweilers are second in popularity, for the same reason.)

After about a year of living alone, Rae recalls, her aunt Wilma in Tennessee got wind of the fact that she was on her own. "Out of no-where my aunt and my cousin showed up. I looked out the window and I'm like, 'Who the hell is banging on the door?' I hadn't seen them in years. So I went down there and I opened the door . . . And when they walked in and seen that I was there by myself, nobody else was there, just the dog, they . . . went immediately right back down to Tennessee and told my sister, 'You need to go up there. Something's going to end up happening to your sister. She's too young to be by herself.'"

So Mary Lou and her husband begrudgingly moved up north to care for Rae. These new guardians "snatched me out of that house pretty quick" (to evade the child welfare authorities) and moved into an apartment that had no heat or running water. It was all they could afford. That first winter, Rae got so sick she was hospitalized twice for pneumonia. Two of her brother-in-law's friends also moved in, an ex-con who had served time for murder and a man Rae believed was a paranoid schizophrenic. Then Mary Lou "started acting like my mother" and ran off, leaving Rae alone in the apartment with the three men for about a year. Finally, Rae's mother signed over custody of her daughter to a friend in Cleveland who was willing to take Rae in, as long as Rae's Social Security checks were turned over to her. The woman evicted Rae the moment she turned eighteen and those checks stopped coming.

After bouncing around from place to place, Rae, now twenty-one, met the man with whom she would conceive her only daugh-ter, Azara. Donny has never worked regularly. He lives rent-free with his mother, sister, cousin, and cousin's girlfriend in a three-bedroom house owned by his grandparents. He and his sister score cash by selling plasma twice a week, but Rae and Azara see none of that money. For years, he has talked vaguely about enlisting in the army, and he has turned the garage into a gym where he works out constantly — at least when he isn't sleeping or playing video games on a big TV he mounted on the wall.

Rae laments, "It wasn't even a month after we met that I ended up getting pregnant." At first, Rae moved in with Donny in an effort to form a stable environment for their coming child, but things were rocky right from the start. "When I was pregnant, I found out he was screwing around with somebody else. I left, but after Azara was born, I came back like an idiot and got played two different times."

Stung by his infidelities, Rae moved in with her friend Danielle, herself a mother of three, and a group of other childhood friends who were sharing a house on a street where virtually every other property was burned-out. When the water and power were shut off in that house and a woman was raped in the abandoned garage next door, she decided it wasn't a safe place to raise a child.

Once again, she was back with Donny. Over the years, she's tried to live with him several more times, but these stints have always ended in disaster. Even when she was pregnant, she was relegated to the house's unventilated basement, down a long flight of stairs. Violence was an everyday occurrence. Once, Donny smashed her cell phone against the wall. On another occasion, he dislocated her jaw ("I had to like, literally, like force it to go back in"). Another time, she got into a fight with Donny's mom, who demanded that she turn over her SNAP card as rent (even though no one in the home paid rent to the grandparents who owned the house). The last time she was living there, Rae says, Donny "grabbed me by my throat . . . then he choked me to the ground and tried to kill me." But it wasn't until Donny admitted to having slept with a fifteen-year-old girl that Rae decided she had to leave the house for good. "I don't think I've decked anybody harder in my life . . . And I'm like, 'If I get called in court, I'm telling them that your custody should be stripped.'"

After that, Rae found herself on the move again, and she is once again back living with George and Camilla. Now four years old, Azara is a bright and cheerful girl who loves the Nickelodeon cartoon *Dora the Explorer* and is always disassembling her toys to see how they work. Since the last time Rae and Azara lived with George and Camilla, they have taken in three boarders. Initially, the entire group rented a three-bedroom house on Cleveland's east side, in what they refer to as "the hood." When a gunman opened fire just down the block, injuring thirteen children, they decided it was time to move back to Rae's childhood neighborhood, the Stockyards.

"I wouldn't let my dog live in conditions like this," one friend remarked after visiting Rae at their new place.

From the outside, the nature of this home is hidden: no slouching rooflines, unlike so many of the other houses in the neighborhood. Uniform gray metal siding—the indestructible type from the 1970s—gives it a look of solidity. It is a classic Victorian farmhouse—two stories, with the second-floor bedrooms carved out of the eaves. The house sports a large front porch with scarred, yet unbroken, floorboards. Out back is every parent's dream: a fenced-in yard. This one is littered with broken glass and an old tire, but it is full of potential as a play space for Azara, with enough room for the backyard garden that Rae has always dreamed of.

The day after the move, the porch is filled with junk. An old leatherette couch that was damaged beyond repair during the move is jammed into the back corner of the U-Haul truck, its stuffing escaping everywhere. A few black plastic bags filled with clothes are propped up against it. Their labels read size XXL, so they must belong to George and Camilla's boarder Big Art, who stands more than six foot five and weighs roughly 265 pounds. Art is only sixty years old, but he can't get around without a walker. He lets the commotion swirl around him while he sits on the porch steps, curbing his two dogs on their rusted chains. One dog clearly has a skin disease — his nose and forehead, plus parts of his back, are hairless and covered with bloody scabs. These are not pets for petting, unless you are Art. To him they are the only family he's got.

It's Big Art's smell and appearance that give the first clues to what lies within the relatively solid exterior of this home. As he scratches the heads of his dogs, who run up and down the stairs to the porch, passersby find it hard not to stare. There is a large, hairless knot on the top of Art's head that is over an inch tall and an inch in diameter. He's entirely bald, so there is no covering it up. Broken blood vessels form dense webs under his eyes, almost making it look as if he has two shiners. He usually doesn't wear shoes because it's hard to fit them over his swollen feet — an effect, he believes, of one of the forms of cancer that ail him — and his curled-over, yellow toenails are more than an inch long. He's worn the same khaki work shirt and matching pants for days now, ever since the move, so anyone standing near him is overpowered by the stench of sweat and urine. But he's not the only one who smells; everyone does, at least a little. There's no washer or dryer in the house, and the Laundromat costs money.

Big Art was taken in by his old friends George and Camilla when his incontinence and difficulty walking (Rae says there is cancer in his legs) threatened to land him in a nursing home. Keith, already balding and stooped in his twenties, and his fiancée, Tiffany, blonde and with a penchant for plunging necklines, came to live with the couple when they were evicted and had no place else to go. On the one hand, George and Camilla are heroes — taking in needy friends, perhaps out of the goodness of their hearts. On the other hand, Big Art turns over the $1,300 he receives in government disability to George in exchange for food and shelter. Keith and Tiffany contribute Keith's monthly disability check of $750 and Tiffany's SNAP card. George is adamant that all the money come to him. Rae says that George "believes that he should have the money so he can deal with everything hisself, which I think is his way of scamming people and doing other stuff."

Despite these suspicions, George and Camilla are the closest thing to family that Rae's got, besides Azara. When Rae has a spell of bad dreams, she asks George if Azara can sleep with them, "because I don't wanna wake up in the middle of the night and swing and then my daughter has a messed-up face because I had a dream that somebody attacked me." And when George and Camilla fight, Rae often ends up playing mediator, "because I'm the only one that can get through to [George]." She tells him, "Look, you're about to lose your woman that you've been with for how long because you wanna be stuck-up and keep your pride? Put that shit down in the corner for a minute and go save your relationship."

George, who reads at a first-grade level (his mental limitations are what earn him his own SSI check of $620 a month), relies on Rae to help decipher the bills and get them paid. He cuts her considerable slack on the rent, since she's unemployed, but she does have to turn over her SNAP card. In turn, she tries to make herself indispensable — cleaning, cooking, and looking after Big Art — all in an effort to make sure she can continue to claim the bedroom that she and Azara share, both of them sleeping on a single air mattress that just about fills the tiny room.

Camilla plans the meals. She uses the two SNAP cards she "keeps" for Tiffany and Rae to shop for groceries. These two cards are meant to buy food for four people and can't be stretched to feed seven — not by a long shot. It's George and Rae, the two thinnest and most altruistic members of the household, who go without eating so the others don't go hungry. Rae always makes sure Azara has enough, but she herself may go days without food toward the end of the month. In Rae's mind, this isn't a big sacrifice, because she often doesn't have an appetite anyway. "Like I didn't eat for four days because I wasn't hungry . . . To be honest, I'm so used to it that I don't even feel it anymore. I don't feel it at all anymore." What she can't do without, though, is her cigarettes. George provides cigarettes for all the adults in the household. Beyond the rent and the water and sewer bills, cigarettes constitute the household's biggest single expense.

Inside, low ceilings trap the smoke of five smokers. With only two operational electrical outlets in the home, the floors are covered with an extension cord spaghetti that trips up Azara and her neighborhood friends as they chase each other from room to room. By certain measures, the adults who share this home enjoy some luxuries. Everyone has a cell phone. The house has cable — it was the first thing George had installed. But the first and second floors have no water supply. The kitchen has no functioning stove. Cooking is done on a charcoal grill outside.

To rent the house, George was required to provide evidence that he had turned on the water and electricity in his name — a poor man's credit check for a landlord with only bad tenants to choose from. But between the time the last tenant vacated the house and George and his crew moved in, someone stripped the basement of all its copper piping, no doubt sold at lightning speed to one of the scrapyards lying side by side on 65th Street. The landlord says he has no plans to repair the damage. Should the new tenants try to force him to do something about it? Probably best not to, they decide, given how many people not on the lease are living here. It's not exactly easy to hide Big Art.

Instead, Rae and Camilla, who along with Tiffany are the only adults not on disability, take turns descending the narrow cellar stairs with five-gallon buckets in each hand. They turn on the water long enough to fill them with the stream that spews from the broken pipe protruding from the wall. After filling the buckets, they haul them back upstairs. Endless trips are needed. Both of the toilets need a gallon of water to flush. Drinking water must be secured, for both humans and dogs. Dishes must be washed. Due to his incontinence, Big Art must be bathed at least once a day. (George takes care of this chore.) Azara must be bathed, too. Rainy days are a godsend, as she can simply be sent out to play, letting the rainwater wash her.

Rae and Camilla also take turns in the basement trying to restore water to the rest of the house. They borrowed a Sawzall from a friend and are using it to cut through some PVC piping they found lying around, which they hope can be jury-rigged to replace the missing copper piping and connect to the water line going upstairs. Big Art claims to have done some plumbing in his day, and he coaches them from where he sits atop the cellar stairs. Rae finds his advice less than convincing.

In the end, what makes this house seem most unlivable is its odor. Beyond Big Art's incontinence, beyond the fact that all five adults smoke, beyond the smell of the dogs, beyond the moldy furniture — the house just smells old. It smells like a vacant property. Until recently, when the prior tenant finally forced the landlord to replace the roof, it leaked like a sieve. The waterlogged plaster walls swell up when there is any hint of moisture in the air. The ceilings sag. The little lean-to roof over the kitchen at the back of the house is so low that everyone but petite Rae must crouch down to move around in there. When walked on, the floorboards in the kitchen creak so loudly that they seem to threaten to cave in at any moment.

This house is just one of the dozens of addresses that twenty-five-year-old Rae has called home over the years. In some months and in some places, she has lived below the $2-a-day threshold. At other times, she has been above it, as she is now, courtesy of her housemates' disability checks (which she herself never sees). But whether she has slipped into $2-a-day poverty or is just barely out of it, her circumstances don't seem that different. She's always a boarder, never making enough money to rent a home of her own, even in Cleveland. And always, it is only a matter of months before she determines that the living conditions in her new place are unsustainable. "Change of address" is the lot of the $2-a-day poor.

If Rae McCormick ever filled out an ACE questionnaire, she would blow a hole through the top of the scale. "I've been beat. I've been raped," she reports matter-of-factly. The ACE survey asks whether your family made you "feel special, loved" and was "a source of strength, support and protection." Rae's father made her feel special and loved, it's true, and she's been holding on to that feeling for fourteen years. But since he died, no one in her life has ever made her feel that way. In fact, just the opposite is true.

One of the items on the ACE survey that she may never have seen in her childhood home is "mother treated violently." But that's probably only because Rae's mother abandoned her at age eleven. However, Rae's mother *was* known to take her daughter with her when she rendezvoused with a lover. "I'd be staying at some random guy's house and I'd be sleeping in a chair and she'd be screwing him not even ten feet from me." Where does that fit on the ACE scoring chart?

Exposure to just one ACE event seems to negatively affect a child's life chances, but what about the effect of multiple and repeated occurrences? The ACE researchers reported that "ACEs were not only unexpectedly common, but their effects were found to be cumulative." So the more adverse experiences someone has in childhood, the worse their outcomes are likely to be as an adult. In Rae's case, she has suffered from numerous adverse experiences, many with repeated and prolonged exposure. And those experiences didn't stop when she became an adult. If anything, her circumstances deteriorated further, and that was because she lost the only thing keeping her in her legal guardian's house — the little bit of income support she had.

Rae likely suffers from the effects of what researchers refer to as "toxic stress," defined as "strong, frequent, or prolonged activation of the body's stress response systems in the absence of the buffering protection of a supportive, adult relationship." She is on near-constant high alert — never knowing when a new threat may emerge or an old one may reappear. And she is always dealing with crisis in one form or another. Exposure to toxic stress affects people mentally and even physically. It can impair "executive functions, such as decision-making, working memory, behavioral self-regulation, and mood and impulse control." It "may result in anatomic changes and/or physiologic dysregulations that are the precursors of later impairments in learning and behavior as well as the roots of chronic, stress-related physical and mental illness." Toxic stress can literally wear you down and, in the end, kill you.

Memory loss is very common in people who have been exposed to the conditions Rae has faced. And she certainly has impaired mood and impulse control. She takes medication for her high blood pressure and is going blind in her right eye. She has lost all her teeth. Recently, she reports, "I fucked up my knee. I'm having, like, pains that would, like, literally send most people to the hospital, but because I have a high pain tolerance because of how I used to be a cutter, . . . I can withstand it." The local corner store, just a block down the street, displays photos of a number of neighborhood residents behind the bulletproof glass that separates the proprietor from his customers, including one of Rae at sixteen — a strikingly lovely young woman. Now, at twenty-five, she's aged almost beyond recognition. With all these ailments, she seems like a prime candidate for Supplemental Security Income, or SSI, but she won't apply, "because I don't wanna just sit around." She views herself as a worker. Going on disability would be a disappointment to her father up in heaven. That's something she just couldn't bear.

She deals with the pain by keeping busy. "My stomach is really hurting. You know what? 'Let me get up and move around. Let me do this. Let me do that.' And then the pain will, you know, slowly . . . die off." But if constant activity is the best medication, a close second is smoking. The fact that she would rather go without food than cigarettes points to the extent to which smoking helps ease the chronic pain she's in, whereas food just doesn't. Hunger pangs are mild in comparison to everything else that ails her.

Rae wants to do her absolute best to protect Azara. But the circumstances she finds herself in put her little four-year-old at immense risk. Trauma and the reverberations of toxic stress ripple through generations, from parent to child, sometimes even grandparent to parent to child. Rae's past has boxed in Azara's life chances, which in turn may impinge on those of her own children.

In Jennifer Hernandez's case, her mother, too, was sexually abused, and Jennifer herself wrestles with mental illness. Now Jennifer's daughter, Kaitlin, her "very sweet, very lovable little girl," will carry with her the experience of sexual abuse for the rest of her life. With luck, she will be better off as a result of her mother's resolve to confront what happened in Texas, better off for Jennifer's determination to make José pay for what he did and her efforts to get Kaitlin the help she needed. Maybe with these heroic acts—which cost Jennifer her family's support—she can help Kaitlin break the cycle of trauma that has marked at least three generations of her family.

What Rae wants—more than anything in the world—is two things. First, she wants a job that she can throw herself into, fully and completely. Like Jennifer, she is happiest when she is working. Work is the only place where she can come even close to escaping her demons. So she needs a job with a livable wage, and a job that can act as a source of stability rather than instability. She needs a job like those that so many middle-class Americans go to every day.

Second, she wants a little place for herself and Azara—a place where they can be together, play together, be a family; a place where they can drown out the noise around them. There's nothing that Rae dreams of more than a home of her own—what would be "our first place together as a family." She smiles as she fantasizes about what being on their own would look like for her and Azara. "We can start it all over. We can have our own dinners together. I can play with her more. I don't have to hear, 'Oh, this happened,' and there's screaming in the background, and I can just relax and enjoy being with my daughter." In Rae's mind, getting her own place is the key to building a new life. "When I get my own place, I'll save up money and I'll start getting stuff slowly . . . Azara will come first. After that, then I'll think about furniture and stuff." She'll keep her costs low so she can afford to buy the things they need. "I'll buy some portable frying things you plug into a wall. Yeah, I'll cook dinner like that until I can afford to get what I need." She doesn't know exactly what order other things will come in, but she knows what will be first: "I want to get [Azara] her own Dora [the Explorer] bed." In their current room, Rae says, "I have this Dora [poster] hanging up. In her room at the new house,

I'm hanging that up over her window. So she's gonna have a decked-out Dora room."

Research suggests that if Rae succeeded in getting such a place, her own life, and especially Azara's life, would be much better for it. Would they make it in the end? Would Rae be able to mute her inner rage and hold down a job? Would she be able to keep their little place over time? Or would she flame out and end up back in the basement at Donny's or living with George and Camilla? No one can know for sure.

But what is clear right now is that Rae, in her current circumstances (and in the circumstances faced by families all across the United States), basically has no shot at achieving this dream. She has virtually no shot at getting Azara that room decked out in Dora gear in their own little place. Housing is too expensive, the jobs she might get pay far too little, and there's too little help.

Chapter 4

By Any Means Necessary

THERE IS NO MONEY to be made selling blood anymore, but you can sell plasma, a component in blood that is used in a number of treatments for serious illnesses. Selling plasma is so common among the $2-a-day poor that it might be thought of as a lifeblood. It is legal to "donate" up to two times a week, for which a plasma bank will pay you around $30 each time, $60 total. Jennifer Hernandez says she tried this for a while but gave it up because she couldn't think straight afterward. She can't afford to be off her game given her current circumstances.

In Johnson City, Tennessee, though, twenty-one-year-old Jessica Compton donates plasma as often as ten times a month — as frequently as the law allows. Plasma Biological Services, the local donation center, is located in a one-story white building fronted with plate glass, with the business name spelled out in large red letters. Jessica is able to donate only when her husband, Travis, has time to keep an eye on their two young daughters, Rachel and Blythe. He can do that pretty frequently these days, because he's been out of work since the beginning of December, when McDonald's reduced his hours to zero in response to slow foot traffic. It's nearly February now.

Both Jessica and Travis are of slight build. Travis is a towhead, but Jessica's fair skin and elfin features stand in contrast to a cloud of smoky black hair. Their daughter Rachel, at four, is an electric and precocious child. Blythe, whose blond hair is cut to chin length, making it spin around her tiny face when she shakes her head, is two. She's tiny—too small to walk the one and a half miles to Johnson City's downtown from the family's front door. But mom and dad are constantly back and forth between the apartment and that part of town, seeking a warm spot in the library, with its reading materials, kids' activities, and Internet connection, which is so critical to finding a job. Thus, Blythe virtually lives in the pink stroller the family acquired at the local Salvation Army. Sometimes it's a bed—she takes naps there—and sometimes it's a hideout. She loves to burst forth from beneath the sunshade, hair standing on end with static electricity.

Travis says his mother "dipped out" on his family when he was in third grade. Not long afterward, his father started "drinking alcohol, eating Xanax, smoking crack." By the time Travis reached fourteen, his dad was a full-blown cocaine addict. His mother made a brief reappearance when he was in eighth grade, only to disappear again a few months later. During those years, Travis thought often about suicide. "I hated myself," he recalls.

When Travis was about seventeen, he ran across Jessica's profile on Facebook. "God, she was gorgeous," he says. It took a full month—"forever," in Travis's estimation—for him to convince Jessica to go out with him. Just a few weeks later, "I guess, we fell in love. It was just four months and she was pregnant with Rachel."

With a baby on the way, Travis was desperate to learn a trade, so he enrolled in YouthBuild, a program that offered prevocational training in basic construction skills plus GED courses. And it paid students to attend. Travis got to work on homes being constructed by Habitat for Humanity one week, and he took job training classes the next. He loved the hands-on learning and spun dreams of becoming an architect. It took him a year to earn his training certificate and pass the GED. But after graduation, McDonald's was the only place he could land a job, at minimum wage and part-time hours. Since then, he's had one job after another, but they've all been temporary gigs. Most recently, he was back at the same fast-food joint where he had started, until that ended once again. Right now, walking Jessica to the plasma clinic and back, kids in tow, is the most important job he has.

Upon arriving at Plasma Biological Services, Jessica checks in. A regular donor, she can bypass the initial, time-consuming full-on health screening. Instead, she proceeds to a kiosk, rhythmically clicking the mouse to answer the required questions about her health. "When you get there, they have you fill out . . . twenty-two questions . . . They ask you about your health and, like, if you've had any recent tattoos or been in jail or had any piercings lately . . . Yeah, if you get a tattoo or something, you got to tell them, and then you got to wait like six months and then they let you come back." Travis has too many tattoos and doesn't remember the exact times and places he acquired all of them, details that the plasma center requires. He says he has been told he "need not come by" to donate.

After completing these initial steps, Jessica sits in the waiting room, listening for her name to be called. Then "they take your blood pressure and your temp. And then if everything is okay, you wait and get your finger pricked to test for your iron and your protein and stuff . . . Usually, it be during my time of the month that my iron really goes down." Lately, the iron pills Jessica has tried haven't been working. This terrifies her, because "donating" is the cash bedrock of the family's finances right now. The phlebotomist in charge of the finger pricking has told her that "if the iron pills don't help, [it means] I could be, like, anemic." Anemics are barred from donating.

Today, like other days, she's nervous. What will happen if she is not allowed to give plasma? The family desperately needs the $30. They're now nearly three months behind on the rent. Travis often stands at the kitchen window of their cramped one-bedroom apartment as if transfixed — on the lookout for the sheriff, who might show up at any time to evict them.

Jessica says, "Usually they tell me to wait because my blood pressure is always up. So I usually have to wait. They make you wait an extra ten minutes just to see if it goes down." After failing the test the first time, Jessica sits for a while, taking deep, calming breaths, before getting retested. When asked why her blood pressure nearly always registers as too high initially, she says, "I don't *know!* It just must be stress, being nervous about my iron levels or something."

Once Jessica passes all the tests, she proceeds to the back room, where she's directed to a recliner. ("It's just, like, a big open space with a lot of chairs in there. Like machines and stuff . . . You go back there, and that's when they just hook you up.") Today she has brought along a Nicholas Sparks novel she checked out of the library. "I always bring a book with me." A technician feels around for her vein with a plastic-gloved finger. Once the vein is located, the technician squeezes out some iodine and with a Q-tip begins spreading the thick liquid in a small circle, slowly widening the circle and rubbing the spot for about thirty seconds, staining Jessica's forearm brown. She positions the IV, snaking it around Jessica's wrist and over the inner part of her forearm. A needle, banded in green and with two small flaps like wings, is inserted into the vein. ("I can't ever look at it. I never look at it when they do it. They do it right here," she says, pointing to the obvious indentation at the crease in her arm, which looks somewhat like a drug track line. Many among the $2-a-day poor bear these small scars from repeated plasma donations.)

She then contracts her fist to start the blood flowing, and keeps contracting it at intervals to keep the purplish liquid moving down the tube to the machine that will separate her blood from her plasma. The goldish liquid is extracted and preserved, while her blood and platelets are returned to her system. First an extraction. Then a return. Another extraction. And so on. While it's happening, "you just got to sit there" as the tube flows yellow, then red, back and forth. For the usual person, it takes about forty-five minutes, but for Jessica it takes well over an hour. She is just over the minimum weight of 110 pounds. The procedure takes a toll, she says. "I get tired. Especially if my iron's down, I get, like, *really* tired."

She describes the rest of the process as follows: "Then you go up to the front and you get a slip of paper and they put your money on a card. Then you just go home. It's just like a debit card, like a pre-paid." The ritual takes roughly three hours door-to-door. Even so, the payoff is good, relatively speaking — $10 an hour. As long as her iron, blood pressure, and temperature are okay, she'll donate as often as she is legally allowed. But no one could reasonably think of a twice-weekly plasma donation as a job. It's a survival strategy, one of many operating well outside the low-wage job market.

Before welfare died in 1996, a family of three couldn't live solely on the $360 or so the program provided on average. Just prior to welfare reform, it took roughly $875 to meet such a family's monthly expenses. But families could generally get only about three-fifths of that amount from cash welfare plus food stamps. To make matters worse, when a mother secured a job, she would lose about a dollar in welfare benefits for every dollar she earned. Yet she couldn't afford to rely only on earnings from work in the formal economy. Work paid only a little more than welfare but cost a lot more in terms of added expenses for transportation, child care, health care, and the like. It was more expensive to go to work than stay on the welfare rolls.

Back then, neither welfare nor work alone could bring a poor family's budget into balance, yet the ability to combine them legally was limited at best. How did these single mothers survive? Some gleaned some sustenance through private charities, as Jessica and Travis do now: Goodwill for shelter, as one double-up after another imploded, and the Salvation Army for clothing and that essential pink stroller. In addition, at any given time, almost half of single mothers on welfare were working. Some used a false identity to avoid detection, or hopped from job to job, since short stints wouldn't typically get reported to the welfare office. Those without a formal job did hair, babysat, sold meals, cleaned homes, or occasionally resorted to fencing stolen goods or selling drugs or sex in an effort to bridge the gap between their income and expenses. All told, poor single mothers drew on dozens upon dozens of different strategies to get by.

What's different these days — and what affects the $2-a-day poor

so profoundly—is that welfare can no longer be counted on to provide a floor of cash that families can depend on. Back in the days
before welfare reform, the strategies poor single mothers employed
were hardly get-rich-quick schemes; they provided a few dollars here
and there, often garnered with considerable effort. But when combined with welfare, plus a lot of old-fashioned frugality, these strategies usually allowed for a bare-bones survival. Today, families who
find themselves virtually cashless have no such floor. If the $2-a-day
poor were truly to make ends meet, they would have to find a way to
generate double the amount their pre–welfare reform counterparts
had to produce in addition to AFDC in order to balance their budgets. None among the families featured in this book have managed to
come even close to this threshold, despite considerable effort.

The panoply of survival strategies used by today's $2-a-day poor
are variations on the same tactics poor families used a generation
ago to get by: private charity, a variety of small-time under-the-table
income-generating schemes, and plain old scrimping. Even those
somewhat higher up the income ladder today, who have steady jobs
or other steady sources of income, draw on such strategies from time
to time when the money doesn't quite stretch to the end of the month
for one reason or another. But the degree to which people must resort
to the riskiest strategies—those that can exact a sharp psychological,
legal, and even physical toll—appears to be an order of magnitude
greater for the virtually cashless poor than it is for poor families with
some cash on hand.

Far from being passive victims, many among the $2-a-day poor
take what few resources they have and try to "make the best out of
a bad," as the son of one parent put it. While the circumstances that
they find themselves in may appear wholly un-American, in many
ways their actions and outlooks are as American as they come: often
surprisingly optimistic, creative, family-focused, scrappy, and imbued with a can-do spirit that belies their desperate circumstances.
They may be officially jobless, but they are intently at work. And their

work can be hard, even grueling at times. It is work into which families at the very bottom pour their blood, sweat, and tears, because their survival — and that of their kids — depends on it.

The Work of Survival

Survival strategies come in three forms. The first is taking advantage of public spaces and private charities — the nation's libraries, food pantries, homeless shelters, and so on. Then come a variety of income-generation strategies, such as donating plasma — means for gleaning at least some of that all-important resource that families seem unable to survive without: cash. Finally, there's the art — often finely honed through years of hardship — of finding ways to stretch your resources and make do with less.

Public Spaces and Private Charities

Jennifer Hernandez, both before and after her family's trials in Texas, remains an immensely kind woman, an innovator whose singular focus is the well-being of her kids. She utilizes every resource Chicago's web of private charities has to offer, plus she makes use of the public spaces available to all the city's residents — especially the public library. Before moving to Texas, while she was living at the La Casa family shelter, Jennifer was known for doggedly scanning the sidewalk for flyers and searching for notices taped to message boards, trees, or light posts that advertised free charity events. That's how she found out about the school supplies giveaway at a nearby church and the free dental checkups for the kids offered by a local hospital — free, that is, except for a three-hour wait to be seen. That's why the family was able to take in a free movie down at Millennium Park (not long after attending that outdoor performance of Shakespeare in the Parks). If there's one person in the world who could write the how-to book about surviving on $2 a day by uncovering every resource available from the patchwork of public spaces and private charities in Chicago, it's Jennifer Hernandez. There isn't a free event that she and the kids miss, a free resource they haven't made the most of.

In the La Casa days, despite all they'd already been through, Kaitlin and Cole remained surprisingly open and unguarded. They showed no visible signs of hardship. On outings, they would blithely bounce down the street in front of Jennifer and then double back from time to time, apparently ready for any adventure.

Those days, their walks most often brought them to the neighborhood library, a one-story brick building taking up most of a city block. The building features columns of windows on each side of the entrance, along with columns of glass bricks in the circular lobby, framing scenes that hold meaning for residents of this predominantly Puerto Rican neighborhood. The small library has book collections for everyone in the family, computers with Internet access, and programming for neighborhood children. Nine-year-old Kaitlin would dash through the door (hair bobbing as she went). Greeting the librarian behind the checkout counter, she would ask if she could "do my job." After a warm hug, she would be given a pile of books to shelve, which she would do in short order and with great intensity. Cole would head over to the picture-book section and browse through a number of titles, several of which were well-loved favorites.

The Hernandez family visited this library nearly every day. They couldn't use the Internet because doing so required a permanent address in the neighborhood and Jennifer was too ashamed to get the requisite letter from La Casa explaining that she was a resident there. Instead, while Kaitlin shelved books, Cole lugged book after book over to Jennifer so she could read to him. During the school year, they did their homework there. This library was a second home to the kids. Maybe it was the closest thing to a childhood home they would ever have.

○　　○　　○

Places like the public library where Jennifer, Kaitlin, and Cole found refuge are crucial to the day-to-day survival strategies of the $2-a-day poor. They offer a warm place to sit, a clean and safe bathroom, and a way to get online to complete a job application. They provide free educational programs for kids. Perhaps most important, they can help struggling families feel they are part of society instead of cast aside by it. Sometimes these institutions serve those in need begrudgingly — a library might prefer that it *not* be a rest stop and warming station for the city's homeless people. But other times they attend to destitute patrons with tremendous love and warmth. Kaitlin's friend the librarian gave her more than a job; she gave her a way to contribute, a place to belong.

Beyond these vital public spaces, there are many private charities across Chicago like La Casa that serve the poor day in and day out, operating shelters, food pantries and soup kitchens, free health clinics, job training programs, and educational programs for children and youth. Most of this aid comes not in the form of cash, but rather through in-kind assistance targeting basic needs (such as shelter and food) or direct services (such as health exams and mental health counseling). The forms this aid takes are not just determined by what families seeking help need. Rather, the nonprofits must be conscious of the values of the broader community and of the requirements placed on them by the government agencies, private foundations, and donors who fund the work. Sometimes what is offered fits what a family needs well. Sometimes it doesn't.

As Jennifer could tell you, private charities come in all shapes and sizes. There are the big players like the Salvation Army, Catholic Charities, and Goodwill. La Casa, with programs all over the west side of Chicago, is a midsize agency. There are also small outfits that may be operating on a wing and a prayer. Many of these are run out of the basements of houses of worship, which can sometimes become sanctuaries in their own right. Some charities are run by trained social workers, while others are staffed by long-term volunteers with no credentials, just a drive to help that comes from their faith, their life experiences, or the goodness of their hearts. Some agencies have predictable days and hours of operation that someone like Jennifer can count on, while others are open only sporadically, depending on the funding and the supply of ready volunteers.

Private charity in America is often viewed as the little engine that could. It chugs along admirably, providing billions of dollars in aid to the poor each year. And its efforts are valuable — the support that philanthropic organizations provide is part of what makes the lives of America's $2-a-day poor different from those of the desperately poor in developing countries. Although charity is not absent in the developing world, there are far more dollars per person flowing to the American poor. Yet even in America, and even for those who are most adept at gleaning all that private charity has to offer, it can't even begin to replicate, much less replace, what the government does. Private charity is a complement to government action, something that bolsters the government safety net.

The availability of private charity is far more limited outside major cities such as Chicago, which has been emblematic of the problem of urban poverty for decades. Yet poverty is actually growing faster outside these large cities than within them. Across the nation, the contours of private charity often reflect local resources. The "haves" — big cities with a lot of wealth, such as Chicago, New York, and Boston — typically have robust nonprofit sectors. Poorer places struggle to find the resources to meet the sea of need there. And in the small towns of the Mississippi Delta, there are precious few charities, if any at all. In Johnson City, Tennessee, in the heart of Appalachia, Travis and Jessica Compton know all too well that there are limited shelter beds. At two of the shelters in town, people bunk by gender. Thus, if a husband and wife with children were lucky enough to get space in either of these, they would be separated at night, with the dad wondering about the safety of the mom and kids as he tried to get some rest. The third shelter makes each family move to a different church basement every night. When Jennifer Hernandez was in crisis in

Abilene, the Salvation Army shelter staff had to empty an office to accommodate the traumatized family. As the geographic mismatch between available charity and the people who require it grows, more struggling families living outside the large urban centers find themselves completely disconnected from help when they need it.

The quality of the services provided by charities can vary dramatically. At the time of her reluctant visit to the west side Chicago Department of Human Services office to apply for welfare, Modonna Harris was lucky to have a slot at one of the city's *good* shelters, one where she and her daughter, Brianna, had a room to themselves with an actual door, and one where the staff treated them with kindness rather than contempt. Some shelters can feel quite unsafe to a vulnerable mother and child with nowhere else to go, especially to those with a history of victimization. Can the staff be trusted? Will they treat you with respect or like scum? And what about the other families staying at the facility? Family homeless shelters take a collection of hurting, desperate families with nothing in common except destitution and a history of bad breaks and abuse, and mix them together over meals and in programs. As a result, sometimes these shelters can be damaging places in their own right.

A few months ago, while living in another of Chicago's family shelters, Brianna developed a little crush on an older boy who was also staying there with his mother. At the time, she remained a surprisingly innocent fifteen-year-old, despite her circumstances, and she enjoyed the attention and distraction of this boy, who flirted with her harmlessly in the halls. But over dinner one night, in front of everyone, the boy asked another girl his own age, "So when you gonna give me some more of that hoo-ha?"

Everyone sitting there knew Brianna had a crush on this boy. Here was someone who had made her feel good during a tough time, and now he was making her feel useless, awful, embarrassed, all in such a crass way. Now everyone knew that the object of Brianna's affection was getting something from this other girl that Brianna was not ready to give, and for which she hadn't even been asked. Maybe in another setting, this would have been just another example of a teenage boy being vulgar. But for Brianna, having not that long ago endured a stint of living with Modonna's mother and a cousin who tormented her daily, this vulnerable, hurting girl lost it. She lashed out at the boy, screaming, throwing things, and swearing. In the aftermath, the shelter asked everyone involved to leave. Within days, Modonna and Brianna found themselves back on the streets, once again in a frantic search for a place to stay.

While this particular shelter sojourn was shorter than usual, virtually no family shelter in the city of Chicago will house a family for more than a few months. Although these shelters have good reasons for such policies—often they are a requirement of the funding they receive, or simply a response to short supply given the demand (too many homeless families and too few beds)—a few months is a very short time for any family with no resources to become self-sufficient. As a result, those experiencing a spell of $2-a-day poverty are liable to find themselves in a never-ending hunt for the next place to live, making it even harder for them to find and keep a job.

What's more, many shelters—in an effort to focus their mission—have strict parameters regarding whom they will help. Some take only women with children under age five. Others require attendance at religious services. Some require that you have recently lost a home, while others mandate a criminal background check. Some have terrific websites, while others are riddled with out-of-date information. Some you can only call, and others you find out about only through word of mouth. Thus, the search for a place to stay can take days of work. And let's say that you finally find a place for which you are eligible and that happens to have room. To get to your new accommodations, you might find yourself traipsing across the city with all your worldly possessions, which is hard to do when you have no money.

Another dilemma faced by parents like Jennifer is that in the world of private charity, kids, and not their moms and dads, are often the focus of whatever aid is offered. Kaitlin and Cole both get regular dental checkups at various clinics and hospitals offering them for free on designated Saturdays. Jennifer is in serious need of a dentist, too, to care for her receding gums. Yet in the early part of the summer of 2012 (just as Jennifer was desperately searching for a job), the State of Illinois slashed funding for adult Medicaid services so that only emergency extractions were covered. Calls to numerous clinics by a professional social worker on Jennifer's behalf identified no dental clinic in the Chicago metropolitan area that would provide any sort of treatment for her without payment.

For the $2-a-day poor, America's private charities are the difference between shelter and no shelter, a meal and no meal, a new backpack for school and none at all. And yet they can provide only an incomplete patchwork of aid, with numerous holes. Even in Chicago, where there are more charities than in many other places, a life dependent on private charity is a life of insecurity.

Income-Generation Strategies

While selling SNAP benefits is rare among food stamp households generally, this is the most common strategy that the virtually cashless poor in our sample resort to in order to generate an even more critical resource — cash. Why and how they do so bears some explanation.

As we've seen, in 2011 there were about 1.5 million households with children in $2-a-day poverty in any given month, based on their cash income. If you count SNAP as income — giving it the same value as cash — that number would be cut almost in half, to about 800,000 households. Comparing the two figures, it is easy to see how important SNAP is in the lives of the extremely poor. If you counted Jennifer Hernandez's monthly food stamp allotment of $500 as cash, she would not qualify as $2-a-day poor. Neither would Travis and Jessica Compton. Clearly, SNAP is one of the most important resources the extremely poor have at their disposal. But SNAP is not the same as cash. One truism about the lives of the virtually cashless poor in this country is that they — like anyone else living here — just can't manage to do without cash. And for that reason, while SNAP may stave off some hardship, it doesn't help families exit the trap of extreme destitution like cash might.

Consider the following scenario. Let's say you were offered a job with a starting salary of $55,000. Coming in to work after a few weeks on the job, you find yourself engrossed in thought about all the things you'll do with your first paycheck. Just then, you happen to pass your boss in the hallway, and she says matter-of-factly, "By the way, $4,000 of your salary is going to come in the form of food stamps." Would you simply shrug your shoulders, reckoning that a dollar in SNAP was the same as a dollar in cash? Or would you be angry? Let's say your boss offers you a choice. Option 1 is that you can take a salary of $55,000 in cash. Option 2 is that you can get $53,000 in cash plus $4,000 in SNAP — a $2,000 raise! Which would you choose? When undergraduate students from various parts of the country are asked questions like this, most (although not all) pick option 1. Most would rather have the flexibility of cash than the added purchasing power.

To understand how SNAP actually works in the day-to-day business of getting by, let's take the exercise a bit further. If you decided to take option 2 — the $53,000 in cash plus $4,000 in SNAP — would you spend $4,000 more on food than you had been spending to begin with? Or would you stop using cash for groceries — using SNAP instead — and spend the cash on something else?

When families enroll in SNAP, most do the latter to some degree: they don't continue to contribute the same amount to buying food as before and instead use that cash for something else. Economists call this "substitution," and it is a relatively common phenomenon. Picture a family of four with full-time earnings of $18,500 a year (roughly $9.50 an hour) and no help from the government. In a typical month, they might have only about $300 left over to spend on food after paying the minimum amounts due on basic obligations such as shelter, transportation, clothing, and utilities. On this budget, the cupboards are nearly bare by week three, save for the cheapest food you can buy — ramen noodles. Mom, dad, and the kids must subsist on a ramen diet until next month's paycheck clears. In America, even full-time, full-year workers earning well over the minimum wage may head a household that runs on ramen, and little else, for a week or more each month.

Now let's say this family decides to apply for SNAP and qualifies for $400 in benefits each month. Do they still spend that $300 in cash on groceries, plus the $400 from SNAP? If they did, it would bring their total food budget up to $700, more than double what they spent before (although still not a huge amount for a family of four). The more likely scenario is that mom and dad—who, given their earnings and the soaring cost of shelter, were probably falling behind on paying for nonfood essentials such as rent and transportation—would increase their food budget to, say, $500 (a 67 percent increase), combining the $400 from SNAP with $100 in cash. In so doing, they could put an additional $200 in cash toward other bills.

Substitution of this kind is a valuable tool for keeping a struggling household going. Cash resources freed up by SNAP not only make it less likely that a household with children will fall behind on rent and utilities, but they also reduce the chances that someone in the house will skip a visit to the doctor because of the cost. Thus, SNAP not only puts food in the stomachs of hungry kids, but it also buffers families from other kinds of hardships. There is a downside to this type of substitution, though. A considerable number of families on SNAP continue to experience what the U.S. Department of Agriculture calls "food insecurity," meaning they run out of food before the month is over. The budgets of these working-poor families are often so tight—and so far in the red—that some level of substitution is needed to avoid eviction and to keep the lights on. For many families, these concerns can outweigh the need to stave off hunger.

Families who substitute in this way aren't breaking the law, not even close. They aren't even doing anything unethical. They are simply reallocating some of the money they had been spending on food to other uses. Yet trading SNAP for cash—the most common strategy used for survival among the families in this book—is a crime, and a serious one at that. The reason the $2-a-day poor do so anyway is that the practice of substitution doesn't work for them. They have no cash to spend on food in the first place. Meanwhile, the need to pay the light bill, or even get the kids new socks and underwear, can seem more compelling than the need to eat in a couple of weeks' time. What's more, it's easier for a family with nothing to get food from another source — such as a food pantry — than to acquire those other things from charities. This is why food stamp "trafficking," though rare among the poor more generally, is common among the $2-a-day poor.

What's so magical about cash? Without it, your activities are restricted. Even if you are among the lucky few to be awarded a rent subsidy, claim government health insurance, and enroll in SNAP — even if you get every in-kind benefit our society might provide — you still lack the $20 in cash to buy an outfit from Goodwill to wear to that job interview, or to pay the bus fare to get downtown. Showing up at a job interview without the proper attire — maybe drenched in sweat after walking several miles on a hot Chicago day — sends the message that you are not taking the opportunity seriously.

Cash is what you need to wash your clothes at the Laundromat rather than in the bathtub at the homeless shelter you call home (assuming you've found a way to acquire some laundry detergent), leaving them to dry stiffly on the shower-curtain rod. Cash is what is required to purchase that new pair of shoes or backpack that can buy your kids a modicum of dignity on the playground or in the school lunch line. A little bit of cash means a little bit of freedom. It allows people the flexibility to purchase what they believe their families need most.

In the summer of 2010, a team of researchers began to study the lives of 150 young adults who had grown up in Baltimore's high-rise public housing projects. As they visited with these young women and men, they noticed there were families who seemed to be living without any regular cash income of any kind. Nineteen-year-old Ashley was one such young mother. Inside an apartment in the Latrobe Homes, where Ashley lived with her mother, brother, an uncle, and a cousin, there was virtually no furniture, only a kitchen table with a broken leg propped up against the wall, a single bar stool, and a mangy couch that looked like it had been fished out of the Dumpster. There was no food in the house and, more important, no baby formula. When asked, Ashley reported that although no one in the house had a job, none got TANF or SNAP—just the rent-free apartment from the housing authority. Ashley, who had just given birth to her first child a few weeks before, was visibly depressed. Her hair was unkempt, and she was having difficulty adequately supporting her baby's head as she rocked the child.

At the conclusion of the interview, the researchers gave the young mother the standard interview stipend of $50 in cash. When they returned to do a follow-up interview just twenty-four hours later, they found that not only was there formula on the shelf, but Ashley had permed and styled her hair and gone to the thrift store for a new outfit. Leaving the baby with her mother, Ashley was now on her way out the door in her new pantsuit to apply for jobs. The little bit of autonomy that $50 had afforded Ashley had apparently sparked enough confidence in her to begin looking for work.

With no cash income to speak of, yet nearly $500 in SNAP benefits every month, Jennifer Hernandez sometimes feels compelled to sell some of her food stamps when she absolutely needs the cash. The last time she did this, it was to buy socks and underwear for the kids. Before that, it was because they needed school uniforms. Trafficking in food stamps is a criminal offense. Jennifer is embarrassed that she has to resort to it. Yet in the end, she does what she feels she has to do. She believes that seeing to her children's needs is more important than keeping to the letter of the law.

Jennifer has some inkling of the legal implications of selling SNAP—she knows it is a crime and that she should by no means get caught in the act. In the fine print on a food stamp application, it is made clear that selling SNAP can result in a felony charge. And the penalty can be stiff. The SNAP application in Illinois (and other states) says that you can "be fined up to $250,000 and put in prison up to 20 years or both" for the offense.

One signal of how strongly a society feels about a particular violation of the law is the maximum sentence that can be imposed on offenders. Possession of small amounts of marijuana carries little legal penalty in most jurisdictions for a first-time offense. Under the U.S. federal sentencing guidelines, a person with a "minimal criminal history" would have to commit an offense at base level 37 to earn up to twenty years in prison. By comparison, voluntary manslaughter earns a base level 29, which could result in nine years in prison. Aggravated assault with a firearm that causes bodily injury to the victim merits only a base level 24, which could yield a five-year sentence. Abusive sexual contact with a child under age twelve also merits a base level 24. Astonishingly, at least in terms of the letter of the law, when Jennifer sells her SNAP, she risks a far longer prison term than the one José was subject to for molesting Kaitlin.

As a practical matter, it is far more difficult to traffic in SNAP than it once was. Back in the days when folks got paper food stamp coupons rather than electronic benefit transfer (EBT) cards, they could easily trade the coupons for cash. But today's SNAP card has your name on it and requires you to enter a personal identification number, or PIN, when you swipe your card at the register, meaning that in most cases you would want to be physically present at a fraudulent transaction. If you were to simply give someone your EBT card and PIN so that he could buy food for himself and then give you cash back, what's to keep the person from using up all your benefits? Do you really want to trust someone with one of your most valuable assets, especially when you already know he is not above breaking the law?

In spite of these difficulties, there are other ways to barter SNAP for cash when the need arises. One relatively simple strategy is to find a family member or friend who will pay you back for groceries you buy on her behalf using your EBT card. Not all among the $2-a-day poor can employ this strategy, for the simple reason that their relatives may be nearly as bad off as they are and don't have any cash either. Others don't have relatives or friends close at hand. Back in Chicago, Jennifer, who by then had pressed charges against José, was on speaking terms with only one relative, an aunt who lived a train and two bus rides away.

People will sometimes stand outside a grocery store and try to solicit strangers to trade cash for SNAP, but they have to do so at a steep discount. If Jennifer were to try this, most of the entering customers would probably ignore her. Some might lecture her. Some might even call the cops, a nerve-racking prospect. But let's say after an hour or so she was lucky enough to find someone who was agreeable. Jennifer and her new partner in crime would enter the store together. The other party would go about filling her cart as usual, but at checkout time, Jennifer would pay the bill using her EBT card. Afterward, Jennifer would be paid the agreed-upon amount for the cart's contents in cash. The going exchange rate in Chicago during the summer of 2012 was roughly 60 cents on the dollar — a good deal for the buyer.

Jennifer has never resorted to soliciting SNAP customers in a grocery store parking lot. It's too embarrassing, plus there is too much risk involved. It seems to her that only drug addicts are desperate enough to trade SNAP for cash in this way. But she does know of another method — a routine that requires the complicity of a merchant who is willing to trade SNAP for a lesser amount of cash. This strategy requires deep local knowledge — you can't just approach a cashier and ask if the store provides the service.

After moving from Abilene to Chicago as a child, Jennifer and her mother settled in the Little Village neighborhood, just south of where La Casa is located. According to Jennifer, the neighborhood is full of little bodegas that, from time to time, engage in SNAP trafficking. But the trade shifts from store to store so that owners can avoid detection. Luckily, Jennifer still has a few contacts in the neighborhood who are in the know and will tell her which store to approach.

The bodega owner will ring through, say, $100 in groceries and charge Jennifer's card that amount. But instead of walking out with the groceries, Jennifer will get, say, $60 in cash. The chief beneficiary of the exchange is not Jennifer but the store owner, who pockets $40 in profit (his price for the risk involved in the exchange). The owners of the Little Village bodegas that Jennifer frequents are smart to be cautious, since this type of trafficking is the kind of SNAP fraud that is easiest for the authorities to detect. What's more, the best available evidence suggests that its prevalence is actually quite low and has decreased over the years. A 1993 audit by the U.S. Department of Agriculture found that such fraud accounted for about 4 cents out of every dollar of food stamps. But this amount fell to around 1.3 cents out of every dollar in 2009–2011. Still, even one egregious example — and they are out there — can make it seem as though the program is awash in fraud.

Like most of the $2-a-day poor, Jennifer tries to reserve most of her food stamps for food, only trading them for cash when important needs, almost always having to do with her kids, arise. No matter what the need, she still feels that selling SNAP is morally objectionable and has at least some sense of the risks. Although selling SNAP may be one of the more common cash-generating strategies practiced by the $2-a-day poor, it is rarely the preferred one.

Many among the $2-a-day poor, including Jennifer, have tried collecting aluminum cans to be recycled for cash. Collecting cans out of the alleys and your neighbors' garbage cans, Jennifer has learned, is unlikely to yield more than eight or ten bucks a day, even when you scour the neighborhood for hours, even if you find every last can. As it turns out, if you want to make any money as a scrapper, you've got to have some basic resources: a place to store the scrap and a truck or van to haul it to the scrapyard.

In the Cudell neighborhood of Cleveland, Paul Heckewelder's backyard is home to a stockpile of scrap — aluminum cans, tin, broken-down air conditioners, and so on — that he hauls to the scrapyard every few months. Paul, who is sixty years old, is an animated, deeply religious evangelical Christian with a sturdy frame and graying, dark blond hair. He usually speaks in a booming voice, but his pitch rises—he even squeaks—when he gets excited. Given his energetic disposition, this happens pretty frequently.

After decades of hardship, Paul came to own several pizza parlors beginning in the mid-1990s and enjoyed nearly a decade and a half among the middle class. But in 2008, after the restaurants went bust, there were several years when his family had no income at all to speak of. Scrapping has been one of the strategies Paul has used over and over again to bring in a few extra dollars. "We save all our cans. So we get about sixty dollars [every time we go to the scrapyard]. That's sixty dollars that would have been dumped in the garbage!"

Paul and his adult son Sam scan the sidewalks on garbage day and sometimes even snatch choice items out of Dumpsters. When the pile in the backyard gets big enough, they take it to the scrapyard. Paul estimates that the current load in the backyard will fetch about $100. "You can get ten, fifteen, twenty dollars from just one air conditioner," he says, holding up the metal inner element of one of the air conditioners he found alongside the road. "You got the part that's the copper, the aluminum. That makes the money."

A little to the south and east of Paul's place, the Stockyards neighborhood, where Rae McCormick lives, is home to a number of popular scrapyards. Along 65th Street just past Clark Street, truck after truck belonging to full-time scrappers—including criminal scrappers who strip houses, even churches, of valuable metals—pulls into the large semicircular driveway of West Side Metals. Some of the trucks are shiny and new, others are beat-up and barely running, but they are all full of metal junk of all shapes and sizes. These vehicles wait to deposit their loads into one of several bays, where each item is weighed and its value assessed. This is probably where the lengths of copper piping from Rae McCormick's basement ended up, leaving the tenants without indoor plumbing.

West Side Metals isn't a place for small-time operators, though, so folks like Paul usually continue south along 65th. On the east side of the street sits a strip mall, formerly anchored by the neighborhood's Kmart, the very one where Rae worked for several years. Currently, there's nothing in the massive big-box space, and its signage has been removed. Only a Payless shoe store, a Subway restaurant, and a few other low-rent businesses survive. Past the white stucco shell that used to house Kmart, a large auto repair shop (specialty: trailer hitches) and an auto wrecking company with a vast scrapyard for auto parts dominate much of the block. On the west side of the street sits the American Scrap Mart. This is where Paul can get 65 cents for each pound of tin and aluminum cans he has acquired, plus extra for whatever else he's scrounged.

Scrapping offers a way to earn some cash, but it requires resources. Few among the $2-a-day poor can make it work as well as Paul does, and even he gets no more than $60 in any given month for doing so. For Jennifer to get that kind of payoff with only a grocery cart at her disposal, she estimates she would have to work at least sixty hours. A place to store the metal and some way to transport it to the scrapyard are assets that are beyond the means of Jennifer and most of the $2-a-day poor. They must look to other strategies and other assets.

In the struggle to generate cash, sometimes the only asset available is your own body. Beyond trading her SNAP or selling plasma, a desperate mother may turn to selling sex. The best available — albeit rough — estimates suggest that a very small percentage of poor single mothers trade sex or sexual favors for money over a year's time. In our small sample, only three parents out of the eighteen families we followed admitted to engaging in sex for pay, but two had teenage daughters who had done so in an effort to help the family survive.

Sex as a survival strategy for those at the very bottom sometimes looks like what you see on TV, with a weathered woman strung out on drugs hanging out on a dark street corner, waiting to sell a john a blow job or sex in one of its various forms in an abandoned building, back alley, or dirty public bathroom. But not usually. More common is the "trading" of sex or sexual favors. In this scenario, a mom might seek out a "friend," probably a man she deems safe, or at least unlikely to get violent. It may be someone she knows from around the neighborhood, or maybe she met him in a bar and he bought her a few drinks. Either way, such a friend is probably not that hard to find. She might invite him home or maybe go to his room, and she might have sex with him or just "take care of him" in some other way. In return, he might pay her phone bill or part of her rent, or even let her and her kids stay with him for a little while.

Over breakfast, Brianna Harris spilled the beans about Modonna's older "friend." This particular morning, Brianna and Modonna were being treated to breakfast, and so Modonna wasn't trying to make a meal out of coffee as she would otherwise do — dumping six creamers and twelve sugars into one mug of joe. "Is our 'guy' still taking care of us?" Brianna asked with a sheepish grin. For the past couple of months, their "guy" had been paying their cell phone bill, plus the fee for a storage unit that was holding all of their things (most shelters don't allow more than one bag per person). What do you do with all your stuff if you have to go to a homeless shelter? Does it get left on the street corner? Even your kid's baby book? Modonna clearly wasn't ready to elaborate on the relationship, except to say that basically, if she takes care of him, he will take care of her and Brianna. She was obviously not proud of the situation, but she might say that she was doing what she needed to do. Certainly, she wasn't a prostitute.

A few months after this meal, after Modonna and Brianna were evicted from a shelter for failing to achieve self-sufficiency in three months' time, they moved in with Modonna's friend. Just days before Christmas, Modonna caught the man looking at Brianna in the wrong way. When she tried to put her foot down, he responded by tossing Modonna and Brianna's belongings out his second-story window onto the street. He shoved them out the door and left them standing in the cold with no place to go, their possessions lying in a tangle around them. It took a full week for them to find stable quarters at a welcoming North Side Salvation Army.

The Art of Making Do with Less

Even accounting for what's made available by the nation's private charities and for the little amounts of cash that can be generated from the various strategies discussed previously, none of these resources can in and of themselves allow a family in $2-a-day poverty to survive. Survival takes more. It requires a stubborn optimism in the face of very tough circumstances. It requires a spirit of determination that can propel someone forward in his or her effort to make do on next to nothing. So beyond private charity and public spaces, beyond selling SNAP, scrap, blood plasma, and even one's body, the primary way the $2-a-day poor cope is to find inventive ways to make do with less. Some have spent years, even decades, in and out of poverty, with multiple spells of living on virtually nothing. For these Americans, the entrepreneurial skills that have been honed by the school of hard knocks are impressive indeed.

During the spring and summer of 2013, after the family pizza business collapsed, Paul Heckewelder's modest residence — totaling about 1,100 square feet on the two main floors, plus an attic and basement — became home to twenty extended family members in addition to Paul and Sarah, his wife of forty years. All of them were trying to survive on Paul's disability check from an old leg injury that limited his mobility.

These were sharply diminished circumstances for the Heckewelder family. In 2007, Paul's three pizza shops had done $1.5 million in sales. He and two of his three sons, Sam and Jonah, had gone into the business together, opening their first store in 2004 in the suburb of Lakewood, just beyond Cudell. That store did well, so in 2005 they opened another, in Sandusky, near the famed roller coaster amusement park Cedar Point. Almost immediately, that store made money hand over fist. So in 2007, Paul added yet another, this time in Amherst, a small city between Cleveland and Sandusky. He recruited his two sons-in-law to share the management duties at this store.

Delivery and takeout were their game, with a trademark special offering two pizzas for the price of one — a way to entice their largely working-class customer base into the store. "My best time economically was when I had the stores," Paul recalls. "I was making $5K a month easily . . . I was making, like, a $10,000 bank deposit each week!" He and Sarah had lived frugally all their lives, so the $5,000 stretched way beyond their needs. The mortgage on the house consumed roughly $700 a month, but other than that, with just the two of them at home, expenses were low — they were no longer supporting five kids. And Paul had always made it a point to pay off the balances on his credit cards and to pay his other bills every month in full, so he had no other debt to speak of. Better still, with the pizza business he could rest assured that two of his three sons plus his two daughters (via their husbands' employment) were provided for. He couldn't control their personal lives, but he had raised his kids to be good workers. He knew they were earning a decent paycheck, because he was the one providing it.

The pizza shops weren't Paul's first business venture. From childhood, entrepreneurship was in his blood. When he acquired a telescope at the age of ten, he set it up right along the ever-busy Lorain Avenue, which traverses Cleveland's west side, and charged passersby 10 cents to look at the moon. "That was a big deal back then! That was before any space program." One night, he recalls, there were so many eager customers in passing cars that he caused a traffic jam. He also remembers with delight the summer night when he and his cousin Peter set about shining shoes, navigating one side of Lorain, all the way from 25th Street, in Ohio City, down to 150th, in Kamm's Corners, then coming back up the other side. It had grown dark — the signal that it was time to go home — but the bars were still open. "We would go in the bars and shine shoes, work boots . . . We were just making too much money to go home — didn't come back until two in the morning, and the whole neighborhood was up worrying . . . Everybody was drunk, so we'd get twenty dollars for shining their work boots! . . . I did that when I was under twelve . . . That was a special night."

At sixteen, while still attending high school, Paul worked in a local steel mill to help with the family's expenses. One day, a large steel beam fell from above, severing his left foot. Even in those days, he had the perspective to know he was lucky — he could have lost his life. After his accident, he had to make his first prosthesis himself. "I made a cast, bought this liquid rubber," and poured it into a mold. Later on, he made another cast from silicone, "before the industry was doing it that way." After several months of claiming workers' compensation, he found that jobs were scarce for a man with one foot and only a high school diploma. Barred from factory work, he and Sarah, then newlyweds, moved to a farm in Amish country, where they got a free place to stay and modest pay working for a local farmer. There, under the farmer's tutelage, Paul became a jack-of-all-trades, learning all kinds of skills to add to his entrepreneur's tool kit. When the farmer retired, Paul was able to parlay those skills into a job as a TV repairman at Higbee's department store. When that trade went bust, he, Sarah, and the kids dipped in and out of poverty for several years as Paul worked odd jobs in construction while pursuing a college degree. Convinced that he would never get ahead without more education, he took a few courses at a time, selling plasma to put enough gas in his car to get to class.

College equipped Paul with the credentials that earned him a five-year stint selling and installing the latest medical imaging equipment in hospitals and clinics all around the world. He began traveling to places such as "Puerto Rico, Philippines, South America. I think I saw all but four [U.S.] states. New York! Nothing is like New York!" Paul loved the travel, loved seeing the world. He picked up quite a bit of Chinese along the way, plus key phrases from a half dozen other languages. But the job meant he was on the road constantly, and by 2004 he had traversed the globe long enough. His kids had come of age largely without his guidance, a fact that he regretted.

Sarah had kept everything together while he was away, and had even homeschooled their five kids. The couple had "gotten saved" in 1979, and homeschooling was a way to try to protect the kids from worldly influences. "[My children] didn't go out [of the house for school] . . . ," Paul says. "They're not full of the world. They love the Lord. They might not be doing the best, [but] I don't care if they're doctors and lawyers, as long as they love the Lord." As his children grew older, however, Paul worried when they married spouses who weren't saved and who had troubles of various kinds. Getting into the pizza business, he thought, would allow him to spend more time with his kids and their families and, he hoped, to shape the direction of their lives.

Paul took out a home equity loan to purchase the first pizza shop from the franchisor, violating a principle he had always held dear: "Not the house. Never the house." He explains, "I didn't do it for my wife. I didn't do it for my kids. But I did it for the pizza store. That was my mistake." Their two-story home, made of brick but covered with faded green siding, was assessed at $70,000 in 2004. Even then, he says, "it wasn't much," referring to the home's worn condition, but he was proud that it was his and was reluctant to go back to owing the bank for it.

With the pizza business, Paul felt he was finally living the life he had dreamed of. Then came 2008. The economy tanked, and he "was losing five thousand a week at some of the stores." First, he sold off the Sandusky location — the one hemorrhaging the most money — using the proceeds to pay back the franchisor what he owed for two of the three stores. The Giant Eagle grocery chain bought out the store in Amherst, but what he made from that sale was only enough to pay off the remainder of his debt on the pizza shops. The Lakewood site finally faltered when the street that it stood on was shut down for more than a year as part of a major road construction project.

Luckily, Paul came out of the fiasco with no debt owed to the parent company. But he wasn't able to pay off the home equity loan. What's more, his home's condition had worsened considerably over the years, and the Cleveland real estate market had virtually collapsed. "Probably with the condition it's in, it's worth fifteen thousand," he says. "I'm stuck with a sixty-five-thousand-dollar mortgage

on a fifteen-thousand-dollar house." Although a government loan re-
payment program recently allowed Paul to cut his monthly payment
from $700 to $250, he finds even that amount a stretch without a job.

The downside of a family business is that if it falls apart, everyone
suffers. Paul had always been the one the rest of the family could
depend on, but "between 2008 and 2010 . . . there was a period there
where I had no income." Without any home equity to fall back on,
he maxed out his credit cards. "I was borrowing from this one to pay
that one. It was a mess." Then "I cashed in my life insurance policy.
I had an investment account from when I worked [for the medical
equipment company]. I cashed that in."

After spending down those funds, the only thing that kept him going was a series of "blessings" he believes were sent by God. During
that period, there were repeated special offerings collected on his behalf by members of his church. Every few weeks during coffee hour,
one of the church elders would hand him a white envelope stuffed
with a few hundred dollars. One week he found a thousand-dollar
check inside. But of equal importance, he says, "the Lord allowed
three accidents on my 2004 [Dodge] Caravan [that were the fault of
the other guy]. I got fifteen hundred [for] one side, then twelve hundred on the next side, . . . a thousand on the next . . . I'd say, 'Lord,
you got one more side, the driver's side!'" Before the fourth miracle
could happen, though, the van went up in smoke, literally. It "ended
up burning up in the driveway . . . The motor caught fire, and we lost
it. No insurance on it . . . just liability."

Church friends gave Paul a used vehicle — a white panel van with
tinted windows that was on its last legs. "Frame [was] totally just
rusted out. You [could] grab the frame with your hands and crumble
it." Rather than complain, Paul simply "welded the frame. I bought a
welder and I got under there and welded some steel . . . Welded it up
good. And the brake line on the one side was jury-rigged, it was all
patched together, and it held together all winter long."

In 2010, just as every resource he had at his disposal had been ex-
pended, Paul was finally approved for Social Security Disability In-

surance. In 2009, he had been diagnosed with diabetes, and his bum leg (which caused chronic back problems) had grown too unsteady to support him for any length of time. Qualifying for disability ensured him access to public health insurance via Medicaid. But when Sarah was diagnosed with cancer in 2011, she had to undergo a year of treatment before she managed to get Medicare (a problem she wouldn't face now, following the expansion of Medicaid in Ohio after passage of the Affordable Care Act). The medical bills accumulated. Paul keeps these bills stacked alongside his computer on his desk. They are nearly a foot high.

Little did Paul know that their trials were just beginning. In the spring of 2013, one son-in-law landed in jail. His pregnant wife (Paul and Sarah's daughter) and their kids moved in with them. Their other daughter was evicted from her home after her husband lost his job at a muffler store. In Cleveland's economy, where the unemployment rate exceeded 10 percent during the summer of 2013, it proved harder than expected for him to find employment, and she moved in along with her kids. One of his son's ex-wives — with kids from several previous relationships — lost custody of all six of her children when she was hospitalized with terminal cancer. When child welfare came calling, Paul and Sarah took them in, too. Then their son Sam's wife deserted him, leaving him with six young kids to care for, including three from her previous marriage. He had to quit his job and become a stay-at-home dad. Unable to pay the rent, he also landed at his parents' home.

To say that the place is overcrowded would be an understatement. Sarah's cancer has confined her to a hospital bed that takes up most of the dining room. The front room serves as a bedroom for four of the kids. The finished portion of the basement houses Sam and his six kids. Five more children and Paul's younger daughter are stuffed into a tiny bedroom on the second floor (doubled up in two bunk beds and a single bed). Paul's older daughter and her family are stashed in the tiny attic. "There isn't a room other than the bathroom where no one's sleeping."

Even with Paul's disability check coming in, with twenty-two mouths to feed, his household income has fallen below the $2-a-day mark. They tried but failed to get additional SNAP for the kids. The caseworker told them they had been denied due to the temporary nature of the living arrangements. Indeed, had the family been completely open about their situation when applying for benefits, the child welfare authorities might have come and taken the kids.

At one point, Paul fell far behind on the humongous water bills that started coming in. "[It] got up to $2,700," he says. The water was shut off for weeks, but he had "a friend we could go to with five-gallon buckets that was for clean water, dishwater." Several times a week, the kids would pile in the back of the panel van, each with a bucket or two in hand, to travel the short distance to the friend's home. There they would fill the buckets and set up a bucket brigade, passing them from hand to hand into the back of the vehicle. Then they would all climb in the van with the buckets for the trip home. For drinking water, "the boys would go to the neighbor's." For baths, sometimes "the kids would go to the pool and get their bath[s]" there. And to flush the toilet, Paul "took the gutter apart, rigged it up over the garbage can, and in just one rain we filled one big rolling garbage can, [toting it upstairs one bucket at a time, and] we used that to flush the toilet!"

Over the six months that Paul's home has housed twenty-two, the family has eaten "a lot of macaroni . . . a lot of peanut butter and jelly." Sam bakes pasta in an industrial-size restaurant pan. At the back of the kitchen, plastic shelving units sit under a window so poorly fitted that you can see light between the frame and the wall. The units buckle under the weight of canned goods gleaned from the local food pantry.

Down the narrow cellar stairs lies the partially finished portion of the basement, home to Sam and his six kids. Always a forward thinker, Paul long ago reserved one corner of the room for a cast-iron pellet stove he bought on Craigslist. He believes it could heat the underground space cheaply in case the power is shut off or there is a widespread power outage. No matter what happens or how cold the winter, his family will stay warm.

In the unfinished portion of the basement, metal shelves and a row of old gym lockers overflow with staples. Most food pantries offer too much in the way of grains and pastas, but not enough meat and fresh fruits and vegetables, he says. Not wanting to waste any of the food he receives, he transfers surplus rice, beans, noodles, flour, cornmeal, and other nonperishables into empty containers of all shapes and sizes—milk cartons, juice jugs, water bottles, and plastic containers that once held kerosene, laundry detergent, or dishwashing liquid—anticipating the future hard times that may come. On the floor, next to the lockers, there is a large picnic cooler filled with about a dozen boxes of instant potatoes.

The unfinished part of the basement also holds the washer and dryer. When the water is on, Paul spends hours here employing a time-consuming conservation technique in order to save money on his water bill. "After it goes to [the] rinse cycle, I take the hose and fill up all these old laundry detergent bottles. That's my next wash load. Then that rinse cycle becomes the wash water for the next load. Saves half the water bill . . . I fill it up, boom, boom, boom, boom! While I'm sitting down there, I can go through five laundry loads [with that water]." When the water wasn't on, the washtub and clothesline in the backyard had to suffice.

"It's good [everyone ended up here] in the summer, because if it wasn't the summer, we would [have had] to do more inside," Paul tells a friend, whom he has apprised of his situation. An eight-foot folding table sits in the driveway on the right side of the house, surrounded by an assortment of plastic chairs. One side is flanked by the backseat from the van (you can get more kids in the van without that seat in it). At one end is a pink-and-green children's picnic table complete with benches, which adds seating for an additional four. "I like it because when they spill their milk, you just hose down the driveway. Like five of 'em generally spill their milk in a meal." This strategy has a downside, however. "Somehow, we are a magnet for rats . . . Rats come from all over the neighborhood. They come out and sit right on the table . . . I take my pellet gun, [and] we have fun using the rats for target practice out of my bedroom window!"

Beyond the dinner table and the big pile of scrap metal, much of the backyard is taken up by a garden that "grew from throwing out spoiling food — cucumbers, tomatoes, spaghetti squash . . . All from the rotted vegetables. Any rotted potatoes we plant, then in November we have another crop of potatoes." The garden provides fresh vegetables to supplement the canned goods, grains, and pastas provided by the food pantry. Survival for the extended family in Paul's home requires that no resource be wasted and no asset go untapped.

Work Without a Job

Is Paul Heckewelder a worker? As of the summer of 2013, it has been about five years since he has held a job, back when he was a proud small business owner. If Paul were to complete one of the official government surveys that captures key statistics about the nation's workforce, he would be deemed "not in the labor force." He isn't employed, and he is no longer looking for a job, in part because his health has deteriorated to the point where he has trouble walking and breathing.

Yet it would certainly be inaccurate to say that Paul has not been working. He has been busy collecting metal for the scrapyard. He's been busy sitting by the washing machine, waiting to catch the rinse water so that he can reuse it in the next load. (When his water was shut off, he was busy rigging up the gutter and garbage can to catch rainwater that could be used to flush the toilet, and driving to his friend's house and making trips to the neighbor's to fill up empty milk jugs with clean water.) He's been busy driving the kids to the local food pantry — to prove just how many mouths they have to feed. And when he hasn't been running back and forth, he's been occupied welding his crumbling van together and buttressing the collapsing floor of his home. None of these jobs can be captured on a résumé or in the U.S. government's official workforce statistics. But this American, who is officially "not in the labor force," is not exactly a couch potato.

Paul's circumstances during his current stint in $2-a-day poverty — he had spells in childhood, as a young adult, and as a middle-aged college student as well — seem relatively good when compared to those of other families whose stories are told in this book. In fact, of all the households included in this study, Paul's is easily the best off. At first, he had assets to tap, even though he used up nearly every penny of them during the years after his pizza shops went bust. His house is badly underwater, yet at $260 a month it still provides the cheapest possible place he could live. Unlike most of America's $2-a-day poor, since 2010 he has had a regular income stream. A disability check of $1,025 can't get him above the $2-a-day mark with twenty-two people living in his home, but it is better than nothing. Plus, it is stable, something he can rely on.

Relatively speaking, Paul is a bit of an outlier among the $2-a-day poor. But in terms of his work ethic, he is the archetype. As his story and the others in this chapter show, the work of survival at the very bottom of America's economic ladder is hard. It's about turning what little you have in the way of assets into cash or goods, or honing your entrepreneurial skills in ways that allow you to make do with less, in an effort to ease the many hardships associated with life on no income.

In big, nationally representative surveys (like the one that provides the hard numbers for this book), families may not always tell researchers (usually government employees) about income from all of the survival strategies described in this chapter. A mom with one child who tells a researcher that she had $120 in income during a particular month might actually have had $180 because she donated plasma twice or sold $100 in SNAP benefits in exchange for $60 in cash. When queried by researchers, a mother may fear prosecution if she reports that she got money from a "friend" in exchange for sex.

Some may simply forget to report the cash they get from collecting aluminum cans—perhaps because it is so irregular or the profit is so small. Others—particularly those who are homeless or otherwise on the move, shifting from the home of one relative to another—may not even appear in big government surveys because they have no stable address. The only way to get a true accounting of the resources of the $2-a-day poor is to spend large amounts of time with them, build trust, and meticulously document their circumstances. But this kind of research is time-consuming. Without millions of research dollars, it is impossible to identify and follow a large random sample of the $2-a-day poor, which would be the only way to paint a reliable national portrait of what they must do to survive.

Critics might say, "Anyone who reports an income below $2 a day in the United States has resources he or she isn't telling us about. This problem is not real." The evidence in this chapter suggests that selling plasma, scrap metal, or one's body may occasionally raise incomes from $2 a day to, say, $3 or $4 a day instead. But this "measurement error" seems far less important than the fact that the number of families who tell government researchers they are living on virtually no cash has grown so dramatically over time. The number of children experiencing a spell of $2-a-day poverty is about the same as the number of kids lifted above the poverty line by the tax credits now extended to the working poor—a program federal taxpayers spend roughly $66 billion on. Also, some of the strategies the $2-a-day poor must resort to actually reduce their resources. When Jennifer Hernandez sells $100 in SNAP, she loses $40 in purchasing power.

Where do we see hard evidence of the rise in extreme poverty among families with children? It is evident in the SIPP, the nationally representative survey that does the best job of capturing the incomes of the poor. It is seen in SNAP administrative records, which show a sharp uptick in the number of families reporting no other form of income save SNAP. In fact, the SNAP estimates match those from the

SIPP survey remarkably closely. Reports in some major cities suggest increased demand for family shelter beds starting in the early 2000s, as well as an increase in the number of families seeking emergency food services that predates the Great Recession. But the best proof of all that the $2-a-day poor exist is that finding people who fit this profile — people like Paul Heckewelder, Jennifer Hernandez, and Travis and Jessica Compton — is not that hard. It can be done in a relatively short amount of time in a number of locales across the country. This virtually cashless form of poverty is out there, even though we wish it weren't. And it has grown.

It would be tragic beyond belief if some segment of Americans lived in conditions comparable to those of the poorest people living in places like Haiti or Zimbabwe. Due to our public spaces, private charities, and in-kind government benefits such as SNAP, this level of destitution is probably extremely rare, if not completely nonexistent here. However, one might argue that some of the families whose stories are told in this book have experienced a level of material want that may approach bare subsistence. Furthermore, to be without cash in America is to be cut off from society, disconnected from the resources that could help you get out of those desperate straits and move ahead. As one expert on global poverty put it, the rise of the virtually cashless poor in the United States may "imply a severe form of poverty in both a practical and intangible sense."

What is true about each of the families in this book is that they would all rather have a real job than engage in any of the alternative forms of "work" described in this chapter. Yet the more employment in the formal labor market proves perilous — with low pay, too few hours, and crazy schedules — the more untenable it is for a parent trying to raise kids. And the weaker the government safety net, the more the informal work described here will proliferate. We know what this kind of economy looks like, because it typifies economies in other, poorer countries all over the world. If the experiences of such countries are any guide, the replacement of a formal economy with an informal one — unregulated and unpoliced — may have a self-perpet-uating effect of pushing the $2-a-day poor further and further out of the American mainstream. Indeed, as the next chapter explains, some parts of our country have already gone much further down this path than others.

Chapter 5

A World Apart

MARTHA JOHNSON RESIDES in a small town of about 2,000 in the heart of the Mississippi Delta. As she holds her grandson in one arm, she pushes open the screen door of her government-built home and steps outside onto her shallow concrete porch to greet the day. From this vantage point, she can see nearly every place that she has ever lived. Across the field bursting with soybeans is the farmhouse where she was born, and just down the street is the small brick abode where her father raised Martha and her siblings with a strict hand after her mother "run out" on them when Martha was just a baby. Ever since she and the father of her youngest child split up for good a decade ago, when she was forty, she has lived in different units in this very apartment complex, which she refers to as "the projects."

The fields that Martha gazes out on are those where her father spent his lifetime as a farmhand. Martha's front porch is so close to these fields, in fact, that on days when the fluorescent-yellow-and-black planes come at dawn to dust the crops with pesticides, they shower her building, too. On those mornings, the sky remains dark long after sunrise. On some early summer days like today, she can sometimes see dirty plumes of smoke rising from red flames all across the horizon as planters burn their fields in preparation for crop rotation. All through the growing season, Martha, her two daughters, and their neighbors complain of a unique local ailment—an upper-

respiratory condition folks refer to as "Delta crud," which many believe is brought on by these farming practices. The symptoms are
wheezing and nausea, sometimes followed by chronic congestion.

Today Martha is dressed in a thin cap-sleeved T-shirt and a pair of
black track pants that end at the knees. Her size-ten feet are clad with
Nike shower shoes. She's nearly six feet tall, with an athletic build,
dark skin, and permed hair ending just below her chin. She has big
eyes, thick brows, a strong jaw, and a wide smile. As she talks with a
friend, her long, strong arms transfer her six-month-old grandson,
who is the size of an average one-year-old, from shoulder to shoulder.

Martha has stable housing thanks to her Section 8 voucher. Her
rent is limited to 30 percent of her official cash income, which runs
only $150 a month for her family of three — now four since the arrival
of her daughter Alona's baby six months ago. Heading back inside her
apartment, Martha steps directly into the unit's sole common space,
the front half of which serves as the living room, while the back wall
makes up the kitchen. Under the window next to the front door sits a
card table choked with blue-and-gold trophies, all carefully arranged.
Trophy tables are prominent features of many homes here in Martha's hometown of Jefferson, because the schools give out so many.
Alona, who has just finished high school and is one of the few in her
class who plans to head to college in the fall while Martha cares for
the baby, reveals that most of them are hers — this one for track, that
one for basketball, another one for soccer. She inherited her mother's
athletic ability as well as her build. Most of the trophies, though, were
given for what she views as the most mundane of accomplishments:
scoring in the proficient range on the math or reading sections of a
state standardized test, or even for school attendance. She isn't much
interested in these.

Later today she'll head to graduation practice, but at the moment
she's got both hands full carrying a papier-mâché volcano that she
and her twelve-year-old sister, Candace, finished the night before.
Alona considers herself a bit of an expert on the volcano homework.

She watched as her older brother and sister constructed their volcanoes. When it was her turn, she relished the opportunity to create her own papier-mâché structure and was sorry to see it erupt with the well-known mixture of baking soda and vinegar. So last night, when Candace was struggling with the assignment, Alona was glad to stay up late to finish it off, long after Candace had given up and gone to bed.

Martha, Alona, and Candace form a close-knit family, eager to help one another in times of need. Unlike many of the homes of the desperately poor, there is an air of contentment here. Things are far from easy, with just $150 a month in cash income between them, but the pain of poverty seems to have been salved, at least in part, by the strength they find in one another.

In Jefferson, one could probably throw a stone in any direction and hit the residence of a family below the $2-a-day threshold. The Mississippi Delta is a world unto itself, with a unique history and a distinctive set of social conditions. The region has always been desperately poor. Even now, nearly fifty years after Robert Kennedy's 1967 visit, delving into the texture of a typical small town in the Delta can be jarring. First, there is the extent of the poverty. In Sunshine County, small cities of just a few thousand like Jefferson record poverty rates of well over 40 percent. Although the nation's child poverty rate is high — about one in five children live in poverty — here the levels can be three times greater than that. In many of the smaller towns of only a few hundred folks, typical household incomes fall below $20,000, and the child poverty rate can surpass 65 percent.

Many consider the Delta to have the richest farmland in the nation — with topsoil running as deep as thirty feet. In an earlier era, local plantations once employed (and before that enslaved) thousands. Lynetta Williams, a neighbor of Martha's, recalls that a few decades ago, local planters would still "take care of you" — to some degree anyway — if you were willing to work. For all the problems back then, she feels that those were better times, because folks didn't need to worry about where they would live or whether they would be fed. Today, she says, that's not a given.

Although Mississippi's social safety net has always lagged far behind that of the rest of the country, AFDC was operational in the Delta by the mid-1960s. In 1970, the program covered only about 30 percent of poor children here, as compared to nearly 60 percent on average across the nation. However, that figure soon shot up as the court cases spurred by the National Welfare Rights Organization broke down discriminatory barriers that states had used to keep blacks off the rolls. By 1990, roughly half of the state's poor kids were covered by AFDC. During those years, desperate parents with no other source of income could claim cash from the welfare office — cash they were entitled to by law (see chapter 1). And many did so. The state had a cash safety net, however modest.

Since the 1996 welfare reform, Mississippi's TANF rolls have seen an astonishing decline, more so than in most other places. As of 1965, the program was serving 83,000 residents, and that number grew to nearly 180,000 at its peak. By 2002, however, the rolls had plummeted to only 40,000, and by the fall of 2014 the figure had fallen even further, to only about 17,000 statewide, around 0.6 percent of the state's population.

In sum, Mississippi, like the rest of the country, is a place where the cash safety net has all but disappeared. This has paved the way for steep growth in the new poverty that has been documented throughout this book — households with children living on virtually no cash income. But what is distinctive about the Delta, along with other rural and semirural places concentrated in the Deep South and Appalachia, is that by the time welfare reform came along, with its new rules around work, opportunities for work had already virtually disappeared for those with low levels of education.

It is not merely the case that welfare reform and the accompanying changes left single mothers at the mercy of the perilous world of low-wage work, as it did in many places. Over the long term, work has been much less available here than it has been in most parts of the country, especially since the mechanization of agriculture. The unemployment rate in this central Delta county has been far above the national average for decades. This was true even during the historic economic expansion of the late 1990s, when the economic needle didn't move here to the extent that it did in other parts of the country. In recent years, the rate of joblessness has been truly staggering. Halfway through 2014, more than 10 percent of adults were out of work and looking for a job (compared to the national rate of 6.3 percent). Most notable, at last available count, more than 35 percent of prime-working-age men were either unemployed or had left the labor force altogether, compared to the national average of just over 20 percent.

The cause of the economic free fall varies from place to place across the Deep South and Appalachia. While the collapse of the coal mining industry is the story in eastern Kentucky, mechanized farming techniques, including today's high-tech, computerized tractors and combines, have allowed the agricultural industry to operate with only a tiny fraction of the workers once required in the Delta. Some of these machines are so fully automated that people say an operator can take a nap while his machine runs the length of a furrow. But it is also true that operating such a machine demands math and computer skills. Therefore, agriculture is not always a viable option for a high school dropout, especially one educated in the Delta, where many local schools earn a C, D, or F rating from the state.

Even among African Americans from around here with the skills to do these jobs, many recoil at the notion of toiling away in the same fields where their great-great-grandparents endured cruel forced labor. One local planter claims that the only way to get enough skilled and willing workers to plant, groom, and harvest his fields is to import them from South Africa. The wages he pays these college-educated guest workers for one planting season — roughly $8 an hour for forty to sixty hours per week — are more than they could make in a full year at home.

You might be able to claim a few hours at the Dollar General or the Double Quick convenience store, staples of many of these towns. There is the occasional Walmart or Kroger grocery store in the bigger cites, but they offer very few full-time positions. A small group of low-skilled individuals find work at municipal buildings or in schools (perhaps as cafeteria workers or bus drivers), but prison inmates are sometimes used for maintenance and janitorial services in these places. There are a few factory jobs in some of the larger cities, the closest of which is a half hour away by car, but most people are too poor to purchase and maintain a vehicle. There are minimum-wage jobs cleaning hotel rooms at the casinos down the road — if you can find a way to get there. Yet even these jobs are harder to come by now. The casino business in the Delta has declined as competition for gamblers has heated up in the region. More and more casinos have sprung up near Memphis, the city where most of the people with real money in the Delta live. All told, the job situation in the Delta can quickly begin to feel hopeless even for the most earnest job seeker, especially if she's hoping for a full-time job.

The legacy of slavery, Jim Crow, and segregation remains thick in places like Jefferson. There are nearly always two sides to these small communities, one white and one black. One is marked by stately red-brick structures shaded by old-growth oaks and outfitted with manicured lawns, sprawling magnolia trees, and the omnipresent crape myrtle. The other side of town teeters. Its tiny wood-frame shotgun-style houses and decrepit trailers sit askew or have imploded altogether. Yards are choked with sunken-in garages, derelict appliances, and junk cars. Narrow porches are lined with old kitchen stools or broken-down living room chairs. Each time a car goes by, which isn't that often, the air fills with dust. The stark contrast between the two sides of town isn't new — it's always been like this.

Many of the old main streets in these Delta towns, built up about a century ago, now sit virtually empty. Jefferson's downtown still has some vitality to it, but just down the road lies another little town with an impressive cluster of red-brick buildings and streets that are utterly still, even on a weekday afternoon. In a third hamlet, a group of old black men spend their afternoons playing cards on the porch of a dilapidated former general store, just as they might have when the town was bustling. Here and there across the county, the carcasses of abandoned schools sit empty, windows busted out, rooflines sagging, lawns choked with weeds. In one, the sun shining in through the broken windows highlights a bird's nest and several old textbooks strewn across the floor. In most of the cities and towns, there are large, empty, unsightly warehouses where cotton was once stored. King Cotton must now compete with the lowly soybean and ethanol-producing corn.

Health care in the Delta ranks among the worst in the nation. Some counties don't even have an ambulance. One person reports that if you want to get your loved one to the hospital, you must drive to the county line and meet the ambulance from the next county over, which is hard to do if you don't have a car. And despite high crime rates, some of the smaller towns lack a single police officer. All of these features impede the possibility of future economic growth. Businesses don't want to locate in a place where the workforce has so little experience and so many prospective workers may be functionally illiterate. What firm could convince its middle management to move there?

These small Delta towns, along with other sparsely populated farm hamlets and derelict mill towns across the Deep South and Appalachia, contain a disproportionate share of the $2-a-day poor. Locales like the Delta have long been among America's poorest places — stops on the "poverty tours" of generations of politicians — due to economic travails evidenced generations ago.

If legitimate means for getting cash — from either welfare or employment — have become increasingly scarce, the infrastructure necessary to earn cash in the informal economy isn't much in evidence either. There are no plasma clinics to be found, and only a few scrapyards in the region's biggest cities. Private charity, which is in greater abundance in rich cities such as Chicago, is noticeably absent here, and many of the public spaces are in disrepair. For the residents of these little towns, the nearest food pantry is often miles away, despite the sky-high poverty. Jefferson's public library, crafted from an abandoned railroad depot, has only a few worn best sellers and a couple of computers on hand. Not surprisingly, you may find it empty even on a weekday in those prime hours just after school, and it's often closed due to the lack of funding.

When the new poverty of those living on $2 a day meets the old poverty of long-term economic stagnation, a whole region can become starved of cash. In places like the Delta, the bite of $2-a-day poverty is experienced on a community level. Under these conditions, a subterranean economy can spring up in place of the formal one, intricately interweaving the lives of the $2-a-day poor, the just plain poor, and even those slightly higher up the economic ladder. This shadow economy springs forth in living rooms, in parking lots, in the checkout line at Kroger, and even inside the legitimate businesses that have managed to survive. At its best, it forges bonds of interdependence that inspire the slightly better-off to aid those who are struggling in ways that speak to the marvel of human goodness. But at its worst, when the new poverty meets the old, it warps human relationships and puts those at the very bottom of society in a position that is ripe for exploitation.

Aside from the crowded trophy table, Martha's apartment is neat and clean, but noticeably bare. There is only a love seat and a couch, and the dozen or so family photos hanging on the wall (some shellacked on antiqued wooden boards) — neither the clutter nor the decor one might expect in a household with two teens and a baby. What stands out most is the wooden dining table that separates the kitchen from the living area. The table reveals Martha's method for surviving on virtually no legitimate source of cash other than the $150 a month in child support she gets from Candace's father. On it, she has neatly arranged an assortment of snacks, some in woven baskets. The offerings are modest — a dozen bags of chips, some cherry- and grape-flavored suckers, a few other varieties of candy. Inside the refrigerator's freezer, though, there are dozens of Dixie cups filled with Kool-Aid, Popsicle sticks taped into place so they stand straight up. All morning, Martha has been checking to see whether the Kool-Aid inside has frozen hard enough to ensure that the sticks will stand upright minus the tape.

At about 10:00 a.m., the first customers come by. A dad wearing a white tank top, jean shorts, and white sneakers is looking to treat his two daughters, about six and eight years old. The fifty-cent Dixie cups he hoped to purchase for the girls still haven't frozen. There are some dollar-size pops in Styrofoam cups left over from yesterday, but he has only $1 and two eager girls, so he'll have to come back in about an hour. Over the next thirteen hours, a similar ritual is repeated over and over again. People knock at the door, and Martha shouts for them to come in. Sometimes parents accompany their kids, sometimes the kids come on their own. Most leave with a special treat.

Martha's business model is simple: buy in bulk, sell for roughly twice the price. Nothing in her store has a sale price of more than $1. The frozen pops yield the highest profit — all they require is Kool-Aid mix, Popsicle sticks, and a supply of Dixie and Styrofoam cups. In the summer, when the neighborhood kids are around all day, she diversifies her inventory some, offering Kool-Aid pickles (Martha's secret recipe: add Kool-Aid mix to the pickle juice, let the pickles marinate for two or three days, and serve) and pickled pigs feet. If she's feeling ambitious and has the supplies, she may offer chitlins, too, the local delicacy made from the small intestines of a pig.

In the bare-bones Delta economy, Martha Johnson has devised a survival strategy that trumps most others in the vicinity, both in terms of the cash it yields and in the lack of a toll on self-respect. In keeping with the biblical parable of the talents, rather than bury her proverbial treasure in the ground, Martha invests the SNAP she receives for herself, her two daughters still at home, and her six-month-old grandchild into a small capitalist enterprise that allows her to provide a minimally decent life for her family in the face of highly precarious financial circumstances. She's spent a decade building up her business, one frozen pop and bag of potato chips at a time.

For Martha, cash is an absolute necessity of life. Her biggest bill is for the utilities, which run about $250 a month on average. She suffers from asthma, so she feels she needs a phone in case of an emergency. She can't afford a smartphone, but she does have a basic flip phone, which costs another $25 a month. She has to keep her grandson in diapers and formula, and Alona, the three-season athlete, in athletic shoes. She must provide school uniforms for the girls. Her goal is to ensure that there is toothpaste and toilet paper in the bathroom and laundry soap to wash the clothes. With the tiny profit she makes on her store—plus a little bit of help here and there from Alona's boyfriend, the part-time Walmart employee whom Martha calls "my angel"—she brings her meager budget into balance. A good day at the store yields $20 in profit for thirteen hours of work, an hourly wage of less than $1.50. If she has a good day every day for an entire month, her proceeds can reach $600. In reality, though, she usually nets only about $400.

Running a little store out of the front room of her apartment is, in many ways, the perfect job for a woman who is too sick to hold down a job but not quite sick enough to qualify for disability benefits. Even outside the path of crop dusters, the health conditions of many poor folks in the Delta are abysmal, and Martha is no exception. The other trophy table of sorts in her home is her bedside dresser, where eight pill bottles stand in a row. Two are for hypertension, two for anxiety, one for the blood clots in her legs and feet, and so on. She's been to the Social Security office to file for disability, but she's been denied. They have told her she's healthy enough to work as a hotel maid, even though there are no hotels anywhere nearby. Even if she could get to a hotel, trying to work such a job doesn't seem realistic to Martha: after about twenty minutes on her feet, they swell up like grapefruit.

Like many of Jefferson's residents, Martha does not own a car, and there are no buses or public transportation of any sort. There is also no place in town to buy groceries, just the Double Quick, the Dollar General, and a tiny restaurant and general store. To acquire products for the store, she must travel to a larger city a twenty-minute car ride away. For transportation, she relies on "Miss Clark," a neighbor lady who lives down the road. On these outings, their first stop is the local butcher, who sells snacks in bulk, as well as pigs feet and chitlins. Then they are on to Walmart or Kroger.

Dorothy Clark is one of the Delta's just plain poor, kept well above $2-a-day poverty by her government disability check, yet she still struggles to raise her three children. She supplements her disability by using her van as a gypsy cab. Miss Clark's neighbors keep her busy driving back and forth to "town." Passengers pay their $30 fare in cash or SNAP. Occasionally, she drives folks around for free due to an abundance of Christian charity. Martha, a fellow churchgoer and close friend, is often the beneficiary of her generosity. Without Dorothy Clark's kindness, the profit margin of Martha's store would be perilously low.

Others in the taxicab business are a bit more hard-nosed. Up in the hamlet of Percy, a town of about three hundred a few miles away, Loretta Perkins uses her "little raggedy car" to transport folks where they need to go, but she never fails to charge a fee. "Nobody even gets in my car unless we go right to the gas station and they fill up the tank with gas," she says. She is available every day but Tuesday, which she calls "National Highway Patrol Day," due to the high number of patrol cars on the road that day of the week. Miss Perkins never drives on Tuesdays because she has no license plate for her vehicle, no insurance, and no driver's license.

In the informal economic system that has arisen in these towns, most people are poor or nearly so, like Dorothy Clark. But some are poorer than others, like Martha. Some have a little cash but not much in the way of SNAP. Some get a large infusion of SNAP each month—though not necessarily enough to make it through—but no cash. Both groups can benefit by engaging in SNAP trafficking, though the strategies used here are a little different from those used by folks up north in Chicago. Here everyone knows everyone else, so finding a business partner who's got some cash but no SNAP is often as simple as going next door. In the typical exchange, those with cash get their groceries for half price. The going rate for a dollar of SNAP is just 50 cents here, rather than the 60-cent rate in places where far fewer folks are involved in trafficking. Those trading SNAP for cash may not be happy about the exchange rate, but with so much SNAP and so little cash in the local economy, it is a buyer's market.

Up in Percy, Alva Mae Hicks is raising ten children under the age of eighteen, plus she has three more who are a little older. She worked on and off as a hotel maid for several years, taking a shuttle van to Greenville each day. For the past decade or so, she hasn't held a job. These days, she couldn't possibly afford child care for all her kids, not to mention that the fee for the shuttle to work now costs $15 a day, a quarter of her potential gross pay. With such a large family, Alva Mae has to go above and beyond selling SNAP to have any chance of keeping her household going. Just this past year, she struck on a new strategy that may help fill the gap a little.

With no job, Alva Mae can't take advantage of the refundable tax credits that the federal government uses to buttress the wages of low-wage workers. While she may not be employed, she does have relatives a few towns over who are, but they don't have any children whom they can claim as dependents. She also has family over in Jonesville — just a hop, skip, and a jump from Percy — whose kids are grown. Recently, one of her relatives offered to buy one of her kids' Social Security numbers for $500. Alva Mae then sold two more to other kin, reaping $1,500 in cash for her household — which currently contains *twenty-one* people. These relatives can "carry" the child whose Social Security number they purchased as a dependent on their taxes and collect the refundable tax credit for which neither they nor Alva Mae is eligible. Last year, Alva Mae used the proceeds from these transactions to buy a used car — mostly so she could visit the food pantry in a nearby town. This turned out to be a poor investment. Just two months later, the car broke down, and Alva Mae has no money to fix it.

It is not possible to tell how common this practice is in the Delta. No family in any of the other three places included in this book (Chicago, Cleveland, and Johnson City, Tennessee) admitted to selling their kids' Social Security numbers at tax time. But conversations with residents across the central Delta suggest that the strategy may not be uncommon. In all likelihood, those who buy the right to claim a child as a dependent on their taxes make out a lot better than those who sell that right: a single person making minimum wage who claims two children can boost her tax refund by more than $5,000. Still, if these examples are any guide, the cash windfall that comes to the region at tax season — with its hefty refunds for the working poor with dependent children — may be shared by workers and nonworkers, parents and nonparents, alike.

Formal Economy, Shadow Economy

At the turnoff from the highway that leads to Percy sits the small town's busiest, and most notorious, enterprise. Salvatore's, a nondescript red-brick and plate-glass 1970s structure, is a white-owned liquor store and bar with an attached but shuttered convenience mart complete with two nonfunctioning gas pumps. The gas station and convenience mart have long since closed, likely casualties of the Double Quick convenience stores that have sprung up here and there along the highway. But the liquor store and bar remain the town's most popular sites for socializing, especially after sundown. Indeed, people come from miles around. Mr. and Mrs. Salvatore do a brisk business, selling alcohol to be consumed both on and off the premises.

During the day, sunlight reflects off the hundreds of beer cans and liquor bottles that have been tossed into a deep ditch along the main highway fronting the property. Sometimes the bottle heap reaches a foot high. The owner is occasionally (though rarely) pressured by the city to clean up around the place. It's hard to put any kind of pressure on Salvatore when he controls one of the town's three remaining businesses, plus virtually all of the rental properties around town. According to one resident, "He own [*sic*] Percy. There's maybe only four or five houses that somebody actually owns here. About ninety percent he owns."

Salvatore rents out a set of generations-old sharecropper shacks he's hauled from the field and plunked down by the main highway. Each has been repaired to some degree, but according to one former tenant, the insides still smell of decades — maybe even a century — of decay. You can rent one of these places for about $200 a month. For as little as $150, you can move into one of Salvatore's collection of barely inhabitable mobile homes, some lacking any source of heat. These shacks and trailers form a ragged necklace around the intersection that marks the entrance to town. Their condition makes the weed-eaten, derelict Section 8 development where Alva Mae Hicks and Loretta Perkins live seem desirable by comparison.

The other two businesses in Percy are run by relatives of the Salvatores. At the Percy Diner, the "diner" part consists of a Formica table and four metal chairs with vinyl seats tucked back by the beverage coolers chilling cans of Coca-Cola. The coolers are the only modern touch to the place. Here, Miss Carol takes orders from the almost entirely black clientele, while Mr. Mike works the grill, dishing up hamburgers ("everything on it" means tomatoes, red onions, a piece of lettuce, and lots and lots of mayonnaise), Philly cheesesteaks, and the like.

Kitty-corner to the diner is Valentine's General Store. Its white proprietor was mayor of Percy for nearly thirty years before losing an election to a black man who used to sweep his floors. Valentine's sells hot dogs, sandwiches, sodas, chips, cupcakes, and Ding Dongs at lunchtime. Loaves of Wonder bread sit on the shelf ready for purchase. Anyone using SNAP here must beware, though. Some locals say that if purchasers aren't paying attention, the Valentines may add a little something extra for themselves when they ring through groceries on SNAP cards.

Of course, if someone were to catch Mr. or Mrs. Valentine cheating them out of their food stamps, they would have little recourse. Percy has no police force. Such an offense probably wouldn't even register with the county sheriff's office, which has plenty of violent crime to deal with. Some years ago, Percy town officials tried to hire a semiretired cop from a larger town nearby to patrol the streets part-time. According to one local resident, after just one night on the job, the new hire called an emergency meeting with the city council to ask, "What part of the law do you want me to enforce?" Reportedly, the officer claimed that if he were to enforce the law in full, he was quite certain that most of the town's residents would be imprisoned by week's end. After getting some guidance from the council, he went back out on the streets for a second night. The next day, he quit.

In the evenings, and especially on the weekends, trucks, with their radios blasting, fill the parking lot at Salvatore's. People come to drink, dance, and play pool. It's the only source of entertainment in the immediate vicinity. According to one nearby resident, "It's like you're going by a football stadium or something like that, where everybody's out and about, tailgating, something like that. Just like everybody doing different stuff up there, everybody's dancing, they got their cars out there, they got bottles flying. That stack of bottles comes from somewhere. It comes from all these people." Shanea Robinson, who lives in one of Salvatore's trailers located just across a small bayou from the store, claims that out back there are "drugs and oral sex and all that stuff." All this activity makes Salvatore's a prime place for a mom desperate for some money—a respectable mom by day—to meet a john and "go for a ride" when a bill needs to be paid.

Especially at Salvatore's, but pretty much everywhere else, too, it's all but impossible to tell where the formal economy ends and the shadow economy begins. Although it's nothing like prostitution, Martha Johnson's little store, for all its virtues, is still an illegal enterprise. Every time she purchases inventory using her SNAP card, she commits a crime. Not revealing her "income" to the housing authority, not to mention the IRS, is also a crime. Operating a business without a license? That's yet another offense. Dorothy Clark and Loretta Perkins operate informal taxi services, the latter without a license plate, insurance, or even a driver's license. In addition to selling her SNAP every month, Alva Mae Hicks has sold some of her kids' Social Security numbers, defrauding the IRS.

Yet one might argue that these activities are more in line with conventional morality than what goes on in many of the town's legal enterprises. There is no way of telling whether Mr. and Mrs. Valentine really cheat people out of their SNAP whenever the opportunity presents itself. But the heaps of liquor bottles that collect in the ditch fronting Salvatore's seem to broadcast the owner's contempt for his customers to those passing by. Salvatore's "legal" pool hall and liquor store are the most fertile ground for vice that Percy has. And Mr. Salvatore is a notorious slumlord. Sure, the places are cheap, but stepping inside, you have to wonder whether most of them are worth any rent at all.

What is the price of the world apart that has arisen in these Delta cities and towns? What happens when a community starved for cash forges a shadow economy that threatens to overtake the formal one — and the two become commingled, almost indistinguishable from each other? Does it become that much harder for a community to right its collective course, to return to a formal system with rules by which people play? The old poverty was linked to an economy based on exploitation of the worst sort. But there were still jobs to be had. Then, for a time, there was a cash floor that kept families with children above a certain threshold. Now there are neither jobs nor a cash safety net. And a place that has experienced entrenched poverty for decades has met a new poverty of the deepest sort.

Growing Up in a Sea of $2-a-Day Poverty

Tabitha Hicks, Alva Mae's daughter, was in sixth grade when a rookie corps member of Teach for America (TFA) was assigned to her classroom. After graduating from a prestigious East Coast university, Mark Patten was offered a high-paying consulting job, but at the very last minute his heart said he was supposed to be somewhere else.

Sixth grade with Mr. Patten was like nothing the students in his class had experienced before. Tabitha looks back on this time fondly. "Normally when you have a teacher, he just give you free grades. You just go and you be the teacher's pet, you just get a free 100. But with Mr. Patten, you had to do the work and stuff. And I kind of liked that," she says. Mr. Patten also was the first to notice that something was wrong with Tabitha. She reports, "It was in sixth grade, I think. And I think I had, like, a lot going on, I didn't focus in class. I do my work, but it was, like, to a certain point. I couldn't see! I didn't have glasses or anything."

One evening, when eleven-year-old Tabitha — small-boned and thin to the point of emaciation — was standing in front of the stove in her mother's kitchen making macaroni for her younger siblings, Mr. Patten knocked on the apartment door. She was holding a baby in her left arm, resting on her hip. Another baby sat in a nearby high chair, and a toddler was asleep on the couch. Six other children, all younger than Tabitha and all separated by about a year in age, hovered around the stove, waiting for their meal. Alva Mae was out running errands, and Tabitha was in charge of the house. What a time for her teacher to show up! "I was embarrassed, because there are a lot of kids, and I was trying to cook and I was cleaning, and I had the baby on my hip, and I told my little brother to answer the door, and he came back and said, 'Hey, there is a white man at the door!' I was like, 'Who that?' And I went to the door, and it was Mr. Patten!"

By the time of this visit, Tabitha had been evading her teacher's request to come to the house to meet her mother for quite some time. "He kept saying he was gonna come 'cuz my grades [were bad], he wanted to meet my mom, and stuff like that. I kept making excuses, like, 'My mom stay gone! She gonna be out of town. She don't *ever* be home!' And he showed up at the house and she was gone and I had the baby on my hip. I didn't want to let him in!"

Eventually, she opened the door, and to Tabitha's surprise, within minutes all of her younger siblings had warmed to Mr. Patten's presence. "I let him in, and he was, like, totally comfortable. He sat on the couch and he played with the kids, and it was, like, different! The kids was loving him, jumping on him, he was playing with them and stuff like that! And he was talking to me about getting my glasses. I couldn't [see the blackboard]. Talking to me about [if that's] why I wasn't focusing in class and all that. He talked to me about what I wanted to do in life . . . I kept thinking he was going to stop talking to me because I was babysitting — my mom had all them kids! I thought he was going to think I didn't have no potential in me."

Never before in Tabitha's memory had a white person crossed the threshold of their home. And this particular white person acted in a way that was totally contrary to expectations. "Well, living in Percy, it's some Caucasian people but it's not a lot. And the ones that we have, they're basically, you know . . . They look at you like the kids is nasty!"

Tabitha had learned what to expect from white folks from her interactions with the owners of Percy's general store. She says, "They can be friendly sometimes, but it's only if you can be showing them that you have, like, an education . . . They don't call [my brothers] by their name . . . They say 'Hey boy.' . . . Like he'll say 'boy,' and my brother, he'll say, 'My name is Stephen.'"

Despite years — even generations — of knowing one another, precious few pleasantries are exchanged between the white folks and black folks in town. To eleven-year-old Tabitha, this made Mr. Patten's behavior completely enigmatic. "So I came home [with my glasses], my mom, everybody was happy and stuff. And then it was, like, [Mr. Patten and I] got closer because he started taking the kids to the dentist and stuff, the eye doctor, all my other brothers and sisters! It was, like, he was there for everybody! Like we'd tell him about our problems, like even my mom called him sometimes. It's not normal for [someone like] him to be that close to our family!"

Further visits by Mr. Patten revealed that Tabitha's nearsightedness was only the tip of the iceberg. Poverty was like a millstone around his young student's neck. The most obvious manifestation of this poverty was in the extreme overcrowding. After giving birth to five children by Tabitha's father — who moved to Biloxi to work on the oil rigs just after Tabitha was born — Alva Mae fell for a much younger man about the time Tabitha turned three. Cliff, who was only sixteen to her twenty-six, was a brutally abusive drug addict who worked as a farmhand for a local planter. He wielded nearly complete power over Alva Mae. She gave birth to eight of his children in almost as many years. By the time Tabitha had turned ten years old, there were thirteen children at home. Over the next few years, several of the older children left, formed families of their own, and then bounced back at regular intervals due to money troubles, sometimes bringing their kids or lovers with them. Although Cliff has been ordered by the court to pay child support of $107 a week, he does so only sporadically. Other than that, Alva Mae and the kids see none of his money. Cliff is cruel. His own children loathe him. He has been known to beat Alva Mae until her face is covered in blood, and he manipulates his family in ways clearly calculated to cause deep psychological wounds. He has an official address elsewhere but is often in the home.

Between Tabitha's sixth- and ninth-grade years, only Alva Mae and ten of her thirteen children had the legal right to live in their government-subsidized apartment. At times, however, up to twenty-four people could be found packed into the unit. "It's a three-bedroom apartment," Tabitha says. "So it was very hard, because . . . basically you slept wherever you wanted to lay your head. Some of them slept on the couch, some of them slept on the floor. Eight of us slept in the bed. But there's like only two beds in the house. So it was really hard. My mother, she would put the covers over us. She would set us in the bed. Like, she had to put the bed against the wall for more support. She just pack us all into the bed. We just lay straight. We try not to complain, because, you know, basically we see our mom going through this and it's painful, it's depressing to her, and then we don't want to bring it to anyone's attention."

Mr. Patten had rocked Tabitha's world just by caring enough to show up at her home one day and then by arranging trips to the eye doctor, as well as medical and dental appointments for her siblings. Then he and a couple of other TFA teachers organized a spring break field trip to Washington, D.C. "My first time out of the Delta. First time out of the Delta, I went to Washington, D.C. It was a lot of us that hadn't been out of the Delta. It was, like, the majority of the school. It was only fifteen of us [that got to go], and it was so exciting and I was so happy . . . My mom was kind of skeptical. 'What? You going out of town with those white men?' They trusted [them], but they was still [nervous]."

As they prepared to leave for the nation's capital, the teachers learned that hardly any of the children had more than one change of clothing, underwear, or socks. A trip to the nearest Walmart—with funds from a few generous donors—provided the provisions needed to get the kids through the week they would be away. Tabitha had even less than the rest. "That was stressful, 'cuz I was, like, everyone gonna judge me, and I was, like, I didn't want anyone to know that we didn't, like, have clothes or anything. Because, like, what my mom said, 'What goes on in the house stays in the house.' We . . . didn't really have no clothes, just wore the same uniform over and over again . . . Basically, that was normal to me. Not that it was normal and I was happy or anything like that. I knew that it was not a good thing, but I was so used to it!"

The trip was the highlight of Tabitha's young life. "It was so exciting. We were on an airplane! Saw the White House, the Washington Monument . . . It was so cool because a lot of white people actually were the ones would talk to us." It was a shock to have white folks addressing her and the other kids in a friendly manner. Also on this trip, many of the children saw an elevator for the first time. Initially, some of them didn't believe that the box behind the doors could actually transport them from one floor to another. They honestly thought it was some sort of joke that the teachers were playing on them.

At the end of the trip, a strange melancholy fell over the band of sixth graders. As they boarded the plane, "everyone was so mad at Mr. Patten 'cuz we was, like, 'You take us all the way out here, you show us *this,* and then you take us back to the Delta where there's *nothing?*'" Once they were back home, it would be back to "waking up every day, not having enough food, sleeping with seven of us, it was, like, seven, eight of us in the bed and the rest of them on the floor. And sometimes a week or two we go without the lights, and then just the feeling, like, you're just starving."

What does it feel like to be that hungry? Tabitha pauses, then says, "Well, actually, it feel like you want to be dead. Because it's peaceful being dead. Going through seeing your little brother and them, you know, wake up crying, and then [them saying] they don't want to go through this anymore . . . And then my mom, she saying she don't want to go through this anymore. It's like really hard because you wake up some days in the dark. And just go for two weeks, three weeks [without lights, heat, or air-conditioning]. [When] stamp day rolls around again, [my mom] sell the stamps and that's how the lights get back again."

Tabitha spent her seventh-grade year, the year after the D.C. trip, hungry. Same with her eighth- and ninth-grade years. Finally, in the tenth grade an opportunity arose. Her gym teacher messaged her on Facebook and said he had been watching her for years, waiting for her to "mature." "Since you were real young," he wrote. He wanted to meet — in secret — at his house after school. He promised food.

Tabitha was deeply conflicted about the teacher's offer. What if accepting it meant that she might finally be able to sleep at night without gnawing hunger pains, afraid that if she moved to clutch her empty stomach, she'd be evicted from the bed she was sharing with seven siblings, forced to sleep on a rug she knew had been fished out of the Dumpster? What if going along with the gym teacher meant she would finally be able to concentrate in school? She was so afraid of disappointing Mr. Patten. Maybe she could even sneak some of the food she was given into her backpack so she could stop her four-year-old brother from crying himself to sleep at night.

Tabitha's dilemma was made worse by the fact that in Percy, conventional morality is often turned upside down. Most grown-ups in this little town claim to be God-fearing; you can almost take that for granted. But what was Tabitha to make of the fact that Mr. Valentine, the store owner who called her brothers "boy" just to show he could, was the town's former mayor, its chief public servant? How was she supposed to think about the fact that her next-door neighbor, who attended the local Baptist church and sang in the choir, was also known to walk the half mile to Salvatore's on a Friday (payday for the farmhands) whenever her family was really desperate to get the power back on? After socializing for a while, she would disappear into a beat-up truck with some guy, the two of them heading off down the road. Forty-five minutes later, the truck would roll back into the parking lot, kicking up dust as it came. She would reemerge from the passenger side, straightening her hair and rearranging her clothing. Once more, twice more, as often as it took to make sure the light bill got paid.

How was Tabitha supposed to come to terms with the fact that it was a teacher — a man in a role she had been taught to respect — who was the one offering her special attention in the form of sex after school in return for a full stomach? If a teacher said it was okay, could it really be so wrong? Besides, could she say no to a teacher?

Tabitha shudders, recalling the liaison that lasted seven months. "He said he had been watching me. Watching me! Since I was young! Like I was *meat!* He was watching me all that time." Finally, Tabitha, fraught with guilt, sought out Mr. Patten, who was no longer teaching at her school but had chosen to stay in the area after his stint with TFA was done. She told him what was going on. She blamed herself.

Mr. Patten tried to convince her that a sixteen-year-old could not consent to a sexual relationship with a grown-up, especially a teacher.

Acting on his instructions, Tabitha reported the gym teacher to the county attorney and the high school principal. At first, nothing happened. Finally, after Mr. Patten insisted, the teacher was removed from his post, although they gave him other work at the school. To date, there has been no criminal prosecution by the county attorney. In fact, there has been no response from his office at all. Tabitha has four sisters under her who will go to the same high school. The thought of this man claiming another victim from among them keeps her awake at night.

Alva Mae and her ten children living at home constitute the "official" SNAP assistance unit. She gets $1,600 in food stamps each month, but she has no cash to pay the utility bills (electricity, water, and sewer), to buy clothing, and so on. In a climate where the temperature has ranged from 9 to 109 degrees in just the past six months, it is clear that electricity is essential to heat and cool the apartment. The thirteenth of each month, when the family's SNAP card gets replenished, always feels celebratory. But with bills that can only be paid with cash, the relief is short-lived. When asked how much of their monthly SNAP gets sold, Tabitha says, "She sell enough to get the light bill paid. So if the light bill comes to three hundred dollars, she take . . . enough out to get three hundred dollars left over." (At the Delta's going rate, it takes $600 in food stamps to yield $300 in cash.) Then "whatever other bills she has [she'll sell more]. But the food stamps don't last because of it."

Somehow, this serious-looking young woman, now eighteen, has been able to see the larger picture and feel moral indignation rather than resignation. Her weight, still so low, is a testament to what it has cost her and her brothers and sisters to live for so many years among the $2-a-day poor. When asked how long the food each month lasts, she says, "It only last a week or two — maybe a week and a half, *if* we eat one meal a day . . . The kids, they so, they so, emotional [about it]. My little sister in the room, and she just crying. My little brother in the room, and he just crying, like, it's sad . . . They cry because they compare their life to someone else. Like, a lot of my little sisters and brothers and them say they wish they wasn't alive. And it's sad because when my [older] brother died . . . I remember my little brother and them breaking down, and . . . my little brother said, 'I wish I was Mike, too. I wish *I* was dead.'"

When Tabitha was sixteen and her older brother Mike was twenty-two, he went to visit their oldest sister, who was in the army and stationed in Knoxville, Tennessee. One Saturday, "he and his friend decided to go [cliff diving]. Well, we seen the video. They [made] a video 'cuz they was just having fun. It's [a place] on a river . . . that used to be a park. But [in the river], it was rocks or something on the bottom."

At this point, Tabitha pauses, lowering her voice as if revealing a secret. "I think he's happy. I *know* he's happy. That's what I tell my little brother and them. I just don't want for them to feel that *they* should go there. That they should do something to hurt theyselves. Me personally? [I think he did it on purpose.] Yes. 'Cuz in the video he went to a corner and he prayed. In the video, [his friends] say, 'Hey man, what you doing over there praying and stuff?' And he put his hands together, he say a prayer and he just run and jump off, and his body just *float*. And you see it, he had a white shirt on. He just was gone."

One might think that her brother's death or her liaison with the gym teacher was the low point of Tabitha's young life. But according to her, that moment had to do with Cliff. It came in the fall of her junior year. Alva Mae and Cliff were fighting, and Tabitha intervened to protect her mom. "I jumped in it like I always do. I jumped in it, and then I was like, 'You're not gonna hit her, not in front of the kids,' because the girls gonna think, you know, that's how men love them, is to take a hand to them . . . Then he pushes me, [holds a gun to my head], and says he's gonna kill me."

With the attention drawn off her and onto Tabitha, Alva Mae fled to Salvatore's, with Cliff following in pursuit as soon as he realized she was gone. Tabitha and her siblings trailed behind him at a safe distance, intent on protecting their mother. At Salvatore's, several patrons had to pull Cliff off Alva as he tried to beat her to a bloody pulp. After the fight was over, Cliff presented Alva Mae with an ultimatum. Tabitha says he told her mother, "'You need to make a choice, me or [Tabitha]. Before tonight, one [of] us is leaving.' And [my mom] was like, 'Well, Tabitha, what do you think about staying with your friend for a while?'" Tabitha's mother had chosen Cliff over her. "And I knew at the time what she was saying. So I just broke down and started crying."

Now Tabitha was virtually homeless. Mr. Patten found a boarding school in Memphis that had scholarships and helped her apply. By January, when she was first interviewed for this book, she was living in Memphis, with her own bed to sleep in, only one roommate, and three meals a day.

Her struggle isn't over, though. "When I'm alone, I'm thinking about [home]. Well, then it's kinda hard. Well, it is hard. 'Cuz then, when I call my mom and [say], like, 'What you doing,' and just to hear the *pain* in her voice?" She says, though, that "every time I look in my little sisters' and brothers' eyes . . . they're proud of me, like if no one else is proud of me, I know my little sisters and brothers [are] proud of me. That's why I said, when I graduate, my mom don't have to come, [but] every one of my siblings *have* to be there. They *have* to be there. Like, if one of them just don't come, like, I would be sad . . . Like it would be a waste of time. Like I want them to see me graduate. But the scary thing is that I'm scared what if I don't make it in college?

"Like, my sisters have always seen other kids who get up and fail. That's why they don't want to get up, because they always seen someone fail. I tell them, 'You got to get all As and Bs!' and they say, 'Why get all As and Bs and I fail this test?' In the house we so scared of failing. *I'm* scared about failing. When I care about something, I give it my all. I care about going to college, so I'm trying to give it my all.

But what scares me is that the family I come from has *no money!* We have no money, so [how am I going to go to college without even one cent]?"

Tabitha's experiences — and the intense hunger and material deprivation that she and her siblings have suffered — reveal the sickening underside of the shadow economy that has sprung up in these little Delta towns. Those trading SNAP for cash might be able to keep the lights and heat on, but doing so virtually guarantees that someone — probably everyone — in the house will go hungry. Hunger, in turn, may put mothers and children at risk of demeaning and dangerous sexual liaisons. To put it simply, not having cash basically ensures that you have to break the law and expose yourself to humiliation in order to survive. And when some among the community leadership — teachers, shop owners, public officials — prey on the poor by charging too much for decrepit trailers or by offering food or vital cash in exchange for sexual favors, the line between good and bad blurs even further, especially in the eyes of a child.

There are certainly many good folks, black and white, in these Delta towns. The loving, supportive bond that is so palpable in Martha Johnson's home is the kind that most American families hope for in their own. Dorothy Clark may be struggling herself, but she is still willing to lend a hand to her fellow parishioner Martha. In Jefferson, a group of business owners have launched — and help fund, out of their own pockets — a small after-school program that has boosted student achievement among participants, helping several to go on to college. There are many good teachers, principals, and public officials to be found in the Delta, too. But how is even the most caring educator supposed to cope when confronted with so many hungry children arriving each morning at school, a school whose state rating is a D? What resources does the current mayor of Percy, the first black mayor in the city's history, really have at hand to change the living conditions of his constituents, given the lack of jobs and basic public infrastructure? What examples of good government has he seen to guide him?

By no stretch of the imagination is the Mississippi Delta representative of the rest of the United States. There's no place in America that has the Delta's history or its particular constellation of challenges. Our country's original sin of slavery lives on here more palpably than in many other places. The degree to which the economy has broken down — in spite of some of the richest farmland in the world — is an order of magnitude greater, perhaps, than in any other region of America. As such, our account of $2-a-day poverty in the Delta might be seen as an outrageous outlier that should be discounted.

In fact, however, according to U.S. Census Bureau estimates, there are more than twenty other cities and towns that are even poorer than Jefferson. A number of these places are located in Appalachia and the Deep South, including Mississippi, Louisiana, Kentucky, Tennessee, and the Carolinas. They are places you've probably never heard of, with names such as like Tchula, Cullen, Sneedville, and Munfordville.

A deeper look into these Census Bureau statistics reveals that all across America, there are thousands of struggling cities and towns. Many of these places, and the rural regions where they are located, are hidden from view in pockets of the country that other Americans have largely forgotten. In these communities, too, the formal economy has all but disintegrated, and the social safety net — both public and private — is threadbare. To visit these impoverished regions is to experience what Lyndon Johnson and Robert Kennedy did fifty years ago, when they were visibly shaken by the conditions there. With so many of their citizens cut off from any legitimate access to a cash income, these places may seem unrecognizable as part of "America." And yet they are America, as much as any other place in the country.

Though these forgotten places are indeed a world apart, much of what the extreme poor in other regions experience is reflected in the experiences of these families, too. In the central Delta, welfare is just as dead as it is in the rest of the country, if not more so. The affordable housing crisis and the perils of doubling up are also richly evident in the Delta. So is the stubborn spirit of those with nothing to survive by any means necessary. But a key difference between other places and the economically distressed small towns and rural regions concentrated in the Deep South and Appalachia is the combination of a virtually nonexistent cash safety net and the virtual lack of any formal-sector jobs. In these places, the impact of $2-a-day poverty — a shadow economy that may all but supplant the formal one — can be felt on a community, not just an individual, level.

With virtually no work, no cash safety net, and a shadow economy that erodes many aspects of "community," the impact on children can be especially severe. Tabitha Hicks would be the first one to tell you that were it not for Mr. Patten, she would still be hungry three weeks out of the month. She might have gotten pregnant — perhaps by her gym teacher. She could have dropped out of school. It would have been easy to enter adulthood with as little hope as her mother had, even before all the hope had been beaten out of her by a violent partner like Cliff.

Yet the Delta's children are not alone in feeling the keen fallout from life among the $2-a-day poor. At this writing, three of the parents who appear in this book have a child who has attempted suicide. Another — Tabitha's older brother Mike — may have successfully ended his life. Yet another, only age nine, is being treated with antipsychotic drugs because he threatened his sister with a knife. Two of the girls whose families we describe have ended up selling their bodies in exchange for food and money. One had to be treated for multiple sexually transmitted diseases at age fifteen. Certainly, this is too high a price for children to pay.

Conclusion: Where, Then, from Here?

BEFORE EXPLORING STRATEGIES that will lift up the $2-a-day poor in a radically different way than has been done before, it's worth revisiting recent welfare history. We've seen that David Ellwood's 1988 manifesto, *Poor Support*, called for replacing welfare, not just reforming it. He turned a spotlight on a portion of the poor who rarely got any attention — or much help — from the government: the working poor. Ellwood believed that by shifting the social safety net to support those who worked but remained in poverty, America could design a form of poor support that would avoid the criticisms lodged against welfare. In the 1990s, President Clinton and Congress acted on Ellwood's ideas and bolstered the well-being of working-poor parents dramatically through tax credits that provided a substantial pay raise in the form of a wage subsidy. The largest of these programs, the Earned Income Tax Credit (EITC), is now generous enough to lift more than 3 million children above the poverty line each year. Millions of struggling working families have been made much better off as a result of these changes, a triumph of social policy.

Ellwood's conclusion — that welfare must be replaced, not just reformed — was based on a crucial insight: any program so out of sync with American values was doomed to fail. He made the case that four values were especially important: the "autonomy of the individual," the "virtue of work," the "primacy of the family," and the "desire for and sense of community." The old welfare system was portrayed, if unfairly, as supporting the opposite — indolence and single parenthood. Because of this, Ellwood argued, virtually everyone disliked the program. Many hated it — even many of its claimants.

An unintended consequence of abolishing AFDC has been the rise of $2-a-day poverty among households with children. But though welfare reform may have been the cause of this increase, reverting to the old welfare system is not the answer. The flaws of that system were too deep. Ellwood's basic premise remains as true today as it was twenty-five years ago: any response to the rise in $2-a-day poverty must be in line with America's values. This is not merely an argument about political feasibility. The primary reason to strive relentlessly for approaches that line up with what most Americans believe is moral and fair is that government programs that are out of sync with these values serve to separate the poor from the rest of society, not integrate them into society. The old welfare system had the virtue of providing a floor of cash income for those in need, but it exacted a heavy price. To be a welfare recipient was to wear a scarlet letter in the eyes of your fellow Americans. The old welfare system separated its claimants from the mainstream. It may even have created a class of outcasts forced to trade their sense of citizenship for relief.

The ultimate litmus test we endorse for any reform is whether it will serve to integrate the poor — particularly the $2-a-day poor — into society. It is not enough to provide material relief to those experiencing extreme deprivation. We need to craft solutions that can knit these hard-pressed citizens back into the fabric of their communities and their nation.

With this in mind, we propose a radical return to the central idea that was behind the 1996 welfare reform: work opportunity is vital and must be at the center of a multipronged strategy to help the $2-a-day poor. The Personal Responsibility and Work Opportunity Reconciliation Act of 1996 — welfare reform — delivered on the "personal responsibility." It ended widespread reliance on cash welfare. But for too many, it failed to deliver on work opportunity.

Our approach to ending $2-a-day poverty is guided by three principles: (1) all deserve the opportunity to work; (2) parents should be able to raise their children in a place of their own; and (3) not every parent will be able to work, or work all of the time, but parents' well-being, and the well-being of their children, should nonetheless be ensured.

All Deserve the Opportunity to Work

Everything we've learned about the $2-a-day poor suggests that it is typically the opportunity to work that is lacking, not the will, and that ensuring work opportunity would do no end of good. For Rae McCormick and Jennifer Hernandez, work is what keeps the problems of mental distress and family dysfunction at bay. The routine, the ability to get lost in one's work, may have a certain healing power.

There's no getting around the fact that there aren't enough jobs — much less ones with adequate pay, hours, and stability — to go around. The solution is a robust program of job creation — one that goes beyond anything America has undertaken since the Great Depression.

Government-subsidized private sector job creation is one way forward. Recently, the federal government sponsored a promising short-term subsidized jobs program through something called the TANF Emergency Fund. States that chose to participate were allowed to use TANF dollars to provide employers (mostly in the private sector) with incentives to hire unemployed workers, targeting those on TANF or those who were in a spell of extended unemployment. Each state was given considerable leeway to design the program however it saw fit, often in close collaboration with employers. Across the District of Columbia and the thirty-nine states that took part in the program, employers created more than 260,000 jobs with an invest-ment of only $1.3 billion dollars. Roughly two-thirds of participating employers said they created positions that would not have existed otherwise, and the businesses that took part expressed, on the whole, eagerness to participate in such a program in the future. Further, many participants remained employed after the subsidy ended, and those who had experienced significant trouble finding work espe-cially made gains. Researchers who studied the program noted that it garnered "widespread support from employers, workers, and state and local officials from both ends of the political spectrum."

Creating a subsidized jobs program modeled on the TANF Emer-gency Fund would be one way to improve the circumstances of America's $2-a-day poor. These individuals tend to be at the end of the hiring queue for a multitude of reasons and would likely benefit from an approach targeting workers who have the greatest challenges finding work. A program that included some support services could be particularly effective. In Michigan, a program called Community Ventures not only helps place individuals in jobs but also goes fur-ther by providing a set of services that make it easier for workers to stay in those jobs, such as assistance in arranging transportation or child care in a pinch. Imagine if Rae McCormick had had a resource like this when the truck had no gas and she couldn't find a way to get to her job at Walmart. Including a caseworker who can counsel workers when conflict arises or advocate on their behalf might make a program like this especially valuable. What if Modonna Harris had had someone to advocate for her when her cash drawer came up $10 short, or if Jennifer Hernandez could have gotten counseling about the laws governing overtime work and pay when she was working double shifts at Catalina? Perhaps her family's sojourn to Texas could have been avoided. Such work support programs could even be paired with mental health services. With the routine and structure that a job provides, and with access to quality mental health services, it seems possible that Jennifer and Rae might be able to really get a handle on their mental health challenges.

Some argue that stimulating private sector job growth doesn't go nearly far enough. Harvard economist and former Clinton treasury secretary Larry Summers predicts that among working-age American men, one in six could be out of a job due to changes in technology even when the economy has fully recovered from the Great Recession. If that trend continues, he says, in a generation "a quarter of middle-aged men will be out of work at any given moment." Economists Carl Frey and Michael Osborne of the University of Oxford estimate that jobs are at a high risk of being automated in nearly half of all occupational categories. If these predictions are correct, the seemingly endless hunt for work won't just be the lot of the $2-a-day poor; many in America will be joining them.

If that is the case, we need to think bigger. Much bigger. If the private sector isn't up to the task of producing enough jobs, one could make a strong argument that government itself ought to create a substantially larger share of the jobs than it does now — jobs like those provided by the Works Progress Administration during the Great Depression. Certainly, there is ample work to be done in our communities. The nation's infrastructure is badly out-of-date in many places — often crumbling, sometimes downright dangerous. The National Park Service and state and local park districts are underfunded; this limits hours and upkeep. Safe, stimulating day care centers — the kind of environments our toddlers and preschoolers require to thrive — are too few. We need many more after-school programs for school-age children. There are too few tutoring programs. There is too little elder care. Our public libraries, pools, and recreation centers — vital institutions for the safety and well-being of our children — sometimes limit their hours due to lack of funding. Trash litters our rural byways and our city streets. There is a widespread need for treatment centers for the chemically addicted and shelters for the homeless. There is enough to do.

In addition to increasing the number of jobs, we need to improve the quality of the jobs available for Jennifer, Modonna, Rae, Travis, Jessica, and the others described in this book. Since the mid-1990s, the country has relied on tax credits to make up for low pay. But a detailed look at the budgets of taxpayers who claim the EITC shows that even those who are stably employed for much of the year can't make ends meet each month on their wages alone. As a result, a significant portion of their tax refunds go to paying off debt accrued over the course of the year. A large share of their tax refund is, in effect, claimed by creditors, who sometimes charge interest at rates as high as 30 percent.

The most straightforward way to improve the payoff of low-wage work is to raise wages. Americans, on the whole, like the idea of increasing the minimum wage, and all signs suggest they would support a substantial increase in it. Some states and cities have grown impatient with Congress and have enacted higher state and local minimum wages through legislation or by popular referendum. These changes offer fertile ground for research. Seattle's minimum wage will rise to $15 an hour for large employers over the next few years. Is such a rate sustainable? The jury is out and will be for some time to come. But most economists now agree that the minimum wage could be raised to at least $10 per hour without driving down the supply of jobs to a meaningful degree, and that doing so might modestly boost economic growth. All of the adults we have written about in this book have worked for less than $10 per hour for much or all of their working lives. Boosting their wages may make their personal circumstances less precarious, which in turn may make it easier for them to stay in their jobs and avoid falling into a spell of extreme destitution.

For those who actually find work, low hourly pay is not the only issue plaguing the $2-a-day poor. Researchers estimate that American workers lose billions of dollars each year to what is referred to as "wage theft"— clear violations of labor standards that include paying less than the minimum wage, forcing employees to work off the clock, and failing to pay mandated overtime rates (like what happened to Jennifer Hernandez at Catalina). If one tallied all of the losses suffered by victims of robberies, burglaries, larcenies, and mo-tor vehicle thefts combined, the figure wouldn't even approach what is taken from hardworking Americans' pockets by employers who violate the nation's labor laws. And the victims are generally the most vulnerable among us.

Insufficient hours and unstable schedules are huge problems. Many low-wage employers choose not to hire entry-level workers full-time, or even to provide stable part-time hours. Unpredictable work schedules multiply the deleterious impact of low pay and too few hours. There's plenty of evidence that on-call shifts, zero-hour workweeks, variable scheduling, and temporary contracts — practices that skirt worker protections and make it difficult to qualify for un-employment insurance — are all too common. Policy proposals aimed at improving conditions for low-wage service sector workers include provisions for minimum or guaranteed hours — perhaps thirty-five hours per week for full-time workers and twenty-five hours for part-time workers. Policy makers would have to look hard at how to design these regulations so as not to tie the hands of workers and firms too much. But a rule that could make an immediate impact would be one requiring employers to post schedules at least three weeks in advance. More predictability at work — and in the family's finances — might bring more stability to the lives of those who other-wise might be prone to fall into $2-a-day poverty.

Legislation can help, but we, as consumers, can also make a dif-ference with our dollars. To do so, we need better sources of infor-mation about which employers treat their workers well — or poorly. Casting a bright light on poor working conditions, and on their con-sequences for parents and kids, may catalyze the public's approba-tion, and there's evidence that it could lead to real change. In 2014, the *New York Times* reported on the deleterious impacts of Starbucks's "just-in-time" scheduling practices on one mother of young children. The resulting uproar compelled the chain to pledge that it would re-vise its procedures. In the early months of 2015, Walmart announced that it would raise wages for its associates to $10 per hour by 2016 and change its scheduling practices so that workers will get at least two and a half weeks' notice of their shifts. These changes appear to have been spurred at least in part by public criticism over the low wages the company offers and the precarious schedules it often imposes on workers. Could drawing more attention to such practices create a race to the top among low-wage employers, especially as the labor market tightens? The nation needs an index of retail firms that offers information on how each one treats its low-level workers — pay, working conditions, scheduling practices, the proportion of employees working full-time — that consumers can use to make decisions about where to shop.

Can firms afford to treat their workers better? New research shows that when workers are treated well, they work harder and more productively, delivering value to investors and customers alike. Fewer things get mis-shelved or priced incorrectly, both major sources of lost profit in the retail sector. When workers are treated better, they might in turn treat customers better, too, leading to more sales. Market Basket, a successful grocery store chain operating in New England, starts employees off at $12 an hour and offers health insurance and paid sick leave to everyone. Wegmans, another regional grocery store chain, QuikTrip convenience stores, and Southwest Airlines are all profitable while treating their employees well. Each firm differs, but as a group they tend to pay higher-than-average wages, rely more heavily on full-time workers, employ more stable scheduling practices, offer more fringe benefits, and invest in their workers through on-the-job training. And their workers seem to perform better because of it.

What is different about these firms — and there are far too few — is not just the pay, hours, or benefits. Market Basket employees say that their CEO, Arthur T. Demoulas, makes it a point to know his employees by name. He attends their weddings and funerals. When he was fired by his board of directors in a turf battle over control of the family-owned company, workers went on strike in protest. They weren't risking their jobs for increased wages or benefits. They were risking their jobs for their boss.

In contrast, the relationship between low-wage employers and their employees is badly degraded in too many cases. The decision makers rarely meet the rank and file. Restoring the relationship between employers and employees may be especially critical for the $2-a-day poor, who tend to have complex personal lives that may spill over into their work lives. Only employers who know their employees personally can exercise the discretion to discern whether someone like Rae, the two-time "cashier of the month," has missed her shift because she's a shirker or is a valued employee who has hit a rough patch.

We recognize that not all among the $2-a-day poor will be able to claim opportunities in the workforce without support. Some among them, like Martha Johnson down in the Mississippi Delta, have physical limitations that prevent them from taking many jobs, but are not disabled enough to qualify for disability benefits. Among the families followed for this book, this group was small — most families had a parent who had successfully worked full-time at some point. But without a larger study, we can't say for certain how many among the $2-a-day poor fit into this category. However large this group, they, too, should have a chance to contribute. We need to be creative about work to ensure that everyone can make a contribution and thus find a way to belong. Extending opportunities for supported work, much as we do for some adults who are officially disabled, would offer a middle ground. Another creative option for informal entrepreneurs like Martha are the small business "incubators" that have sprung up all over the country helping to formalize the "brown"— informal yet not illegal — economy. A food incubator, for example, might provide access to a professional kitchen that's up to code, allowing Martha to produce her Kool-Aid pickles and market them on grocery store shelves.

Parents Should Be Able to Raise Their Children in a Place of Their Own

We believe that, at the very least, all Americans willing to work full-time throughout the year should be able to maintain a place of their own. Rae deserves to have that place where she can "just relax and enjoy being with my daughter," where she can give Azara the "decked-out Dora room" she's been dreaming of.

Since 2000, more and more Americans have found that the price of an apartment is out of their reach. Those concerned about the affordable housing crisis often focus a spotlight on rising rents. Clearly, a few million additional government rental subsidy vouchers would help. In addition, there is a place for investment in the building or rehabbing of more affordable housing. There's actually already an underutilized mechanism in place at the federal level that could help with this—the National Housing Trust Fund. The NHTF is supposed to act as a pot of money that could be tapped by states to help support the building of affordable housing developments. Yet the recent housing crisis derailed efforts to fully fund the NHTF, and the federal government has yet to build the program up. One idea to fund such an initiative is to limit the home mortgage interest deduction on mortgage values above a certain level, perhaps half a million or a million dollars, in effect shifting a subsidy away from very wealthy families to some of the very poorest ones. Another possible avenue to increase the stock of affordable housing and decrease residential segregation is to reduce the prevalence of discriminatory "exclusionary zoning" regulations. Through such provisions, municipal (often suburban) governments restrict what kind of housing can be built in a community—such as by prohibiting apartment buildings or setting large minimum lot sizes—so as to limit the supply of housing available to low-income families.

Rising rents are certainly a big part of the problem, but the concurrent fall in renters' incomes has outstripped the rise in prices by a factor of more than two to one. And while exploitation certainly exists, even nonprofit housing providers find it difficult to deliver housing to the poor for much less than it costs in the private market. Many smaller landlords and real estate investors, especially the mom-and-pop operators who provide the bulk of the nation's housing, report profit margins that are perilously slim.

It follows, then, that part of the solution to the affordable housing crisis is to increase the incomes of renters. By ensuring the opportunity to work, and by taking strides to improve wages and guarantee hours, we can alleviate at least some of the pressure. In no state today does a full-time job paying minimum wage allow a family to afford a one- or two-bedroom apartment at fair market rent. But a family with a full-time earner making $15 an hour can afford a two-bedroom apartment at the fair market rent in twenty-two states and can come very close in another four.

Interviews with landlords of low-income renters in three cities offer at least anecdotal evidence that these investors factor in the job and income instability of their prospective tenants when setting rents. If a landlord anticipates that she'll be able to collect rent in full and on time for only two-thirds of her tenants, she may factor that into the prices she charges. In the summer of 2014, some landlords with units in the tougher sections of Cleveland said they could count on getting only about 50 percent of their rents paid on time in a given month. Most attributed the problem to the unstable earnings of their tenants. Even if some tenants might pay up eventually, in other cases the landlord will have to forgo rent for a month or more while evicting the current tenant and finding a new one. If these considerations do indeed factor into rental prices, it follows that ensuring work opportunity might well provide benefits that trickle up to landlords, allowing them to make apartments available at lower prices.

Government housing subsidy dollars could be redirected to cover more eligible households if a greater number of families with housing subsidies earned more. Currently, subsidized renters must put 30 percent of their net income toward rent. Researchers found that roughly

45 percent of non-elderly, nondisabled housing subsidy holders re-ported no earnings in 2010. What if even one-third or one-half of these households instead earned net incomes of even $15,000 a year? The total savings could conceivably reach into the billions. If these dollars could then be reallocated to alleviate the housing burdens of a greater proportion of the poor, the United States would make even more progress toward closing the gap between income and rents.

Sometimes Work Won't Work

One very good piece of news about the $2-a-day poor is that most have a recent history of work. Seventy percent of children in $2-a-day poverty live in a household where someone has worked in a formal job during the year, while only about 10 percent are in households that have claimed TANF. The high level of attachment to work in the formal economy indicates that ensuring work opportunity and increasing the quality of low-wage jobs will be a sufficient safety net for most of this population, much of the time.

But we do need a program that can provide a temporary cash cush-ion, because no matter what strategies we implement, work—even supported work—will sometimes fail. Factors not related to the avail-ability of jobs can throw families into crisis, especially those whose lives are sometimes overwhelmingly complicated. In difficult times, they need a real safety net to catch them. In-kind benefits such as SNAP and Medicaid offer a lifeline to families in these straits, but they just aren't the same as cash. They don't offer the flexibility of cash—the kind of flexibility that the stories in this book have shown to be so crucial. For many of our families, their downward spiral into $2-a-day poverty might have been reversed by a timely infusion of cash.

Right now, we don't have a functioning cash safety net to catch people when they fall. Thus, too many families at the very bottom feel compelled to secure a modicum of cash by trading their SNAP. This isn't good for them, and it's not good for society. Beyond the fact that it's illegal, it's a waste of government money. When Jennifer Hernandez decides she must sell some of her SNAP to buy socks and underwear for her kids, or when Alva Mae Hicks trades away her SNAP to pay the utility bill, they lose a whopping 40 to 50 percent in purchasing power. And as a result, they and their children go hungry.

In many cases, a relatively small infusion of cash might be all it would take. Since most families work, perhaps something called a "family crisis account" might be built on top of the EITC — something that families could tap a finite number of times over a given period to help them bridge the gap during a crisis. Credits could be earned with work effort and banked until needed. The key would be that families would be able to access these resources quickly, in a pinch, without having to cut through too much red tape. One idea is to provide those claiming the EITC the option to "save" some of their refund — to have it disbursed at intervals throughout the year rather than in a lump sum at tax time — and offer them incentives to do so. That way, when families hit a rough spot or face a sudden crisis, they have a self-made safety net to draw on.

Providing the ultimate safety net is the role that Temporary Assistance for Needy Families is supposed to play, but it hasn't proved to be up to the task. Part of the reason TANF isn't doing its job is that it is a block grant given to the states, which have broad flexibility as to how they spend the money. This means that they have plenty of reasons to keep families off the rolls, because if they do, they get to use the money for other, related purposes. Of the $16.5 billion the federal government transfers to states for TANF, more than $11 billion is siphoned off for other uses, sometimes to fund a state's child welfare system. Strained state budgets are thus eased. TANF has become welfare for the states rather than aid for families in need.

Beyond eligibility rules and other formal restrictions on who qualifies, there's evidence that some prospective applicants may be "diverted" from applying for aid in unauthorized ways. After nearly a year without employment, a desperate Rae McCormick swallowed her pride and finally took a trip to the welfare office to apply for

TANF. She says she was told, "Honey, I'm sorry. There are just so many needy people, we just don't have enough to go around." Rae's visit to the welfare office is not the only evidence of this kind of behavior. In Georgia, one study found suggestive evidence that the state welfare commissioner's oft-repeated phrase, "Welfare is not good enough for any family," may have led caseworkers to actively discourage families from following through on their applications.

Rather than providing short-term aid that families can gain access to quickly in a pinch, TANF offices in nearly every state require applicants to jump through numerous employment-related hoops before they can be deemed eligible, including attending an orientation, making an employment plan, registering for employment services, or engaging in hours of job search activities. For those who do manage to get on TANF, stringent work requirements must then be met — typically thirty hours a week of work for a private employer or at a community service job — the latter in return for only a couple of hundred dollars' worth of benefits each month. Ironically, this work may put them no closer to finding a "real" job.

Even for those who receive TANF, its cash value, though never high, is now very, very low — so low that it doesn't bring a family's income even to half the poverty line in any state. In thirty-two states plus the District of Columbia, TANF benefits for a family of three with no other income are now below 30 percent of the poverty threshold. In sixteen states, the maximum payment is below 20 percent of the poverty line. And in one state, Mississippi, TANF benefits are so low they wouldn't even lift a family above the $2-a-day threshold. One can imagine that very low benefit levels could easily lead a prospective applicant to conclude that it is just not worth the trouble to apply.

Even taken together, though, these factors cannot fully explain why struggling families aren't getting TANF. The main problem is that prospective applicants are failing even to show up at TANF's doors. With the rolls so small, information about what TANF has to offer is presumably less likely to spread. If our families' stories are any guide, many people may not even know about the program, or may dismiss the idea of applying for it for any number of reasons. When we asked Travis and Jessica Compton, in Johnson City, Tennessee, why they hadn't applied for TANF, they asked, "What's that?" Modonna Harris had heard they just didn't give it out anymore. In some parts of the country, even the advocacy community seems to have given up on the program. "We don't talk about TANF anymore," Atlanta's food bank advocacy and education director Laura Lester told *Slate* in 2012. "We don't even send anybody in to apply, because there's just no point."

What would happen if states were incentivized to spend a far greater proportion of what they received from the federal government for the TANF program on basic cash assistance? While welfare has never been in line with America's core values, help for the poor has. Americans' sense of, and desire for, community—one of the core values Ellwood pointed to in *Poor Support*—mandates that we help those who, through no fault of their own, can't help themselves. While there is no going back to AFDC, helping TANF fulfill its mission—as a temporary hand up—is a worthy goal, one that most Americans may support if the overarching direction of antipoverty policy is to ensure work opportunity for all.

For generations, welfare served to separate the poor from the rest of society. It robbed people of their dignity, their sense of self-worth. Now welfare is dead. Now it is not the receipt of cash benefits, but the lack of any cash at all, that serves to separate the $2-a-day poor. Without cash, they can't meaningfully participate in society. Furthermore, no American should have to resort to the lengths they must go to in order to generate that critical resource. Most Americans cringe at the idea of fellow citizens having to spend hours scrounging for aluminum cans or to take iron pills to ensure they can donate plasma twice a week—just to keep their families barely treading water. Selling your SNAP, your kids' Social Security numbers, or your body are strategies that the $2-a-day poor believe are immoral, not merely illegal. Parents should not be forced to cast aside strongly held notions of right and wrong simply to keep their kids in socks and underwear.

In our search for a model — an antipoverty program that incorporates rather than divides — we need not go very far. We can find it in our own made-in-America revolutionary approach to helping the working poor. This is the other half of the idea David Ellwood took with him to Washington back in 1993: to replace welfare by expanding a tiny refundable tax credit that had been on the books since 1975. As it turned out, however, the most revolutionary aspect of the EITC was that it managed to fold the poor back into society.

How did it do so? In-depth interviews with 209 EITC claimants in the Northeast and Midwest in 2007 showed that while TANF receipt confers stigma and shame, claiming the EITC gives people dignity and restores their pride. First, the EITC is tied to employment. Second, tax credits are included as part of your federal tax refund — along with wages that were overwithheld. This lends the impression that the government benefit is "earned," a just reward for hard work. Third, you don't have to go to a welfare office to apply — an address that in and of itself connotes stigma. Instead, roughly 70 percent of EITC beneficiaries find their way to a professional tax preparation firm such as H&R Block, Liberty Tax Service, or Taxman. There you are not a supplicant. Instead you are a customer, there to claim your tax refund like any other American.

In particular, it is the treatment they receive at H&R Block that the EITC's claimants wax most eloquently about — part of why they are willing to fork over roughly $200 for the service. "I've got people!" was a common refrain among those interviewed, parroting the popular H&R Block slogan. Upon entering the front door, claimants are welcomed with a smile: "How can we help you?"

We are not arguing here that the EITC is a solution to $2-a-day poverty. But it does offer a critical lesson in how antipoverty policy ought to be crafted. Too often, America has gone down the road of trying to shame those in need. We've put up barriers. We've made people jump through hoop after hoop—all based on the not-so-subtle presumption that they are lazy and immoral, intent on trying to put something over on the system. TANF is a perfect example. Yet research shows that the intrusive treatment people typically receive at the welfare office can undermine their confidence in government and erode political participation. It stands to reason that this kind of treatment could also erode the very confidence that is so necessary for pulling yourself out of $2-a-day poverty. Shame may act as a barrier to claiming that little bit of cash that might stop a downward spiral. As a nation, the question we have to ask ourselves is, Whose side are we on? Can our desire for, and sense of, community induce those of us with resources to come alongside the extremely poor among us in a more supportive, and ultimately more effective, way?

As the stories told in this book show, the circumstances of the $2-a-day poor are worlds apart from the experiences of most Americans. Many among them feel that they are forced to do things that they believe are morally objectionable—actions that further separate them from the rest of society—just to get by. And the experience of surviving a spell of extreme destitution often leaves deep physical and emotional wounds—wounds that further serve to separate, not incorporate. For the rest of her life, Rae McCormick will be hiding the fact that she has no teeth, cupping her hand over her mouth when she laughs. And from now on, Tabitha Hicks will carry with her the experience of being lured into a sexual relationship by her high school gym teacher with the promise of food.

Yet despite all they've been through, despite the abuse and trauma, the hunger and fear, despite the anger they carry with them at what they have endured, many of the everyday experiences of the $2-a-day poor are—truly—American to the core.

After a visit with Travis and Jessica Compton in their small one-bedroom home in Johnson City, Tennessee, one thing that stays with you is little Blythe's delight when she pops out of that pink stroller —"Boo!" Nearly toppling over with laughter, she is happy and confident in her parents' care.

On the Near West Side of Chicago, Kaitlin and Cole Hernandez are outfitted in matching khakis and polo shirts. You can't help but notice the bounce in their step as they walk down North Avenue ahead of their mother, Jennifer, toward their favorite public library.

Deep on Chicago's South Side, Susan and Devin Brown take joy in watching little Lauren toddling along while holding the edge of their old couch, in awe of how those big brown eyes and that one-toothed smile can utterly captivate.

Brianna Harris loves to match her mother Modonna's steps as they stride side by side. They smile at each other while doing so, even while enduring another spell among the $2-a-day poor, this time living at a Salvation Army shelter on Chicago's North Side.

Among Paul Heckewelder's enormous brood in Cleveland, the grandkids who have been living on virtually nothing for months are endearingly curious. With no cable TV in the house, they have nearly depleted the public library up the street of its books. Shawnee, age twelve, reads tomes about the origins of the universe, while several of her male cousins vie for the latest science fiction find. When Shawnee overhears her granddad describing the family's many ingenious approaches to their struggles, she quips, "It's like pioneer days!"

Just down the road, in Cleveland's Stockyards neighborhood, Rae McCormick's daughter, Azara, sees that her mother is upset. She walks across the empty lot next to their house, plucks the tiny flower of a clover in the median between the sidewalk and the street, and solemnly presents it to her mother. Rae picks her up, laughing. The two then smile and rub noses. It is their little ritual.

Clearly, there is much to cherish here — much worth protecting and nurturing.

Acknowledgments

$2.00 a Day was a deeply collaborative work. Both authors contributed equally, and authorship is listed alphabetically.

We owe a great debt to the many people who advised us on this project. Andrew Cherlin, Stephanie DeLuca, Robert Francis, Meredith Grief, Barbara Kiviat, Tim Nelson, Susie Shaefer, Timothy Smeeding, and Elizabeth Talbert all read the full manuscript and offered comments. Scott Allard, Jessica Compton, Mary Corcoran, Sheldon Danziger, Indi Dutta-Gupta, Peter Edelman, Paula England, Philip Garboden, Leigh Gibson, Suzanne Marcus, Alexandra Murphy, LaDonna Pavetti, Wendell Primus, Anna Rhodes, Julie Ribaudo, and Marci Ybarra all read chapters, or portions of chapters, at various points and were crucial to this effort.

Thanks go to Tessa Boudreaux, Brian Corbin, Jason DeParle, Matthew Desmond, Herbert Gans, Ron Haskins, Julia Henly, Sandy Jencks, Susan Lambert, Jodie Levin-Epstein, Elizabeth Lower-Basch, Barbara Morgan, Harold Pollack, Wendell Primus, Barbara Sard, Isabel Sawhill, Kristin Seefeldt, Harry Shaefer, Jack Shaefer, Marjorie Shaefer, Arloc Sherman, Luke Tate, Ian Reed Twiss, Debbie Weinstein, and Bruce Western for wise counsel. We also thank participants of a seminar at the Council of Economic Advisers for valuable comments on the SIPP research that informed this project. All opinions voiced in this book belong to the authors alone and do not represent any of the individuals listed, as do any mistakes and omissions.

Without our students and research staff, this project would not have been possible. In particular, we thank Melody Boyd, Michael Evangelist, Robert Francis, Vincent Fusaro, DeMarian Hampton, Saundra Kelley, Bethany Patten, and Elizabeth Talbert, who made major contributions at multiple stages of the work. Some of our close research collaborators cannot be mentioned by their real names in order to protect the identity of the respondents, but our thanks go out to you as well. Patrick Leonard, Rick Rodems, Pinghui Wu, and students in courses at the Harvard Kennedy School, the University of Michigan School of Social Work and Gerald R. Ford School of Public Policy, and the Johns Hopkins University Department of Sociology also contributed to this work.

Research costs were largely borne by internal appropriations to Edin from the Harvard Kennedy School and Johns Hopkins University and to Shaefer from the University of Michigan School of Social Work. Some of Shaefer's time on the SIPP research that informed this work was supported in part by the National Science Foundation under Grant No. SES 1131500, and in part by a cooperative research contract (58-5000-0-0083) between the National Poverty Center at the University of Michigan and the U.S. Department of Agriculture, Economic Research Service, Food and Nutrition Assistance Research Program. The ERS project representative is Alisha Coleman-Jensen. The views expressed are those of the authors and not necessarily those of any funding entity.

We are completely indebted to our respondents, who gave so generously in telling us their stories. We would have been entirely lost were it not for our agent, Lisa Adams, and editor, Deanne Urmy, who always challenged us to dig deeper into the material of the book, and shaped and honed our prose. Thanks also to Barbara Jatkola for excellent copyediting. Our spouses, Tim Nelson and Susie Shaefer, both provided tremendous support throughout the process. Finally, three of our four children, Bridget Shaefer, Kaitlin Edin-Nelson, and Marisa Edin-Nelson, made field trips out to join us while we were on location at various field sites, while the last, Michael Shaefer, was held in one arm during some of the book's writing. Their presence made the work all the more meaningful.

Notes

Introduction

page

xiv *welfare recipients:* See Kathryn Edin and Laura Lein, *Making Ends Meet: How Single Mothers Survive Welfare and Low-Wage Work* (New York: Russell Sage Foundation, 1997).

xvii *any given month:* H. Luke Shaefer and Kathryn Edin, "Extreme Poverty in the United States, 1996 to 2011" (Policy Brief No. 28, Gerald R. Ford School of Public Policy, University of Michigan, February 2012), http://www.npc.umich.edu/publications/policy_briefs/brief28/policybrief28.pdf. See also H. Luke Shaefer and Kathryn Edin, "Rising Extreme Poverty in the United States and the Response of Federal Means-Tested Transfers," *Social Service Review* 87, no. 2 (2013): 250–68. Since publication of these reports, we have updated our baseline estimates through mid-2013, and they remain consistent. See H. Luke Shaefer and Kathryn Edin, "Understanding the Dynamics of $2-a-Day Poverty in the United States," *RSF: A Journal of the Social Sciences* (forthcoming).

a decade and a half: Shaefer and Edin, "Extreme Poverty"; Shaefer and Edin, "Rising Extreme Poverty."

xviii *50 percent increase:* Shaefer and Edin, "Rising Extreme Poverty."

rise of $2-a-day poverty: For a more detailed accounting of these other indicators, see the end of chapter 1.

xx *"City of the Big Shoulders":* Carl Sandburg, "Chicago," *Poetry,* March 1914, 191–92.

The Truly Disadvantaged: William Julius Wilson, *The Truly Disadvantaged: The Inner City, the Underclass, and Public Policy* (Chicago: University of Chicago Press, 1987).

xxi *"America's Most Miserable Cities"*: Kurt Badenhausen, "In Pictures: America's 20 Most Miserable Cities," Forbes.com, February 18, 2010, http://www
.forbes.com/2010/02/11/americas-most-miserable-cities-business-beltway
-miserable-cities_slide.html.

  pockets of deep need: Appalachian Regional Commission, "Economic Overview of Appalachia — 2011" (n.p., n.d.), http://www.arc.gov/images
/appregion/Sept2011/EconomicOverviewSept2011.pdf.

  "hardest places to live": Alan Flippen, "Where Are the Hardest Places to Live in the U.S.?," *New York Times*, June 26, 2014, http://www.nytimes
.com/2014/06/26/upshot/where-are-the-hardest-places-to-live-in-the-us
.html?action=click&contentCollection=The Upshot&module=Related
Coverage&region=Marginalia&pgtype=article&abt=0002&abg=0.

xxii *government housing developments*: While it is still possible to supplement one's earnings with a vegetable garden or a "cash crop" such as tobacco in the region's rural areas, we found that those who have migrated into Johnson City and the other population centers largely rely on the cash economy to survive, just as in Cleveland and Chicago.

  "the most southern place": James C. Cobb, *The Most Southern Place on Earth: The Mississippi Delta and the Roots of Regional Identity* (New York: Oxford University Press, 1994).

xxiii *"sleeping on grates"*: Ian Fisher, "Moynihan Stands Alone in Welfare Debate," *New York Times*, September 27, 1995, http://www.nytimes.com
/1995/09/27/nyregion/moynihan-stands-alone-in-welfare-debate.html.

1. *Welfare Is Dead*

1 *Welfare Is Dead*: For this chapter, we completed in-depth interviews with Peter Edelman, Ron Haskins, Wendell E. Primus, and Isabel V. Sawhill, all of whom played important roles as public officials in the events surrounding the 1996 welfare reform. We also drew on an in-depth interview with David Ellwood that Edin conducted for a previous research project. Edelman is now a professor of law at the Georgetown University Law Center (also known as Georgetown Law). He served as counselor to Health and Human Services Secretary Donna Shalala and then as assistant secretary for planning and evaluation, Department of Health and Human Services, in the Clinton administration. Ron Haskins is now a senior fellow at the Brookings Institution and served as majority staff director for the Subcommittee on Human Resources, Committee on Ways and Means, U.S. House of Representatives (1995–2000), and before that as welfare counsel, Republican staff, of that subcommittee (1986–1994). Wendell E. Primus is now senior policy adviser to Minority Leader Nancy Pelosi, U.S. House of Representa-

tives, and served as deputy assistant secretary for human services policy, Department of Health and Human Services, in the Clinton administration. Isabel V. Sawhill is now senior fellow in economic studies at the Brookings Institution and served as associate director at the Office of Management and Budget during the Clinton administration. David Ellwood is now dean of the John F. Kennedy School of Government at Harvard University and served as assistant secretary for planning and evaluation, Department of Health and Human Services, in the Clinton administration (1993–1995).

2 *she relented:* In Illinois in 2012, it was possible to apply for cash aid online. But after completing the online form, you could expect to wait a few weeks before getting an appointment to see a caseworker. If you showed up in person, you had a chance to see someone that day. Since seeing a caseworker was essentially the first step in applying for benefits, it made the most sense just to go down to the office and stand in line.

4 *eligibility criteria:* Alix Gould-Werth and H. Luke Shaefer, "Do Alternative Base Periods Increase Unemployment Insurance Receipt Among Low-Educated Unemployed Workers?," *Journal of Policy Analysis and Management* 32, no. 4 (2013): 835–52; H. Luke Shaefer, "Identifying Key Barriers to Unemployment Insurance for Disadvantaged Workers in the United States," *Journal of Social Policy* 39, no. 3 (2010): 439–60; Government Accountability Office, "Unemployment Insurance: Factors Associated with Benefit Receipt" (Washington, DC, 2006); Government Accountability Office, "Unemployment Insurance: Low-Wage and Part-Time Workers Continue to Experience Low Rates of Receipt" (Washington, DC, 2007).

making at Stars: Illinois's "replacement rate" for unemployment insurance captures the ratio of the average of the claimant's weekly unemployment benefits to the average of the claimant's previous weekly wages. It has hovered around 40 percent (or below) in recent years, even lower by some calculations ("UI Replacement Rates Report," Employment and Training Administration, U.S. Department of Labor, http://workforcesecurity.doleta .gov/unemploy/ui_replacement_rates.asp).

7 *today's cash welfare program:* In calendar year 2013, preliminary estimates show there were an average of 4.0 million individuals per month receiving benefits from Temporary Assistance for Needy Families (TANF) or related state supplementary payments (SSP) programs ("Caseload Data 2013," Office of Family Assistance, U.S. Department of Health and Human Services, May 23, 2014, http://www.acf.hhs.gov/programs/ofa/resource/caseload -data-2013). As of July 4, 2013, the U.S. Census Bureau estimated that the U.S. population was about 316 million. This works out to about 1.3 percent of the U.S. population being on TANF in any given month. Also note that what we as a country spend on TANF makes up just a tiny fraction of the federal budget. Out of every $100 spent by the U.S. Treasury, less than 50

cents goes to this program. (The TANF block grant is set at $16.5 billion. In 2012, total federal expenditures were around $3.5 trillion.) What's more, the average state spends less than 30 percent of the money set aside for TANF (both federal and required state funds) on basic cash assistance for poor families. The rest of the money allocated to the program has been diverted to other uses, such as child care subsidies, child welfare protection (e.g., the foster care system), job training, and marriage promotion programs. This information comes from Liz Schott, "Policy Basics: An Introduction to TANF" (Center on Budget and Policy Priorities, Washington, DC, December 4, 2012), http://www.cbpp.org/cms/?fa=view&id=936.

Just 27 percent: Schott, "Policy Basics: An Introduction to TANF."

postage stamp collectors: "A Hobby for Everyone," American Philatelic Society, n.d., http://stamps.org/A-Hobby-for-Everyone.

3.8 million: See the following sources for TANF caseloads: for 2012, http://www.acf.hhs.gov/programs/ofa/resource/caseload-data-2012; for 2014, http://www.acf.hhs.gov/programs/ofa/resource/caseload-data-2014; for earlier years, http://archive.acf.hhs.gov/programs/ofa/data-reports/index.htm. For adult workforce participation, see "Characteristics and Financial Circumstances of TANF Recipients, Fiscal Year 2012," table 30, http://www.acf.hhs.gov/sites/default/files/ofa/tanf_characteristics_fy_2012.pdf.

8 *above the $2-a-day mark:* Shaefer and Edin, "Rising Extreme Poverty."

how desperate the need: Some states take an active role in perpetuating this, using "informal diversion practices" that "dissuade people from completing the TANF application process, whether intentionally or not" (Heather Hahn, Olivia Golden, and Alexandra Stanczyk, "State Approaches to the TANF Block Grant: Welfare Is Not What You Think It Is" [Working Families Paper No. 20, Urban Institute, Washington, DC, August 2012], 15, http://www.urban.org/UploadedPDF/412635-State-Approaches-to-the-TANF-Block-Grant.pdf). Florida, for example, requires that applicants engage in work activities for 30 hours before receiving aid.

than ever before: Peter Ganong and Jeffrey B. Liebman, "The Decline, Rebound, and Further Rise in SNAP Enrollment: Disentangling Business Cycle Fluctuations and Policy Changes" (NBER Working Paper No. 19363, National Bureau of Economic Research, Cambridge, MA, August 2013), http://www.nber.org/papers/w19363.

9 *Democrats and Republicans alike:* Republican support for refundable tax credits like the EITC has diminished some as the credits have grown in size.

had no work: For a review of the changes in federal means-tested programs, see Shaefer and Edin, "Rising Extreme Poverty," and Yonaton Ben-Shalom, Robert Moffitt, and John Scholz, "An Assessment of the Effectiveness of Anti-Poverty Programs in the United States," in *Oxford Handbook of the*

Economics of Poverty, ed. Philip N. Jefferson, chap. 22 (Oxford: Oxford University Press, 2012).

her low earnings: We estimated Modonna's tax liability using Internet TAX-SIM, Version 9.3 (http://users.nber.org/~taxsim/taxsim-calc9/index.html). We estimated Modonna's SNAP benefit using the Illinois SNAP Eligibility Calculator and assuming fair market rent for her apartment at $894 per month (http://fscalc.dhs.illinois.gov/FSCalc/). The 36 percent pay raise was based on her net income.

11   *as long as it did:* See David Ellwood, *Poor Support: Poverty and the American Family* (New York: Basic Books, 1988), and R. Kent Weaver, *Ending Welfare as We Know It* (Washington, DC: Brookings Institution Press, 2000).

a historical accident: See Christopher Jencks, *Rethinking Social Policy: Race, Poverty, and the Underclass* (Cambridge, MA: Harvard University Press, 1992), and Jason DeParle, *American Dream: Three Women, Ten Kids, and a Nation's Drive to End Welfare* (New York: Viking, 2004).

off the rolls: See Deborah Ward, *The White Welfare State: The Racialization of U.S. Welfare Policy* (Ann Arbor: University of Michigan Press, 2005), and Weaver, *Ending Welfare.*

12   *The Other America:* Michael Harrington, *The Other America: Poverty in the United States* (1962; repr., New York: Simon & Schuster, 1997); quotation appears on p. 182.

Johnson declared: Lyndon Johnson, State of the Union address, 1964, http://www.pbs.org/wgbh/americanexperience/features/primary-resources/lbj-union64/.

measure whether someone was poor: A quick and dirty measure was swiftly adopted, based on the work of Mollie Orshansky, a research analyst at the Social Security Administration. The Orshansky measure is determined by tripling the cost of a minimally nutritious diet for a family. It is based on findings from the time stating that families spent about a third of their income on food. A family's cash income is then compared to this threshold. This formula is the basis of the official poverty measure that has been used by the federal government ever since.

13   *"really good-looking":* Peter Edelman, *Searching for America's Heart: RFK and the Renewal of Hope* (Boston: Houghton Mifflin, 2001), 49.

"three hours behind schedule": Ibid., 57.

14   *in its own right:* The period also saw the first major federal effort to increase work among recipients, which consisted of a carrot and a stick. The carrot allowed recipients to keep a larger fraction of their benefits when they worked, although far from all of them. The stick was that states were allowed to drop able-bodied recipients who refused to register for new, state-sponsored work programs. Yet without any real funding dedicated

by the federal government to support such work programs, cash-strapped states enrolled only a small number of people, neutralizing the impact of the effort.

drops considerably: Our student research collaborator Bethany Patten analyzed historical data from the General Social Survey, administered by NORC and publicly available at http://www3.norc.org/GSS+Website/. See also Tom W. Smith, "That Which We Call Welfare by Any Other Name Would Smell Sweeter: An Analysis of the Impact of Question Wording on Response Patterns," *Public Opinion Quarterly* 51, no. 1 (1987): 75–83.

"destroyer of the human spirit": Franklin D. Roosevelt, State of the Union address, January 4, 1935, http://www.fdrlibrary.marist.edu/daybyday /resource/january-1935/.

reduced their work effort somewhat: Robert Moffitt, "Incentive Effects of the U.S. Welfare System: A Review," *Journal of Economic Literature* 30, no. 1 (1992): 1–61. See also Sheldon Danziger, Robert Haveman, and Robert Plotnick, "How Income Transfers Affect Work, Savings, and the Income Distribution: A Critical Review," *Journal of Economic Literature* 19, no. 3 (1981): 975–1028.

15   *the next decade:* Stephanie J. Ventura, "Changing Patterns of Nonmarital Childbearing in the United States" (NCHS Data Brief No. 18, National Center for Health Statistics, Hyattsville, MD, May 2009), http://www.cdc.gov /nchs/data/databriefs/db18.pdf. See also "Trends in Non-Marital Birth Rates: The Rates of Non-Marital Births Have Increased," NHMRC Fact Sheets and Research Briefs, National Healthy Marriage Resource Center, n.d., http://www.healthymarriageinfo.org/research-and-policy/marriage -facts/index.aspx.

for the dole: Charles Murray, *Losing Ground: American Social Policy, 1950–1980* (New York: Basic Books, 1984).

driven by welfare: Moffitt, "Incentive Effects"; Robert Fairlie and Rebecca London, "The Effect of Incremental Benefit Levels on Births to AFDC Recipients," *Journal of Policy Analysis and Management* 16, no. 4 (1997): 575–97.

16   *heard from the crowd:* Josh Levin, "The Welfare Queen," *Slate,* December 19, 2013, http://www.slate.com/articles/news_and_politics/history/2013/12 /linda_taylor_welfare_queen_ronald_reagan_made_her_a_notorious _american_villain.html.

profile in Slate: Levin, "The Welfare Queen."

was white: Our student research collaborator Vincent Fusaro, a doctoral student in social work and political science at the University of Michigan, analyzed data from the harmonized version of the March Current Population Survey (CPS) Supplement from 1968 to 1995 (Miriam King, Steven Ruggles, J. Trent Alexander, Sarah Flood, Katie Genadek, Matthew B. Schroeder, Brandon Trampe, and Rebecca Vick, *Integrated Public Use*

Microdata Series, Current Population Survey: Version 3.0 [machine-readable database] [Minneapolis: University of Minnesota, 2010]). He produced annual estimates of the demographic characteristics of AFDC recipients. In only one year was the proportion of household heads receiving AFDC who were black slightly above 40 percent. In every year between 1968 and 1995, a majority of the recipients were white.

increased long-term poverty: Murray, *Losing Ground.*

17   *"spider's web of dependency":* Ronald Reagan, State of the Union address, February 4, 1986, http://www.presidency.ucsb.edu/ws/?pid=36646.

"poverty won": Quoted in Nicholas Lemann, "The Unfinished War," *Atlantic Monthly,* December 1988, http://www.theatlantic.com/past/politics/poverty /lemunf1.htm.

18   *the public sphere:* For a more detailed description of Ellwood, see DeParle, *American Dream.*

crisis or transition: David Ellwood and Mary Jo Bane, "The Dynamics of Dependence: The Routes to Self-Sufficiency" (prepared for the Office of Planning and Evaluation, U.S. Department of Health and Human Services, Washington, DC, June 1983). Ellwood and Bane compared long-term welfare recipients to the small number of chronically ill hospital admits who end up claiming a disproportionate share of the hospital's beds simply because they are there longer.

could ever survive: Ellwood, *Poor Support.*

19   *Murray's claims weren't credible:* Sara McLanahan, Glen Cain, Michael Olneck, Irving Piliavin, Sheldon Danziger, and Peter Gottschalk, "*Losing Ground:* A Critique" (Special Report No. 38, Institute for Research on Poverty, University of Wisconsin–Madison, August 1985); Christopher Jencks, "How Poor Are the Poor?," review of *Losing Ground: American Social Policy,* by Charles Murray, *New York Review of Books,* May 9, 1985, 41–49; Ellwood, *Poor Support.*

into conflict: Ellwood, *Poor Support,* 6.

"a temporary setback": Ibid., 238.

20   *admired the professor's work:* Sarah Halpern-Meekin, Kathryn Edin, Laura Tach, and Jennifer Sykes, *It's Not Like I'm Poor: How Working Families Make Ends Meet in a Post-Welfare World* (Berkeley: University of California Press, 2015).

front and center: DeParle, *American Dream.*

21   *"you're out":* Joel F. Handler, "'Ending Welfare as We Know It': Another Exercise in Symbolic Politics" (Discussion Paper No. 1053-95, Institute for Research on Poverty, University of Wisconsin–Madison, January 1995), http://www.irp.wisc.edu/publications/dps/pdfs/dp105395.pdf.

"pure heroin": DeParle, *American Dream,* 4.

"independence and dignity": William J. Clinton, Address Before a Joint Ses-

sion of Congress on Administration Goals, February 17, 1993, http://www
.presidency.ucsb.edu/ws/?pid=47232.

22   *"be in poverty":* Ibid. ·
     "make work pay": Halpern-Meekin et al., *It's Not Like I'm Poor.*
     going to look like: DeParle, *American Dream.*
     ever had on AFDC: Halpern-Meekin et al., *It's Not Like I'm Poor.*

23   *would be working:* Weaver, *Ending Welfare.*

24   *make welfare reform a reality:* Ron Haskins, *Work over Welfare: The Inside
     Story of the 1996 Welfare Reform Law* (Washington, DC: Brookings Institu-
     tion Press, 2006).
     block grants: Ibid.

25   *for work or not:* DeParle, *American Dream.* In addition, states would gain
     new abilities to impose harsher sanctions on families (including penal-
     ties that resulted in the loss of their cash benefits) if they failed to meet the
     state's work or other requirements.
     using federal funds: States could continue to support families who had
     reached their lifetime limit, but the state would have to pay for the aid
     entirely by itself.

26   *he would veto them:* Clinton would veto welfare reform bills twice. Clearly,
     he vetoed the first bill because of what he viewed as damaging changes to
     the Food Stamp Program and Medicaid, among other things. The reason he
     vetoed the second bill is not as clear; some argue it looked fairly similar to
     the final bill he signed.
     "national government": Marian Wright Edelman, "An Open Letter to Presi-
     dent Clinton," op-ed, *Washington Post,* November 3, 1995.
     "almost 11 percent": 141 Cong. Rec. S16,466 (daily ed. Nov. 1, 1995) (statement
     of Sen. Moynihan).

27   *more than a year and a half:* "Presidential Approval Ratings — Bill Clinton,"
     Gallup, http://www.gallup.com/poll/116584/presidential-approval-ratings
     -bill-clinton.aspx.
     "quit the next day": Peter Edelman, telephone interview with author, Janu-
     ary 20, 2014.

28   *"what I'm thinking":* Ibid.
     "over the legislation": Barbara Vobejda and Judith Havemann, "2 HHS Of-
     ficials Quit over Welfare Reform," *Washington Post,* September 12, 1996.
     "particular rebuke": Alison Mitchell, "Two Clinton Aides Resign to Protest
     New Welfare Law," *New York Times,* September 12, 1996.

29   *"this autumn":* Robin Toner, "New Senate Push on Welfare Revives Tensions
     in Both Parties," *New York Times,* September 9, 1995.
     "soup kitchens": Peter Edelman, "The Worst Thing Bill Clinton Has Done,"
     Atlantic Monthly, March 1, 1997.
     "best for the country": Bill Clinton, "How We Ended Welfare, Together," op-

ed, *New York Times,* August 22, 2006, http://www.nytimes.com/2006/08/22 /opinion/22clinton.html?_r=0.

unprecedented increase: Ron Haskins, "Welfare Reform, Success or Failure? It Worked," Point CounterPoint, *Policy and Practice,* March 2006, http: //www.brookings.edu/~/media/research/files/articles/2006/3/15welfare% 20haskins/0315welfare_haskins.pdf.

30   *no researcher could discern:* Robert A. Moffitt, "From Welfare to Work: What the Evidence Shows," executive summary, *Welfare Reform & Beyond* (Policy Brief No. 13, Brookings Institution, Washington, DC, January 2002), http://www.brookings.edu/~/media/research/files/papers/2002/1 /welfare%20moffitt/pb13.pdf. According to Moffitt, "A recent review of these studies conducted by the U.S. Department of Health and Human Services indicates that the employment rate among welfare leavers is approximately 60 percent just after exiting welfare."

"welfare leavers" remained high: Maria Cancian, Robert Haveman, Daniel R. Meyer, and Barbara Wolfe, "Before and After TANF: The Economic Well-Being of Women Leaving Welfare," *Social Service Review* 76, no. 4 (2002): 603–41; Sheldon Danziger, Colleen M. Heflin, Mary E. Corcoran, Elizabeth Oltmans, and Hui-Chen Wang, "Does It Pay to Move from Welfare to Work?," *Journal of Policy Analysis and Management* 21, no. 4 (2002): 671–92; LaDonna A. Pavetti and Gregory Acs, "Moving Up, Moving Out, or Going Nowhere? A Study of the Employment Patterns of Young Women and the Implications for Welfare Mothers," *Journal of Policy Analysis and Management* 20, no. 4 (2001): 721–36.

had risen substantially: Rebecca M. Blank, "Improving the Safety Net for Single Mothers Who Face Serious Barriers to Work," *Future of Children* 17, no. 2 (2007): 183–97; Pamela Loprest, "Disconnected Families and TANF" (OPRE Research Brief No. 2, Urban Institute, Office of Planning, Research and Evaluation, Washington, DC, November 2011); Lesley Turner, Sheldon Danziger, and Kristin Seefeldt, "Failing the Transition from Welfare to Work: Women Chronically Disconnected from Employment and Cash Welfare," *Social Science Quarterly* 87, no. 2 (2006): 227–49.

during the mid-2000s: Note that Ron Haskins tried to call attention to this worrying trend in a 2001 column in the *Washington Post.* He and coauthor Rebecca Blank wrote that research "shows there is a group of mothers and children at the bottom of the income distribution who are worse off as a result of welfare reform" (Ron Haskins and Rebecca Blank, "Revisiting Welfare," *Washington Post,* February 14, 2001). Going even further in 2004, Haskins argued that "the evidence of increased hardship among families at the very bottom of the income distribution should signal that welfare reform has not worked for all families and that researchers and policymakers should focus attention on these floundering families" (Ron Haskins,

"Welfare Reform: Success with Trouble Spots," *Eastern Economic Journal* 30, no. 1 [2004]: 125–33).

31   *no other income:* "Characteristics of Supplemental Nutrition Assistance Program Households," annual report by fiscal year, Supplemental Nutrition Assistance Program (SNAP) Research, Food and Nutrition Service, U.S. Department of Agriculture, http://www.fns.usda.gov/ops/supplemental -nutrition-assistance-program-snap-research.

37 million Americans in 2009: Estimates of emergency food program utilization come from Feeding America's "Hunger in America" national reports. Historical estimates were provided by Feeding America research staff. The most recent report, "Hunger in America 2014," was excluded because of changes in the study's methodology, but it can be found at http://help.feed ingamerica.org/HungerInAmerica/hunger-in-america-2014-full-report.pdf.

soured in 2001: Nancy Smith, Zaire Dinzey Flores, Jeffrey Lin, and John Markovic, "Understanding Family Homelessness in New York City: An In-Depth Study of Families' Experiences Before and After Shelter" (Vera Institute of Justice, New York, September 2005), http://www.nyc.gov/html/ dhs/downloads/pdf/vera_Study.pdf.

1.3 million in 2012–2013: Estimates taken from National Center for Homeless Education, *Education for Homeless Children and Youth Consolidated State Performance Report Data,* http://center.serve.org/nche/pr/data_comp.php.

don't explain the trend: Dan Bloom, Mary Farrell, and Barbara Fink, "Welfare Time Limits: State Policies, Implementation, and Effects on Families" (Manpower Demonstration Research Corporation, n.d.), http://www.mdrc .org/sites/default/files/full_607.pdf.

32   *process is so time-consuming:* Hahn, Golden, and Stanczyk, "State Approaches."

young children: Edin and Lein, *Making Ends Meet.*

benefits from the program: Ellen K. Scott, Andrew S. London, and Kathryn Edin, "Looking to the Future: Welfare Reliant Women Talk About Their Job Aspirations in the Context of Welfare Reform," *Journal of Social Issues* 56, no. 4 (2000): 727–46.

2. Perilous Work

36   *roughly $645:* We estimated Jennifer's tax liability using Internet TAXSIM, Version 9.3.

$960 per month: Fair market rent for the Chicago-Joliet-Naperville, Illinois, metropolitan area ("Individual Area Final FY2012 FMR Documentation," Fair Market Rents, U.S. Department of Housing and Urban Development, http://www.huduser.org/portal/datasets/fmr.html).

39   *hardest-hit cities that year:* Mary E. Podmolik, "Surge in Foreclosure Auctions Shows Chicago-Area Market's Pain," *Chicago Tribune,* February 6, 2013, http://articles.chicagotribune.com/2013-02-06/business/ct-biz-0206 -foreclosure-auctions-20130206_1_foreclosure-auctions-foreclosure -activity-initial-foreclosure-filings.

42   *during the year:* Shaefer and Edin, "Understanding the Dynamics."

43   *out of poverty:* Our student collaborator Vinçent Fusaro analyzed data from the harmonized version of the March Current Population Survey (CPS) Supplement for 2012 (reporting on 2011) and 2013 (reporting on 2012) (King et al., *Integrated Public Use Microdata Series*). The sample was restricted to respondents between the ages of eighteen and sixty-four who were currently employed for either salary or wage income. Self-employed workers were excluded from the analysis. Among all wage and salary workers in 2012, 22.5 percent were hourly workers with a wage of $11.50 per hour or less, roughly the pay rate needed to raise a family of four with a full-time worker above the poverty threshold. We did not include involuntary part-time workers with higher hourly rates whose annual earnings wouldn't raise them above the poverty line, so this might be considered a lower-bound estimate. See also John Schmitt, "Low-Wage Lessons" (Center for Economic and Policy Research, Washington, DC, January 2012), http://www.cepr.net/documents /publications/low-wage-2012-01.pdf, who came up with a similar estimate.
concentrated in the service sector: Françoise Carré and Chris Tilly, "America's Biggest Low-Wage Industry: Continuity and Change in Retail Jobs" (CSP Working Paper No. 2009-6, Center for Social Policy, McCormack Graduate School of Policy Studies, University of Massachusetts Boston, December 2008), http://www.umb.edu/editor_uploads/images /centers_institutes/center_social_policy/Americas_biggest_low-wage _industry-_Continuity_and_change_in_retail_jobs.pdf. See also Drew Desilver, "Who Makes Minimum Wage?," *Factank: News in the Numbers,* Pew Research Center, September 8, 2014, http://www.pewresearch.org /fact-tank/2014/09/08/who-makes-minimum-wage/.
retirement plans: Schmitt, "Low-Wage Lessons."

44   *projected to grow, not shrink:* "Industry Employment and Output Projections to 2022," *Monthly Labor Review,* December 2013, http://www.bls .gov/opub/mlr/2013/article/industry-employment-and-output-projections -to-2022-1.htm. See also Rebecca Thiess, "The Future of Work: Trends and Challenges for Low-Wage Workers" (EPI Briefing Paper No. 341, Economic Policy Institute, Washington, DC, April 27, 2012), http://s2.epi.org /files/2012/bp341-future-of-work.pdf.

45   *set workers up for failure:* Susan J. Lambert, Anna Haley-Lock, and Julia R. Henly, "Schedule Flexibility in Hourly Jobs: Unanticipated Consequences and Promising Directions," *Community, Work & Family* 15, no. 3 (2012):

293–315; Arne L. Kalleberg, "Precarious Work, Insecure Workers: Employment Relations in Transition," 2008 presidential address, *American Sociological Review* 74 (February 2008): 1–22; Susan J. Lambert, "Passing the Buck: Labor Flexibility Practices That Transfer Risk onto Hourly Workers," *Human Relations* 61, no. 9 (2008): 1203–27.

46   *week to week:* Lambert, Haley-Lock, and Henly, "Schedule Flexibility"; Center for Law and Social Policy, Retail Action Project, and Women Employed, "Tackling Unstable and Unpredictable Work Schedules: A Policy Brief on Guaranteed Minimum Hours and Reporting Pay Policies" (n.p., n.d.), http://www.clasp.org/resources-and-publications/publication-1/Tackling -Unstable-and-Unpredictable-Work-Schedules-3-7-2014-FINAL-1.pdf; Susan J. Lambert, Peter J. Fugiel, and Julia R. Henly, "Precarious Work Schedules Among Early Career Employees in the US: A National Snapshot" (research brief, EINet, University of Chicago, August 27, 2014), http: //ssascholars.uchicago.edu/work-scheduling-study/files/lambert.fugiel .henly_.precarious_work_schedules.august2014.pdf. The last study is the first nationally representative accounting of schedule unpredictability among early-career workers. They found that 47 percent of part-time hourly workers got only one week or less of advance warning of their work schedules. Nearly one in two black non-Hispanic workers in hourly jobs reported advance notice of a week or less. They also found employee control over the timing of work hours to be uncommon and fluctuating work hours to be quite common.

even to zero: Lambert, "Passing the Buck."

"on-call" shifts: Stephanie Luce and Naoki Fujita, "Discounted Jobs: How Retailers Sell Workers Short" (Murphy Institute, City University of New York, and Retail Action Project, 2012), http://retailactionproject.org /wp-content/uploads/2012/03/7-75_RAP+cover_lowres.pdf.

reduced as a result: Lambert, Haley-Lock, and Henly, "Schedule Flexibility."

52   *identifiably black or white:* Marianne Bertrand and Sendhil Mullainathan, "Are Emily and Greg More Employable Than Lakisha and Jamal? A Field Experiment on Labor Market Discrimination," *American Economic Review* 94, no. 4 (2004): 991–1013.

53   *relative to whites:* For descriptions of both studies, see Devah Pager, *Marked: Race, Crime, and Finding Work in an Era of Mass Incarceration* (Chicago: University of Chicago Press, 2007).

54   *wildly inaccurate:* Persis S. Yu and Sharon M. Dietrich, "Broken Records: How Errors by Criminal Background Checking Companies Harm Workers and Businesses" (National Consumer Law Center, Boston, April 2012), http://www.nclc.org/images/pdf/pr-reports/broken-records-report.pdf.

61   *average low-wage job in America:* Andrew Leigh, "Who Benefits from the

Earned Income Tax Credit? Incidence Among Recipients, Coworkers and Firms," *B.E. Journal of Economic Analysis & Policy* 10, no. 1 (2010): 1–41.

62 *opens in a community:* David Neumark, Junfu Zhang, and Stephen Ciccarella, "The Effects of Wal-Mart on Local Labor Markets," *Journal of Urban Economics* 63 (2008): 405–30.

occupied their properties: Jessica Silver-Greenberg, "Invasive Tactic in Foreclosures Draws Scrutiny," *New York Times,* September 9, 2013, http://dealbook.nytimes.com/2013/09/09/invasive-tactic-in-foreclosures-draws-scrutiny/; Ben Hallman, "Safeguard Properties Internal Documents Reveal Rampant Complaints of Thefts, Break-ins," *Huffington Post,* April 29, 2013, http://www.huffingtonpost.com/2013/04/29/safeguard-properties-complaints_n_3165191.html; The People of the State of Illinois v. Safeguard Properties, LLC, http://illinoisattorneygeneral.gov/pressroom/2013_09/SAFEGUARD_PROPERTIES_COMPLAINT_09-09-2013_15-51-37.pdf. There is no public record of a change in the status of the lawsuit as of the date of this writing.

3. A Room of One's Own

66 *essential expenses:* "Who Needs Affordable Housing?," U.S. Department of Housing and Urban Development, n.d., http://portal.hud.gov/hudportal/HUD?src=/program_offices/comm_planning/affordablehousing/.

according to HUD: Ibid. See also Althea Arnold, Sheila Crowley, Elina Bravve, Sarah Brundage, and Christine Biddlecombe, "Out of Reach 2014" (National Low Income Housing Coalition, Washington, DC, 2014), http://nlihc.org/sites/default/files/oor/2014OOR.pdf. Fair market rent is set at "the dollar amount below which 40 percent of the standard-quality rental housing units are rented" ("Fair Market Rents: Overview," U.S. Department of Housing and Urban Development, http://www.huduser.org/portal/datasets/fmr.html).

69 *in Abilene:* To protect them from being identified, we have changed the city in Texas where the Hernandez family went.

72 *local Salvation Army:* Remember that we have changed the city in Texas where the Hernandez family went to protect them from being identified. In Abilene, according to a program representative, the Salvation Army does have rooms where families can stay together, but as of the fall of 2014, they have to pay a small fee after five nights in residence. Also, a couple has to produce their marriage license to stay in a room together.

73 *less extreme poverty:* Shaefer and Edin, "Understanding the Dynamics."

74 *nearly 70 percent:* Joint Center for Housing Studies of Harvard University,

"The State of the Nation's Housing 2013" (Cambridge, MA, 2013), http:
//www.jchs.harvard.edu/sites/jchs.harvard.edu/files/son2013.pdf.
less affordable as a result: Stephen Malpezzi and Richard K. Green, "What
Has Happened to the Bottom of the US Housing Market?," *Urban Studies*
33, no. 10 (1996): 1807–20; John M. Quigley and Steven Raphael, "Is Housing
Unaffordable? Why Isn't It More Affordable?," *Journal of Economic Perspec-
tives* 18, no. 1 (2004): 191–214.
fell 13 percent: Joint Center for Housing Studies of Harvard University,
"America's Rental Housing—Evolving Markets and Needs" (Cambridge,
MA, 2013), http://www.jchs.harvard.edu/sites/jchs.harvard.edu/files/jchs
_americas_rental_housing_2013_1_0.pdf.

75　*deemed "substandard":* Ibid.
notorious landlords: Phillip Morris, "The Brown Brothers Are Splitting
Their Ribs Laughing at Cleveland's Housing Court," Cleveland.com, July
15, 2011, http://www.cleveland.com/morris/index.ssf/2011/07/the_brown
_brothers_are_splitti.html.
maintenance costs very low: Interviews conducted by a research team led by
Edin, Stefanie DeLuca, and collaborators.

76　*reduce housing instability considerably:* Michelle Wood, Jennifer Turnham,
and Gregory Mills, "Housing Affordability and Family Well-Being: Results
from the Housing Voucher Evaluation," *Housing Policy Debate* 19, no. 2
(2008): 367–412.
the Reagan administration: According to Marian Wright Edelman and Lisa
Mihaly ("Homeless Families and the Housing Crisis in the United States,"
Children and Youth Services Review 11, no. 1 [1989]: 91–108), federal funding
for housing assistance for those in poverty was drastically reduced over the
course of the 1980s.

77　*rental subsidy:* Will Fischer, "Research Shows Housing Vouchers Reduce
Hardship and Provide Platform for Long-Term Gains Among Children"
(Center on Budget and Policy Priorities, Washington, DC, January 25, 2013);
Joint Center for Housing Studies of Harvard University, "The State of the
Nation's Housing."

78　*nausea, vomiting, and headaches:* Jan Gibertson and Geoff Green, "Good
Housing and Good Health? A Review and Recommendations for Housing
and Health Practitioners" (Affordable Homes Strong Community Sector
Study, Housing Corporation and Care Services Improvement Partnership,
UK Department of Health, n.d.), http://www.pewtrusts.org/en/~/media
/Assets/External-Sites/Health-Impact-Project/Good_housing_and_good
_health.pdf.

79　*history of sexual abuse:* Shanta R. Dube, Robert F. Anda, Vincent J. Felitti,
Daniel P. Chapman, David F. Williamson, and Wayne H. Giles, "Childhood Abuse, Household Dysfunction, and the Risk of Attempted Suicide

Throughout the Life Span: Findings from the Adverse Childhood Experiences Study," *Journal of the American Medical Association* 286, no. 24 (2001): 3089–96. See also "Prevalence of Individual Adverse Childhood Experiences," Centers for Disease Control and Prevention, n.d., http://www.cdc.gov/violenceprevention/acestudy/prevalence.html.

greater risk of such experiences: Child Trends DataBank, "Adverse Experiences: Indicators on Children and Youth" (Child Trends, Bethesda, MD, July 2013), http://www.childtrends.org/wp-content/uploads/2013/07/124_Adverse_Experiences.pdf.

related to the child: Julia Whealin and Erin Barnett, "Child Sexual Abuse," National Center for PTSD, U.S. Department of Veterans Affairs, n.d., http://www.ptsd.va.gov/professional/trauma/other/child_sexual_abuse.asp.

housing instability: Rebecca Cohen, "The Impact of Affordable Housing on Health: A Research Summary," in *Insights from Housing Policy Research* (Center for Housing Policy, Washington, DC, May 2011), http://www.nhc.org/media/files/Insights_HousingAndHealthBrief.pdf.

87   *an ACE questionnaire:* Quotations from the questionnaire are from "Prevalence of Individual Adverse Childhood Experiences."

88   *"found to be cumulative":* "Origins and Essence of the Study," *ACE Reporter,* April 2003, http://acestudy.org/yahoo_site_admin/assets/docs/ARV1N1.127150541.pdf.

      "toxic stress": Jack P. Shonkoff, Andrew S. Garner, and the Committee on Psychosocial Aspects of Child and Family Health, Committee on Early Childhood, Adoption, and Dependent Care, and Section on Developmental and Behavioral Pediatrics, "The Lifelong Effects of Early Childhood Adversity and Toxic Stress," technical report, *Pediatrics* 129, no. 1 (2012): e232–e246, http://pediatrics.aappublications.org/content/129/1/e232.full.pdf.

4. By Any Means Necessary

97   *on the welfare rolls:* Edin and Lein, *Making Ends Meet.* This information is based on repeated in-depth conversations with hundreds of low-income single mothers across the country about how they balanced their budgets.

98   *one reason or another:* For more information on this topic, see Mariana Chilton, Jenny Rabinowich, Amanda Breen, and Sherita Mouzon, "When the Systems Fail: Individual and Household Coping Strategies Related to Child Hunger" (paper commissioned by the National Academies of Sciences Child Hunger Symposium, Washington, DC, April 2013), http://sites.nationalacademies.org/DBASSE/CNSTAT/DBASSE_081775.

101   *who fund the work:* Judith A. Lewis, Thomas Packard, and Michael D.

Lewis, *Management of Human Service Programs*, 5th ed. (Belmont, CA: Brooks/Cole, Cengage Learning, 2012).

102 *bolsters the government safety net:* What's more, recent trends have blurred the lines between private charities and government. Many nonprofits are, in fact, now funded in large part by government contracts. Few of these could survive on the donations of generous individuals alone. For more on this topic, see Scott W. Allard, *Out of Reach: Place, Poverty, and the New American Welfare State* (New Haven, CT: Yale University Press, 2009).
reflect local resources: Ibid.

105 *only emergency extractions were covered:* Abby Goodnough, "Sharp Cuts in Dental Coverage for Adults on Medicaid," *New York Times*, August 28, 2012, http://www.nytimes.com/2012/08/29/health/policy/hard-to-grin-while-bearing-cuts-in-medicaid-dental-coverage.html?pagewanted=all&_r=0.
food stamp households generally: Richard Mantovani, Eric Sean Williams, and Jacqueline Pflieger, "The Extent of Trafficking in the Supplemental Nutrition Assistance Program: 2009–2011" (Nutrition Assistance Program Report, Food and Nutrition Service, U.S. Department of Agriculture, August 2013), http://www.fns.usda.gov/sites/default/files/Trafficking2009.pdf.

107 *because of the cost:* H. Luke Shaefer and Italo Gutierrez, "The Supplemental Nutrition Assistance Program and Material Hardships Among Low-Income Households with Children," *Social Service Review* 87, no. 4 (2013): 753–79.
keep the lights on: Kathryn Edin, Melody Boyd, James Mabli, Jim Ohls, Julie Worthington, Sara Greene, Nicholas Redel, and Swetha Sridharan, "SNAP Food Security In-Depth Interview Study: Final Report" (Nutrition Assistance Program Report, Food and Nutrition Service, U.S. Department of Agriculture, March 2013), http://www.fns.usda.gov/sites/default/files/SNAPFoodSec.pdf.

110 *for molesting Kaitlin:* For the federal sentencing guidelines, see "Sentencing Table," http://www.gwtfirm.com/documents/Federal-sentencing_grid .pdf; and United States Sentencing Commission, "Offense Conduct," chap. 2 in *Guidelines Manual*, November 1, 2013, http://www.ussc.gov/guidelines -manual/2013/2013-index.

112 *in 2009–2011:* Mantovani, Williams, and Pflieger, "The Extent of Trafficking."

114 *over a year's time:* Edin and Lein, *Making Ends Meet.*

126 *extended to the working poor:* Center on Budget and Policy Priorities, "Policy Basics: The Earned Income Tax Credit" (Washington, DC, December 4, 2014), http://www.cbpp.org/files/policybasics-eitc.pdf.
survey quite closely: Shaefer and Edin, "Understanding the Dynamics."
the early 2000s: Smith et al., "Understanding Family Homelessness."
predates the Great Recession: See Feeding America's "Hunger in America" national reports.

127 *"intangible sense"*: Laurence Chandy and Cory Smith, "How Poor Are America's Poorest? U.S. $2 a Day Poverty in a Global Context" (Policy Paper No. 2014-03, Brookings Institution, Washington, DC, August 2014).

5. A World Apart

129 *A World Apart:* We called this chapter "A World Apart" to pay tribute to James C. Cobb's seminal work on the Mississippi Delta, *The Most Southern Place on Earth.* Chapter 6 of that work shares the same title.

131 *well over 40 percent:* American Community Survey, U.S. Census Bureau, http://www.census.gov/acs/www/about_the_survey/american_community _survey/.
were covered by AFDC: "Section 7. Aid to Families with Dependent Children and Temporary Assistance for Needy Families (Title IV-A)," table 7-10, http://aspe.hhs.gov/98gb/7afdc.htm.

132 *only about 17,000 statewide:* For caseload data, see "Data & Reports," Administration for Children and Families Archives, U.S. Department of Health and Human Services, http://archive.acf.hhs.gov/programs/ofa/data -reports/index.htm.

133 *mechanization of agriculture:* Cobb, *The Most Southern Place on Earth.*
just over 20 percent: The unemployment rate is taken from the Local Area Unemployment Statistics series, Bureau of Labor Statistics, http://www.bls .gov/lau/. The ratio of employment to population is taken from the American Community Survey, based on a three-year county average, 2011–2013.

135 *worst in the nation:* Olga Khazan, "The States with the Worst Healthcare Systems," Atlantic.com, May 1, 2014, http://www.theatlantic.com/health /archive/2014/05/the-states-with-the-worst-performing-healthcare-systems/ 361514/. According to rankings by *U.S. News & World Report,* of the 14 hospitals in the Delta, none met its standards for a strong performance ("Best Hospitals in the Mississippi Delta," *U.S. News & World Report,* n.d., http: //health.usnews.com/best-hospitals/area/ms/the-mississippi-delta).
disproportionate share: Shaefer and Edin, "Understanding the Dynamics."

155 *even poorer than Jefferson:* Based on household income, using data from the American Community Survey.
if not more so: Most people here know all about the mechanics of TANF. The place is just too small, and the need too widespread, for such secrets to be kept. But that doesn't mean welfare is alive. Martha Johnson and most of her desperately poor neighbors and friends have never even applied for TANF. Each gives her own reason. For Martha, it is the low payoff relative to the toll on her self-respect she believes applying would involve. She would rather toil for less than $2 an hour selling treats out of her little store.

156   *evident in the Delta:* Beyond her gypsy cab service, Loretta Perkins gener-
ates cash by taking boarders into her subsidized unit — usually SSI recipients
who aren't lucky enough to have a housing subsidy and don't get enough
cash from the government to get by. Her current tenant is a severe schizophrenic whose behavior can become so erratic and threatening when she's
off her meds that she strikes terror into Miss Perkins's four young children.
When Alva Mae Hicks's older children return home in the face of economic hard times — when they can't continue to maintain a home of their
own — they must come face-to-face with Cliff.

Subsidized housing appears to be somewhat more plentiful here than in
other regions. The annual inspection that Section 8 units must pass ensures
that a unit rented to someone with a voucher will remain in reasonable
condition (though at this writing, several of the windows in Alva Mae's unit
are covered with plywood, having been broken on various occasions when
Alva Mae tried to lock Cliff out of the house and he simply came through
the glass). But for those without subsidies, the housing that is available and
affordable may be barely habitable by U.S. standards.

Conclusion: Where, Then, from Here?

157   *above the poverty line each year:* Center on Budget and Policy Priorities,
"Policy Basics: The Earned Income Tax Credit."

158   *"sense of community":* Ellwood, *Poor Support,* 16.
many of its claimants: Ibid., 3–4.
for relief: This is nothing new. As the work of the late historian Michael
Katz has shown, poor relief, in its various forms, has served to so separate
the poor for centuries (Michael Katz, *In the Shadow of the Poorhouse:
A Social History of Welfare in America* [New York: Basic Books, 1986]).

160   *"the political spectrum":* Anne Roder and Mark Elliott, "Stimulating Opportunity: An Evaluation of ARRA-Funded Subsidized Employment
Programs" (Economic Mobility Corporation, New York, September 2013),
http://economicmobilitycorp.org/uploads/stimulating-opportunity-full
-report.pdf.

161   *"any given moment":* Lawrence H. Summers, "Lawrence H. Summers on
the Economic Challenge of the Future: Jobs," *Wall Street Journal,* July 2,
2014, http://www.wsj.com/articles/lawrence-h-summers-on-the-economic
-challenge-of-the-future-jobs-1404762501.
all occupational categories: Carl Benedikt Frey and Michael A. Osborne,
"The Future of Employment: How Susceptible Are Jobs to Computerisa-
tion?" (paper prepared for the Machines and Employment workshop,

Oxford University Engineering Sciences Department and Oxford Martin Programme on the Impacts of Future Technology, Oxford, UK, September 17, 2013), http://www.oxfordmartin.ox.ac.uk/publications/view/1314.

162 *their wages alone:* Halpern-Meekin et al., *It's Not Like I'm Poor.*

a meaningful degree: Congressional Budget Office, "The Effects of a Minimum-Wage Increase on Employment and Family Income" (Washington, DC, February 2014), https://www.cbo.gov/sites/default/files/44995 -MinimumWage.pdf.

boost economic growth: David Cooper, "Raising the Federal Minimum Wage to $10.10 Would Lift Wages for Millions and Provide a Modest Economic Boost" (EPI Briefing Paper No. 371, Economic Policy Institute, Washington, DC, December 19, 2013), http://s1.epi.org/files/2014/EPI-1010-minimum -wage.pdf.

163 *part-time workers:* Center for Law and Social Policy, Retail Action Project, and Women Employed, "Tackling Unstable and Unpredictable Work Schedules."

revise its procedures: Jodi Kantor, "Starbucks to Revise Policies to End Irregular Schedules for Its 130,000 Baristas," *New York Times,* August 14, 2014, http://www.nytimes.com/2014/08/15/us/starbucks-to-revise-work-scheduling-policies.html?_r=5.

164 *notice of their shifts:* "Walmart to Increase Wages for Current U.S. Workers to $10 an Hour or Higher, Launches New Skills-Based Training for Associates," February 19, 2015, http://cdn.corporate.walmart.com/a1/0e/6fec066e4c f48b9ec4b9f09bcd67/associate-opportunity-fact-sheet.2.pdf. See also Sruthi Ramakrishnan and Nathan Layne, "Wal-Mart, Under Pressure, Boosts Minimum U.S. Wage to $9 an Hour," Reuters, February 19, 2015, http: //www.reuters.com/article/2015/02/19/us-walmartstores-results-idUSKBN 0LN1BD20150219.

where to shop: While no such national index exists, there are some examples of related efforts. The Thrive Index is a checklist for employers to use to evaluate the quality of their lower-wage jobs, focusing on the circumstances of low-wage working women (Olivia Morgan, "Introducing the Thrive Index," Center for American Progress, January 12, 2014, https://www .americanprogress.org/issues/economy/news/2014/01/12/82029 /introducing-the-thrive-index/). See also "2013 Best Companies for Hourly Workers," Workingmother.com, http://www.workingmother.com/best-companies/2013-best-companies-hourly-workers.

investors and customers alike: Zeynep Ton, *The Good Jobs Strategy: How the Smartest Companies Invest in Employees to Lower Costs and Boost Profits* (New York: Harvest Books, 2014).

165 *for their boss:* Alana Semuels, "Power to the Workers: How Grocery Chain

Employees Saved Beloved CEO," *Los Angeles Times,* August 28, 2014, http:
//www.latimes.com/nation/nationnow/la-na-nn-market-basket-ceo-arthur
-t-demoulas-20140828-story.html.

the rank and file: Elizabeth Lauer-Bausch and Mark Greenstein, "Single
Mothers in the Era of Welfare Reform," in *The Gloves-Off Economy:
Workplace Standards at the Bottom of America's Labor Market,* ed. Annette
Bernhardt, Heather Boushey, Laura Dresser, and Chris Tilly (Champaign,
IL: Labor and Employment Relations Association, 2008), 163–90.

166　*affordable housing developments:* See the NHTF website, http://nlihc.org
/issues/nhtf, for the latest updates on the program.

available to low-income families: Patrick Sharkey, *Stuck in Place: Urban
Neighborhoods and the End of Progress Toward Racial Equality* (Chicago:
University of Chicago Press, 2013).

167　*perilously slim:* Philip M. E. Garboden and Sandra Newman, "Is Preserving
Small, Low-End Rental Housing Feasible?," *Housing Policy Debate* 22, no. 4
(2012): 507-26.

in another four: Arnold et al., "Out of Reach 2014."

when setting rents: Interviews conducted by a research team led by Edin.

168　*no earnings in 2010:* Barbara Sard, "Most Rental Assistance Recipients Work,
Are Elderly, or Have Disabilities" (Center on Budget and Policy Priorities,
Washington, DC, July 17, 2013), table 1, http://www.cbpp.org/cms/index
.cfm?fa=view&id=3992.

have claimed TANF: Shaefer and Edin, "Understanding the Dynamics."

small infusion of cash: This was the logic behind the state diversion practices mentioned in chapter 1 notes, yet none of our families had any knowledge of, or prior experience with, such practices, and evidence suggests that
a very small fraction of TANF dollars are spent in this way.

169　*safety net to draw on:* Halpern-Meekin et al., *It's Not Like I'm Poor.*

siphoned off for other uses: This assumes that federal and state funds are
shared proportionally across TANF expenditures.

unauthorized ways: Hahn, Golden, and Stanczyk, "State Approaches."

170　*their applications:* Liz Schott, "Georgia's Increased TANF Work Participation Rate Is Driven by Sharp Caseload Decline" (Center on Budget and
Policy Priorities, Washington, DC, March 6, 2007), http://www.cbpp.org
/files/3-6-07tanf.pdf.

job search activities: Linda Rosenberg, Michelle Derr, LaDonna Pavetti,
Subuhi Asheer, Megan Hague Angus, Samina Sattar, and Jeffrey Max, "A
Study of States' TANF Diversion Programs: Final Report" (Mathematica
Policy Research, Princeton, NJ, December 8, 2008), http://www.acf.hhs.gov
/sites/default/files/opre/tanf_diversion.pdf.

20 percent of the poverty line: Ife Floyd and Liz Schott, "TANF Cash Benefits
Continued to Lose Value in 2013" (Center on Budget and Policy Priorities,

Washington, DC, October 21, 2013), http://www.cbpp.org/cms/?fa=view &id=4034.

171   *"just no point"*: Neil DeMause, "Georgia's Hunger Games," *Slate,* December 26, 2012, http://www.slate.com/articles/news_and_politics/politics/2012/12 /georgia_s_war_against_the_poor_the_southern_state_is_emptying_its _welfare.html.

172   *restores their pride:* Ruby Mendenhall, Kathryn Edin, Susan Crowley, Jennifer Sykes, Laura Tach, Katrin Kriz, and Jeffrey R. Kling, "The Role of the Earned Income Tax Credit in the Budgets of Low-Income Families," *Social Service Review* 86, no. 3 (2012): 367–400. See also Halpern-Meekin et al., *It's Not Like I'm Poor.*
      like any other American: Halpern-Meekin et al., *It's Not Like I'm Poor.*

173   *erode political participation:* Suzanne Mettler, *The Submerged State: How Invisible Government Policies Undermine American Democracy* (Chicago: University of Chicago Press, 2011); Joe Soss, "Lessons of Welfare: Policy Design, Political Learning, and Political Action," *American Political Science Review* 93, no. 2 (1999): 363–80.

Index